WRITE.
PUBLISH.
REPEAT.

The No-Luck Guide to Self-Publishing Success

by Sean Platt &
Johnny B. Truant
(with David Wright)

Sean Platt & Johnny B. Truant's
WRITE. PUBLISH. REPEAT.
The No-Luck Guide
to Self-Publishing Success

Contents

About This Book's Voice 1
About Fiction vs. Nonfiction 3
Our Evil Ulterior Motive 4

PART 1: Prefatory Matters

• Who We Are 8
• Who We Think You Are 27
• Terms You Should Know 38

PART 2: Understanding the Self-Publishing
Landscape

• The Good News and the Bad News 52
• The Discoverability Shift 63
• The List of Truths 71
• The List of Myths 84

PART 3: Preparing Your Books and
Making Readers Love You

• How to Avoid Looking Like an Amateur 102
• Creating Professional Products Part 1:
  Pre-Production 110
        Knowing Your Market 111
        Knowing Your Story 117
        Knowing Your Characters 119
        Knowing Your World 123
        Preparing Your Beats (Fiction) 128
        Preparing Your Outline (Nonfiction) 134
• Creating Professional Products Part 2: Writing 140
        Decide On Your Workflow 141
        Write Fast 144
        Be Consistent and Have a Plan 147
        Use the Right Tools 150
        Shut Out the World 159

• Creating Professional Products Part 3: Editing 162
        Developmental Editing 163
        Line Editing..........164
        Proofreading 165
        Beta Readers 167
        Best Practices for Editing 170
• Creating Professional Products Part 4:
  Post-Production 183
        Covers 184
        Titles 190
        Formatting 195
        Product Descriptions 197
        Pricing 199
        E-Publishing on Multiple platforms 204
        Getting Your Books Into Print 212
        Odds and Ends 216

PART 4: Marketing Your Work

• Gathering Your Tribe 228
        Building Your Own Platform 229
        Deciding on Your Brand and Your USP 235
        Finding Your Peeps 239
        Proudly Alienating Those Who Aren't
        Your Peeps 248
• Building Relationships and Having Conversations 251
        Email 253
        Social Networks 254
        Your Email Newsletter 263
        Podcasting 263
        Blogging 265
        Real Life 268
• Understanding Funnels 272
        What a Funnel Is 272
        Things You Need to Know About Funnels 276
        Calls to Action 280
        Using Free 284
        Upsells, Next Steps, and Bundles 290
• Email Marketing the Non-Sleazy Way 294
        How To Set Up Your List 305
        How to Use Your List 314
        How To Grow Your Email List 318

- All About Reviews 329
     How to Get More Good Reviews 333
     Dealing With Negative Reviews 346
     Things You Should Never Do 352
- Ways to Supercharge Your Marketing 356

PART 5: Thinking Like a New Wave Publisher

- Mistakes That Writers Make (and That Publishers Usually Don't) 375
- Things You Can Probably Stop Worrying About 386
- How To Kill It 401
- Write. Publish. Repeat..........415

APPENDIX: Interviews with Successful Indie Authors

- Hugh Howey 425
- CJ Lyons 432
- David Gaughran 442
- Ed Robertson 450
- Joanna Penn 456

About the Authors

For Robin and Cindy,
who made (and make) it all possible.

WRITE.
PUBLISH.
REPEAT.

The No-Luck Guide to
Self-Publishing Success

by Sean Platt &
Johnny B. Truant
(with David Wright)

The Note Where We Tell You About This Book's Voice

AFTER A YEAR AND A half of producing the weekly *Self Publishing Podcast* and publishing millions of words, Sean and I (Johnny) decided we should create *SPP: The Book*, wherein we'd take the podcast's core philosophies and best tips for crafting a smart, sustainable, and potentially lucrative writing career and set them down in a single bottom-line volume.

Lucky you: That's the book you're holding.

David Wright, SPP's third host, isn't one of this book's primary authors, but he did contribute — and because he's part of our story, his presence is with us on every page. But even with only Sean and I writing, trying to include multiple "voices" in this book proved immediately difficult and totally annoying. The use of "we" also got clumsy fast. To keep things simple and easy to read, I decided to arrogantly wrestle control into my corner and write with my own voice as the primary point of view.

As you read this book, know that all "I" and "me" mentions are Johnny. Like in real life, Sean is all over the place and never shuts up. In this book, he shows up right in the middle of my sentences (LIKE RIGHT NOW). But that would be punishment to suffer through a see-sawing voice. I'm writing the rough draft (like always, because Sean is lazy) so we're writing from my perspective. If you're a podcast listener, you already know all about

Sean's slobber and can clearly see that this is for the best (Johnny's not being mean, I'm still me).

The Note Where We Talk About Fiction vs. Nonfiction

WE'RE PRIMARILY FICTION AUTHORS, SO much of what we say in this book will skew toward fiction writing. But if you're a nonfiction author, take heart! We're nonfiction authors, too (evidence of this is in your hands or on your screen), so we have a ton to say about nonfiction as well.

If you're a nonfiction writer and find yourself in the middle of a section detailing series novels or story narrative, we suggest you keep reading. The best nonfiction is full of story. This book has plenty of story in addition to its how-to, and Sean's book *Writer Dad* is nonfiction crafted around a personal narrative. Even if you ignore the story sections, everything pertaining to pre-and post-production, marketing, editing, the self-publishing process, setting goals, thinking outside the box, and so much more will still apply directly to you.

And remember, if you're having trouble researching your nonfiction book, you can always stick a unicorn somewhere inside it. That way, you can write off factual errors as part of the story.

The Note Where We Describe Our Evil Ulterior Motive

WE'D LOVE TO GET SOMETHING out of the way up front.

This book is chock-full of our best advice on how to build a successful career in self-publishing, or "indie publishing" if you prefer (we totally do). It's a logical, rational, workmanlike approach that has nothing to do with ninja tricks or magic beans. It's not about gaming the system, sliming your way to the top, or getting rich quick. It is, in short, advice that will actually help you get where you most want to go, if you're willing to wear your overalls and get to work (you don't actually have to wear overalls, though Sean's mom would love it if you did). This book is the written version of our *Self Publishing Podcast*, which we record every week and which goes out to thousands of writers who often send us beautiful e-mails about getting unstuck, fighting past their fear, publishing their best work, and starting a journey toward living their dreams.

Most writing examples used throughout this book are our own. This is done for two reasons. First, these are the examples we have. If we're going to describe a product funnel, it makes most sense to tell you how *The Beam*, *Yesterday's Gone* and *Fat Vampire* are organized because we don't know how someone else organized his or her funnel, or how well the approach worked. We also make the point throughout this book that successful indies are, above everything else, smart businesspeople. Yes, they're artists ... but if they're not businesspeople as well, they have little chance competing against the writers who are willing to work at the intersection of art and commerce. This book will tell you everything you need to know in order to become one of those smart businesspeople, but please understand that the book in your hands — in addition to being what we hope is the most comprehensive, absolute best self-publishing guide you'll ever read — *is also a part of our business strategy.* One of the things we want to do with this book is to (wait for it) raise the profile of our other books.

We promise to never actively promote our stuff, and use our books only as examples. We promise to keep things informational and helpful, but as on our podcast, *we will mention them.* Often. Does that seem like a fair trade, using those details to explain how we published more than 1.5 million words and built three successful product lines (with our busy hands in a fourth) in this last year alone? We also discuss the same people throughout the book, either authors we've worked with or had on our show. We put as much of our personal experience as we could in these pages, but it isn't a research project. The book was already sprawling enough. Our experience doesn't begin and end with the three of us, but we can speak with most authority about those projects we know best.

We also swear. Not a lot. Less than on the totally NSFW *Self Publishing Podcast* (someone really should stop us), and less than in most of our books, though not all of them. We don't swear in *Unicorn Western,* except for our made-up word *dagnit.* Nor do we swear in any of the children's literature in production (written under the pen name Guy Incognito). But we do use some four-letter favorites when it makes sense. To do our best work, this book should read as much like we're sitting on the barstool beside you as possible. And if we were side by side, and comfortable, with our children out of the room, we would probably call an asshole an asshole, if he was being an asshole.

Lastly, we *will repeat ourselves.* This can't be avoided. *Write. Publish. Repeat.* is a reference book, and while many authors will want to read it straight through, others won't. You might read it through the first time and then use it only as reference after that. We've written a book that is at least 90 percent strategies to 10 percent tactics (more later on what that means and why it absolutely matters). Each section must stand on its own without being reliant on something you may or may not have read 50 pages before. We've taken great care to curb this as much as possible, but if you're reading straight through, please do expect some minor repetition.

Before we delve in, we'd like to make a request: *If you are the kind of person who will complain and leave bad reviews because we mention our own work in explaining how we do what we do (or swearing, which we are right now telling you we are going to very occasionally do) please close this book and return it now.*

If that's not you, let's get started.

This book might make for one hell of a life-changing ride.

PART ONE:
Prefatory Matters

CHAPTER ONE:
Who We Are

YOU MIGHT BE WONDERING JUST who we are. That's an excellent question. Because, hey, we're about to presume to tell you how to build a successful self-publishing career. If we were in your shoes, we'd want to know where this advice was coming from — i.e., if we had successful indie careers ourselves. We would think long and hard about taking fitness advice from someone who was unfit, smoking cessation advice from a smoker, or wealth-creation advice from someone who was poor.

Along those same lines, there are plenty of people out there talking the self-publishing talk who aren't walking the walk. There are people who make a lot of money teaching people how to become successful writers ... but aren't successful writers themselves. We're not those guys. We're writers, and after a crap-ton of hard effort, we've made this work. We write fiction. We make up stories, and the sales of those stories fill our fridges with food.

Here are the details:

Who Johnny Is

I wrote my first novel in 1999, shopped it for a few years to agents, then gave up on becoming a writer. I accepted the inevitable conclusion that unless you were *very* lucky, you couldn't make a living writing stories. I accepted what seemed to be my best second choice, which was to write things I didn't want to write. That way at least I'd be writing, and some day, after I made enough money and could buy myself some time, I'd go back to writing the things I truly wanted to write, like novels.

At the time, I was getting a Ph.D. in molecular genetics, because *that* made sense with my personality. One day, I decided I hated grad school and work in a lab counting fruit flies (the panic attacks were a big tip that something was wrong) and quit.

Then, much to my conservative wife Robin's delight (can you smell the sarcasm?), I refused to get a real job and started freelancing on a wing and a prayer. I wrote whatever I could find, from brochure copy to ad copy to sell sheet copy to web copy. My sister worked for a company with an internal magazine, and I snagged a gig there writing occasional articles for $300 each. This felt like big money. Eventually, I worked my way up and got a much better gig (still freelance) writing articles about human resources. It was dry like toast but paid well. Some of me died by the month, but bills were paid.

Around 2008, a bunch of my investments imploded, and all of my clients stopped using me. Desperate, I did the most sensible thing I could think of. I started a humor blog. Robin probably thought the most sensible thing would have been to get a job, but that was crazy talk, and she blessedly never even brought it up, knowing my allergies.

My blog made me no money whatsoever. I decided to learn about online business. I began researching, then found some reputable online teachers and started to make some real money selling things that had nothing to do with my blog's topic: at first, website services like blog setups. Looking back, this was all due, again, to writing. I wrote funny stuff, and people liked me. So for some reason, when they needed a blog installed, they came to the guy they liked. I did that for a while, yada yada yada, you don't really care about the details. In the end, I became a pretty well-known blogger who focused mainly on what I called "human potential," which is kind of what Tony Robbins would be if he swore and kicked you in the teeth (for your own good) as he motivated you. I had several posts go viral and built a rather large following. Johnny B. Truant entered his golden age.

If you're thinking I was all over the place (genetics to HR writing to humor blogging to website services to business instruction to rah-rah viral articles), you're half right. Robin loves me, though I totally baffle her, and thinks I'm at least somewhat insane. But while I've flitted from thing to thing over the past five years and have never had a normal job, writing has always been central in everything I've done. I made my connections in the blogging world because I wrote blog posts that those connections thought were awesome, hilarious, or poignant. I got my website clients because they were blog readers and liked me. I was able to sell online business courses very successfully after my web business took off because people were compelled by my writing and persuaded by my transparent, no-bullshit sales copy. I worked with BlogWorld (now called New Media Expo) for a while, running their "Virtual Ticket" online conference, and I got that job because CEO Rick Calvert contacted me after reading a huge blog post I wrote called "The Universe Doesn't Give a Flying Fuck About You" and echoed one of that post's subheads, suggesting we could "do some epic shit" together.

So, when I interviewed Sean for my blog in 2012 about his and Dave's adventures in digital publishing, it made sense that my initial fiction spark was reignited. I'd never stopped writing; I'd just moved my focus into areas where it seemed to work as a one-degree-removed asset. I couldn't make money from my writing, so I was finding ways to use my writing to draw *other* moneymaking opportunities to me. It was working, but once that interview showed me that making money *directly* from creative writing was possible, my old business was a hot potato. Robin was so excited she began losing sleep over our unstable income.

I'd known Sean from the online marketing and blogging world for a few years, but that interview moved us closer. I immediately cleaned up and self-published that first novel I'd written in 1999. *The Bialy Pimps* finally went on sale. I listened to my interview with Sean over and over, then nagged him into a podcast. I joined Sean and Dave to start *The Self Publishing Podcast* in early 2012.

Meeting with two prolific writers every week motivated me. I learned a new style and rhythm and method to my writing, and when I did, the many blocks I'd had after finishing *The Bialy Pimps* (my hard drive is littered with the detritus of many failed novels) vanished. It was my awakening.

I wrote *Fat Vampire*, my second novel, in September 2012. In October, I wrote *Fat Vampire 2*. Something had finally uncorked ... and thanks to Sean and Dave's incessant inspiration, my books were actually selling.

Sean and I teamed up to write collaboratively for the first time with *Unicorn Western*, which grew out of a joke on our "after-hours and pointless" podcast *Better Off Undead*, wherein Dave essentially dared us to write a western without doing research. (Our solution was to put a unicorn in it, hence rendering reality and research moot.) The first *Unicorn Western* was so fun, we wrote another, and another, and another.

I could go into excruciating detail, but it's almost time for me to pass the mic to Sean, so I'll stick to the highlights. Together, we unleashed an inhuman level of production, releasing the entire nine-book, 250,000-word *Unicorn Western Full Saga* in May 2013, followed by our huge sci-fi political thriller *The Beam* in July. In the remainder of 2013, I finished the six-book *Fat Vampire* series on my own. In addition, my and Sean's new publishing company Realm & Sands spat out new titles (*Unicorn Genesis, Namaste, Robot Proletariat,* a Malcolm Gladwell-style social commentary based on the future world of *The Beam* called *Plugged, Cursed,* three six-episode "written sitcom" seasons, the book you're reading now, and more) faster than Eminem spits lyrics. Looking back, our level of production was as stupid crazy as it was awesome. I'm not even counting the collaborative work we did with our friend Lexi Maxxwell, designing and writing the non-sex parts of two of her erotic series: a genre-shattering project in the world of *The Beam* called *The Future of Sex* and a sitcom called *Adult Video*, which we collectively think of as "*Clerks* in a porn shop."

October 2013 was my 13th month of publishing for real, and my 13th month of working my ass off hitting keys. It was the first month of my second full year … but more importantly, it marked the first month in which my publishing income — book sales and nothing else — allowed me to pay all of my bills with room to spare, and hence allowed Robin to finally relax a little.

There's a critical mass thing that happens when you publish the way we discuss in this book, and the mountains of work Sean and I did as 2013 drew to a close was about one thing: *completing product funnels.* We'll go into product funnels in detail later, but for now all you need to know is that complete product funnels, done correctly, are where most of your money will come from. By the end of the year, we had a dozen funnels, all ticking off steadily, day by day.

It took a year of working in overdrive to start making a living doing this, but things have gotten kind of stupid amazing since.

Who Sean Is

This is Sean. I took the mic from Johnny.

I write fast, thousands of words every day for years. Still, I've spent a half hour on this section and am only here, four sentences deep.

I had to start over. It was taking too long. I wrote half a page as Johnny, and it was too weird so I had to scrap it. I've written millions of words as a ghostwriter, so it shouldn't have been a problem, but it felt weird being Johnny talking about me. I have to get used to it; the nature of this book requires me to do it throughout, but I'm here for my bio then I'll fade back into the copy while Johnny maniacally laughs, twirling his mustache and monocle while claiming these pages as his own.

The three of us are like the Super Friends, each bringing something cool to the table that the others need but don't have. Dave keeps countermeasures designed to take Johnny and I down on his utility belt, just like Batman. We share well-tinted shades of overlap and contrast that allow us to create better art in less time, and I wake each day feeling fortunate for my friends and partners.

Johnny's been writing forever in one way or another. Dave's always wanted to. He did have a short stint as an ace reporter — tough writing under tougher deadlines, where his words changed lives, reversed fortunes, and made his city a better, more decent place to live. I've been at it for a few months over five years, though I've written a career's worth of words in that time.

Five years ago I was living in Long Beach, California — same place I'd lived for 30+ years before that. I love Long Beach. It's where I went to school, started my first businesses, met my wife, Cindy, had our two amazing children (actually she did that — my part didn't take too long and was the best sort of fun), bought our house, and lost the house after deciding to gamble it all on a life as a writer. Now we live in Austin, Texas after a three-year stop in Ohio (Johnny's jealous and will be fleeing Cleveland as soon as he's able), and I make my full-time living from fiction.

I started writing on accident. Cindy loves me dearly, but thinks (knows) I talk too much. One day (after a decade of trying) she finally convinced me to start moving my mouth less and my fingers more. She's a fantastic teacher (Houston Unified's teacher of the year before she moved to California and I was lucky enough to meet her) and had always told me I could write. I wrote nothing but letters to Cindy, so I took her compliments as verbal blushing. I was a high school dropout: *I couldn't write.*

Blah blah blah, sorry if you've already read *Writer Dad.* That would make the last couple of paragraphs as redundant for you as the coming few.

We started a preschool when Haley was 4 and Ethan was 1, hoping to spend as much of their first five years together as possible. Ethan went to kindergarten, and our family transitioned. I started writing a little, then a lot. I thought I could write well enough to make our ends meet. Spoiler alert: I couldn't. I sucked, and we lost everything instead.

I started out querying my work — children's poems I wrote for the students at our preschool. But I'm even less patient than Johnny and quit the queries after number one went nowhere. The agency said my vocabulary was too rich for children; I said "Homey don't play that." So I started a blog to gather my crowd and the blog blew up, but I didn't know what to do with the attention. I failed to leverage what I earned, went totally broke, and learned to write sales copy because ramen sucks.

As Johnny said, my heart beats with entrepreneurial blood. The first book I wrote that didn't suck was called *Penny to a Million* (now available under the pen name Guy Incognito). *Penny* is about a fifth-grade kid named Kelly who sells crap on the playground (candy and other assorted junk). I wrote that book without stopping because once upon a time *I was Kelly.* I did the same thing in the same grade. I've always been in business for myself, and can't imagine life lived any other way. I fumbled at the start, writing keyword articles by the 100 at $5 a pop. I was upside down before I managed to flip back, learning to write sales copy that paid enough to save us.

I met Dave two weeks into my online adventure, and we started working together immediately. He suffered through some of those keyword articles with me, but never got into the sales copy. So totally Dave. That man would *rather* write articles for $5 each than "sellout" copy at $1 per word. The only premium words Dave was ever happy with was when we ghostwrote site copy and model descriptions for a swanky international escort agency.

I learned to write sales copy because it paid more than anything else. Because of that copy I met one of the world's best copywriters, and one of my best friends, Lori Taylor. She helped me get better at what I do, and paid for a ton of awesome training that helped me get smarter faster.

I spent a year ghostwriting marketing materials, and learning to write with ever-increasing speed. 2010 came and brought us the Kindle. BOOM: Life changed. Dave and I formed our publishing company Collective Inkwell and started writing fiction like we'd always wanted to, and built our first major success: a serialized fiction series called *Yesterday's Gone*. I thought it was great because it was built around a funnel (where one episode led readers immediately into the next) and Dave thought it was great because it was like Stephen King's six-episode *Green Mile*. Both of us were happy.

We changed the language of our books to "episodes" and "seasons," just like TV, then marveled at the aftermath. It seems so simple, but no one (to our knowledge then or now) had done it before. Episodes and seasons gave our readers immediate shorthand, telling them exactly what to expect (we'll get more into all of this later, it's super important), and our readers rewarded us with buys, and constant support. We took our first series (now up to its fourth season, with another two to go) and built a business publishing fiction each week, positioning ourselves as the AMC, HBO or Showtime of Kindle.

I'd known Johnny for a while, but by the time *Yesterday's Gone* was getting going with its third season, the fiction bug had crawled up his ass and laid eggs. He suggested that we start a podcast. I said that Dave and I had been talking about doing a podcast forever, but couldn't imagine adding one more thing to my plate. Johnny promised that all I would have to do would be to show up and talk (I'm quite good at that) and drag Dave along behind me (I'd been doing that for a few years already), so I agreed.

I have a fantastic creative relationship with Dave. It's easy to build stories together, but very difficult to build a business. I want to build a house, but Dave's suspicious of nails. Like me, Johnny sees life as a lab and loves to experiment with beakers full of instinct. It wasn't too long after the podcast that we scheduled our first collaborative project.

Dave and I landed a two-book deal with Amazon's publishing arm, 47North, forcing me to postpone my work with Johnny. By the time I was finished I was too exhausted to wrap my head around the cerebral project we'd originally planned (we're finally hitting that title in February of 2014). I said I wanted to do something "stupid simple." *Unicorn Western* fit, because before we wrote it we had no way of knowing it would end up so surprisingly complex.

Ever since finishing the first *Unicorn Western* we've hit insane levels of production. A recurring joke on our show is that Johnny's my mistress because he does all the things Dave doesn't want to do. And while that *is* true, there's more to it than that. Systems make me happy, and if you're a writer who wants to get well-paid for your words, you should love systems, too. Working with Johnny isn't a case of one plus one equaling two. It's one and one equaling five or six or seven, depending on the project.

Our partnership works on two levels: First, our work is absurdly compatible. I love doing all the stuff that Johnny doesn't want to do, like world-building and designing basic story layout. Johnny loves writing rough drafts. I love writing them, too (I write a lot of firsts with Dave at the Inkwell) but it's pure magic to make up a story, deliver beats to Johnny, and get back an awesome narrative that I totally love, along with the chance to do the other stuff I really love to do: edit and tweak.

When I first started writing, I wrote like an idiot without even knowing it (it's possible you do, too. So, this part's important). I wrote for *me*, rather than my readers. I *thought* I was writing for them, but I was more interested in how my words sounded than what they said. I've always loved the "music" of language, so when I first started writing I made certain that every sentence sounded like part of my song. After reality slapped me hard, dragged me across a cold concrete floor strewn with broken glass, and dropped me in a ditch I finally learned copywriting, which changed my game for the better in two ways.

In copywriting, no words are wasted. Everything has a point. Your job isn't just to please the reader, it's to keep them on the page. If they stop reading, you lose. If you write copy that doesn't convert, you won't be hired again (at least not by smart businesses). If you can write copy that converts, people will stand in line no matter how much you charge. My friend Lori's been making more than a million dollars a year since her mid-20s *writing copy.* Because it converts. Keeping readers on the page is an art, and no one does that better than copywriters. Without the open loops and rhythms I picked up learning copy, the serials Dave and I wrote together would never have been as strong, or sold as well.

Dave's a natural storyteller, and as we'll revisit throughout this book, a "purer artist" than either Johnny or myself. That's neither good nor bad; it simply is. The three of us are a team, all invested in the others' success, but Johnny and Dave don't write together. I'm the bridge between them.

Johnny's fantastic at bringing my beats to life. I can't imagine anyone ever doing it better. On the other hand, Dave doesn't even *want* my beats, and would rather write them for me. My flow with Dave (much more on flow later) is dictated from project to project, and therefore slow to improve. After five years of writing together we still don't really have a system.

By contrast, Johnny and I are both so systems-oriented that we improve by the project. We're not necessarily getting faster, but we are delivering a better product per hour spent; understanding one another more; fading in and out of one another's work, almost as a single writer. The magic of collaboration — and really, this is a book in itself — is that when done right, there should be long stretches where neither writer knows who wrote what. At the very least (and this is essential), your reader should be clueless that there are two authors behind the words.

Dave and I take great pride in our work because there are times when Dave writes the entire draft, times when I write the entire draft, and yet other times when we're splitting words down the middle. Yet, no reader can tell where one of us stops and the other starts. When they try to guess it's usually wrong. Johnny and I also disappear into one another, but the drafts are always his. We trust one another completely, so Johnny never cares what I add, subtract, or tweak.

This project is different. This one isn't just *in* Johnny's voice, it *is* his voice, which makes it the oddest writing/editing/polishing job I've had since my days as a ghostwriter, and why this small section took me forever to start.

Johnny and I are both here with you through every page of this book. As with all of our work, I'm the invisible hand scrubbing sentences, flipping phrases, and otherwise sharpening Johnny's already remarkable articulation.

We are in this together. We wrote this book to make a difference: to change your life as it continues changing ours. We hope you enjoy it; you're in for a great ride.

Who Dave Is

We won't give you a ton of detail about Dave for two reasons.

First, he's tinfoil hat paranoid. On one of our first shows, Sean made a casual, off-handed comment about [REDACTED], and Dave made us edit it out. He's so paranoid that on one show, we learned that our good friend Dave carries a decoy wallet filled with no cash and bogus credit cards so that if he's ever mugged, he won't take a hit. He's never actually been mugged, but in Dave's world it's always safest to assume the worst because good things never *ever* happen.

The second reason is that this is really our book. Dave helped us out and contributed some amazing interviews. He did the cover design for us, but was working on other (fiction) projects at the time and tends to get very angry when Sean suggests new projects that weren't originally on the docket, such as this one. Fortunately, I'm like Sean's mistress, so when Sean's first work wife, Dave, won't fulfill his needs, he comes to me because he knows I'm as freaky as he is.

What you need to know about Dave — and all I'm allowed to divulge unless I want a letter bomb — is that he has been Sean's writing partner since 2008. They are the original odd couple. Dave is like Dracula, and Sean is Kermit the Frog. Before moving to fiction in 2011, Sean and Dave wrote everything together from small print-on-demand books (before P.O.D. was cool or remotely a good idea) to copy, to ghostwritten books and articles. Dave is the reason that all of Collective Inkwell's fiction is dark, and why there's always at least one child in jeopardy in each of their stories.

Dave is also an artist. Left to his own devices, he would lock himself in his office all day, listen to Tool, drink gallons of Diet Coke, and write stories where happy endings would be crushed for being the rainbows of fancy that they are. Dave likes *Calvin and Hobbes* and ironically agrees 100 percent with 17th century philosopher Thomas Hobbes, AKA "the original goth," who said that human nature was brutal and animalistic and pretty much had nothing going for it when civilization crumbled. Don't go near Dave's house during or after the apocalypse. You'll be shot without hesitation because "It's just safer that way."

Just about everything Sean and I do sales- and marketing-wise is a hair's breadth from evil to Dave, and that's actually the secret, second reason Sean and I wrote this book. Dave can't talk about marketing. He's allergic. We drag him along and make him sell his work with a combination of chains, whips, and tranquilizer darts.

But don't let Dave's lovable curmudgeonliness affect *your* opinion of marketing and sales. You can't just be an artist if you want to be a successful indie. You need to think of yourself as a businessperson as much as you think of yourself as a writer. That's why it's the two of us who love business as much as writing — Sean and I — who wrote this book.

Who The Three Of Us Are Together

This is where the magic happens.

If you read the above, you know our brief history, plus a bonus almost-profile of Dave. More important than knowing who we are as individuals is knowing who we are when we all get together, like the robots that join to make Voltron.

You already know we're the guys behind the *Self Publishing Podcast* (we mentioned it in the previous section even if you missed it in the product description or aren't one of our listeners). We all love the podcast and would love it even if nobody listened. The podcast — or, more importantly, the live brainstorming and masterminding that occurs during the podcast — is *the* reason I figured out how to make my fiction writing pay. The friendships and working relationships among us are the reason that all of us have grown as fast as we have. Without our teamwork, the three of us would be significantly weaker than we are right now.

But why do you care? Why does the value we, as hosts, have found in the *Self Publishing Podcast* matter to you?

Let's stop talking about SPP and discuss the value of a mastermind in more general terms. Or if the idea of a "mastermind group" doesn't resonate with you, just consider it to be a community. We all need support to do our best, right? Of course, we do.

When you know other writers, you can borrow from their tricks and techniques, using what they've learned to benefit yourself and in turn sharing what you've learned to help others. For instance, when our buddy Ed Robertson was on the podcast in late 2013, he told us how he created a box set of the first three books in his *Breakers* series, discounted the whole work to 99 cents, and used that insane deal to drive sales to his fourth book. Ed sold 2,200 copies of the box set in a single day thanks to this technique. His box set *and* the fourth book rode high on the bestseller lists for months, selling seriously impressive numbers of copies. Ed suggested I do the same to promote my *Fat Vampire* series, so I did, making my four-book box set 99 cents with heavy promotion: the move that finally earned me my first truly profitable month.

Aside from the information-sharing, consider the moral support that comes from a group — the simple belief you gain, as a writer working alone, when you see other people successfully doing what you're trying to do. Consider the value of being able to ask questions, lean on each other, and cross-promote.

That's what listeners tell us our podcast gives them. They're not hosts or guests, yet they benefit just the same. Several times each week, we get e-mails from listeners who tell us how we gave them the courage or knowledge to start publishing. Receiving those e-mails — knowing we're making a difference for people like us — is amazing, and incredibly gratifying.

Week by week, it feels like we're building an army. Sean, Dave, and I already think of ourselves as "all for one and one for all," and that's how we make decisions. I don't worry about what's best for Johnny. I worry about what's best for *us*. Sean and Dave do the same. I can think of at least three times when Sean, our best networker, could have easily cashed out on a big deal for himself. He never does. He always tells whoever it is that the rest of us are part of the deal, or there won't be one.

Beyond our trio, we've formed tremendous kinships with our guests and listeners. We told Ed he's Justin Timberlake to our *Saturday Night Live* because he's been on four times, and that makes him part of the family: the strategy and algorithm-hacking guy. C.J. Lyons, who sold 100,000 self-published books per month in 2012, is the family's big-picture strategist and our link to traditional New York publishing. Joanna Penn, who has her own successful writing podcast (*The Creative Penn*), is our family explorer, always bringing back some tidbit we were ignoring: like audiobook production, foreign sales and translation, and pairing on certain projects with a literary agent *after* achieving self-publishing success. Joanna is also the first person who sold us on Kobo, a bookseller we adore today. Joanna was on the Kobo train long before it had earned our attention.

We love the *Self Publishing Podcast* so much because we are truly a community. There are the three of us as hosts, our guests as extended family, and thousands of listeners and readers as our eyes and ears in the world. Our listeners are *constantly* bringing us great information. They're programmers and engineers who give us insights on selling books direct to readers, rather than using an intermediary. They're successful writers who offer insights on things we don't understand. Our listener Shannon

Morgan suggested the title we chose for this book. We love our listeners. They're our biggest champions and helpers, and we always lower the rope once they've helped us to get it untangled enough for them to climb.

We've included this section about our podcast's guests and listeners in the "Who We Are" section for one reason: As you read this book, it's important to understand that you're not just hearing advice from three random writers. You're getting the sorted and sifted "best of" curated from the experience of thousands.

CHAPTER TWO:
Who We Think You Are

SO THAT'S US. NOW: WHO are you?

We'll tell you who we think you might be. And, because we're the ones steering this ship, we'll also tell you who we think you really should be — who you *need* to be — if you're going to make a career out of self-publishing. Because that's what this book is really about: becoming a full-time author who derives enough income from publishing books to support him- or herself and hence doesn't need to do anything else.

While we believe that most writers will benefit from what we have to say, the core audience for this book is writers who would like to build substantial incomes — possibly sideline revenue streams, but ideally quit-your-day-job incomes. That's who we are. Sean and I both have a disease, and it can be terminal. It's called *entrepreneurship*. We literally are unable to see "rational" alternatives to self-employment if they involve working for someone else. We've both been dead broke, and when that happened, it honestly never occurred to us to get jobs. Both of us worked harder on one venture or another while our long-suffering but incredibly supportive wives stood beside us shaking their heads in befuddlement. And while that might seem dedicated in retrospect, it was simply how things were at the time. When we thought about becoming full-time authors with quit-our-day-job incomes, there was no day job to quit. The options were to succeed or starve. So, we know how to scrap. We know how to scramble. We know how to fight for our lives to make a career work, because it lives in the neighborhood of literally true.

If you want to make writing work full time for you, you'll need to develop some of that fire. We don't suggest quitting your job so you have the fear necessary to drive you, and we would never advise anyone to leap with the hope that the net will appear, but you will need a reason to work hard … and to work hard for a long time, often without any real sign of reward. Building a writing career can be maddeningly slow and frustrating, even if you're very dedicated. Neither of us quit because we didn't feel like we had an alternative. You *will* have an alternative (we think you *should*, anyway), so you're going to need another reason to keep publishing once it gets tough — which it absolutely will. It might be as simple as envisioning the compelling future ahead if you keep at it. What will life be like, some day, once you're writing full time? Spend hours with that thought. Days or weeks if you need it. But not too long. Daydreams live outside of reality.

This is where community can be very helpful. If you listen to our podcast, you'll be surrounding yourself with writers every week, and you'll continually hear from and about people who have been able to make it work for them. Belief comes first. Actions that justify that belief come second.

Right now, we'd guess that you're a writer. You could have written a book; you could be in the planning stages of your first one; you could have written several. Plenty of our podcast listeners are already full-time successful authors; you could be that, too. If you're new, you're looking for ways to get started. If you're advanced, you're looking to refine what you already have.

That's a wide spectrum. When we started writing this book, we looked at that range and asked ourselves who we wanted to write for, but realized that we couldn't narrow our focus to a certain *stage* of writer — beginner, middle, or advanced. Building a publishing career is a journey, and it would be a mistake to exclude anyone simply by virtue of how far along they were on that journey. Instead, we decided to narrow our focus to a certain *type* of writer.

Let's break things into categories.

Who This Book Definitely Is For

If you're willing to think of your writing career as a business rather than purely an art, this book is for you. (Caveat: It can and should be both; more on that in a bit.)

If you're willing to think of your books as products (rather than precious soul-babies) and are willing to embrace a strategy that packages and promotes them in the way you'd package and promote a product for maximum appeal, this book is for you.

If you're willing to think of your readers as customers (who behave like customers, meaning they're affected by pricing and market psychology), this book is for you.

If this is starting to sound dry, have heart. Sean and I are both bubbly, optimistic, highly artistic people in addition to smart businessmen. We love our readers, and we *love* writing our stories. When we say you must package your product for maximum appeal, understand that the story *always* comes first and the marketing second. We've seen people who approach writing with the precision of statisticians, adding golfers to their story when golf is a hot trend and hopping on the coattails of every tip and trick even if it means whoring their stories. We're not those guys. But we're also not guys who think that art should speak for itself and that great art will succeed because everyone will see how inherently awesome it is. We believe you should write what you want, but think you should do so within a framework of intelligent strategy, always considering how to reverse-engineer the market's expectations after you're done to get the most bang for your buck. We could say that writing is primary and business is secondary, but that's not entirely true. It's more accurate to say that writing comes first and that business comes second. First and second here aren't about which is more important; they're about chronological order. When you write, your creative mind is in charge, and your business mind needs to get out of the way. But when you're done writing and editing, those two have to flip. Once the book is complete, it's product more than art, and you need to let business dictate how you present it to the world.

This book is for people who are willing to work hard. *Very* hard. It's for people who don't give up. It's definitely for optimists — ideally people so forward-thinking that they're deluded into thinking that things are awesome when everyone else sees them as hopeless. It's for people who believe that "obsession" is a word lazy people use to describe dedication. You can't be dissuaded by naysayers or critics. You must be tough, and gutsy.

You should be the kind of person who would want to write anyway. Someone who loves telling stories. Someone who loves the spark that comes when a story's twist surprises even you, the person writing it. If you're looking for the e-book gold rush and are hoping to cash in on what you see as easy money, please put this book down and go spam people about Viagra and porn. This is not a way to get rich quick by *any* means. This book's ideal reader understands that but doesn't care, because they agree with us: The reward of being able to tell stories every day is worth the effort required to make it happen, no matter how long it takes.

Who This Book Might Be For

You remember Dave, right? We introduced him in the last section. Dave hates sales and marketing. He's not an optimist by any definition of the word. The dude carries a decoy wallet. Dave thinks that at least half of the great strategic ideas Sean and I have are scams, or will be seen by the world as scams. One time, Sean proposed an idea, I cheered it on, and Dave replied that we were going to get in trouble with the Federal Trade Commission. That's not a joke. Dave sweats every bad reader review while Sean and I laugh them off as long as our average is great, and Dave often sends us long, ranting e-mails about how the sky is falling. Dave hates people because he's secretly very kind and sensitive and hence sees the evil in the world as everpresent. He gets it, too. Dave has said that his Meyers-Briggs personality type is "I.T.F-You."

Regardless, this book would be great for Dave if he didn't already know the stuff inside it. There's an excellent chance Sean will make him read it anyway.

It's preferable that a writer who wants to build a significant publishing income be upbeat, optimistic, business- and marketing-minded, bold and fearless, and risk-tolerant, but the one trait that trumps all of those is a willingness to do things that seem best, no matter how uncomfortable they may be. Dave has said he doesn't do well with risk (Sean and I, to our wives' consternation, have no problem with tumbling dice), but in a way his willingness to proceed in spite of his hesitation is much gutsier than what Sean and I do. We're puppies, almost blind to risks because we're so eager. Dave sees the risks and feels the fear and does it anyway. Now, he'll tell you he's had help — Sean has been bludgeoning Dave forward for five years now so it's not like he's had a huge choice — but *he does it.* He allows his art to get stuffed into logical product funnels, where each book leads readers to the next, including into packaged upsells. He tries his best to stick to deadlines so the business can operate *as a business* rather than as a "whenever, whatever" artistic enterprise. He allows advertisement, allows e-mail marketing, and reluctantly turns from troublesome potential readers who aren't truly part of his "tribe."

If you have difficulty doing the things in this book because they conflict with your personality type, yet do them because you agree they make sense for your publishing business (if you're shy but must surface from your shell to sell a tiny bit) this book is probably still for you.

Who This Book Isn't For

This is actually a fairly large group of people. Let's cover them point by point.

Hobbyists

Maybe writing is just a fun hobby for you, and perhaps you'd like to publish something someday because doing so is a dream. You may not have any interest whatsoever in building a business behind your writing, and you kind of just want to know how it all works. If that's you, this really isn't the guide you need. If you want to know the mechanics of digital self-publishing (the details of how to create and publish a file, including which buttons to push), a much better guide is *Let's Get Digital* by David Gaughran. And we love "how to write" books like Stephen King's gem, *On Writing*. We do think that every kind of writer will get some value from this book, but while we do discuss both writing mechanics and how-to, it's minimal. You may find yourself mired in this book.

Artists

I love artists. My dad is an artist, like Dave. But if you *only* want to be an artist and think that business and creativity can't co-exist, this book will only piss you off, and we can't help you sell if you won't embrace a bit of business. We don't believe that anything we do or advise is tantamount to whoring our talent, but pure artists may feel it is anyway. We believe art exists within a definition ("Paint me a portrait using watercolors" is different and more restrictive than "Paint me a portrait"), but you may disagree. Feel free to read on, but you've been warned.

People Who Want Instant Riches or an Easy Button

We have a whole section to follow for these folks if we don't trim the tribe enough right here. If you think you're going to get rich quick or have bought into any of the the e-book gold rush crap, you might as well stop reading now. Let's be clear: You will not get rich quickly; you may not get rich at all; you will not work four hours a week to build your business; you will get nowhere by repurposing public domain content, making collections of existing work, or in any way trying to game a system that doesn't want to be gamed and isn't going to let you, because you're not going to fool a reader more than once, and you deserve to fail if you try. You will also never get by with half-assed work, shoddy editing, cheap or unprofessional covers; you cannot ignore your fans; your business will never operate entirely on autopilot; you cannot publish poorly written stories and expect them to fly on the wings of a catchy title. Those who believe in the gold rush may succeed for a month — two if they're lucky — but banking on it as a long-term career is three orbits past stupid.

Lazy People
See above. We'll say it over and over: *This can be fun as hell, but it will never be easy.*

People Who Want to Please Everyone
We love you guys and gals, because you truly have other people's best interests at heart. But what you must understand is that no matter how hard you try, you *can't* please everyone. You will never write a story that each of even your most devoted readers will enjoy. You can't sell without turning some people away. You can't appeal to Grandma's knitting club while also appealing to the folks who love bloody horror (unless your knitting club is more awesome than ours). We'll discuss speaking to your ideal readers — and, as a consequence, being content with trimming your tribe. Trimming your tribe means deliberately choosing the types of people you want in your readership and not trying to please those outside of it. You'll do the same when you communicate with those readers — via an e-mail list, if you follow our advice. Sometimes you need to choose a direction for your writing, pricing, or business in general, and not everyone will like it. You must be willing to accept that, because if you insist on staying in the middle in order to keep from ruffling feathers, you'll fail. Like Mr. Miyagi said: "Walk on road, hmm? Walk right side, safe. Walk left

side, safe. Walk middle, sooner or later, you get squished, just like grape."

People Who Complain, Make Excuses, or Are Eager to Take Offense

One of the biggest things you'll need to become a long-term, successful, profitable independent writer is an ability to roll with the punches. You have to takes hits, adjust, and keep moving forward. Every so often in the self-publishing world (more often than you'll like, guaranteed) something big changes. When this happens, we hear about it at the *Self Publishing Podcast*, and looking through our listener e-mails and voicemails, you'd think the sky was falling (this is in addition to our regular e-mails from Dave). Amazon will change the algorithms it uses to rank books on the bestseller lists; a big promotional engine will shut down; a service interruption somewhere will result in lost sales. It happens. And when it does, you must be able to look at the big picture rather than sweating details that don't really matter. Yes, it sucked when Amazon started crapping all over free book promotions (more on that later) and hence put a pillow on the face of promotion for many writers, but smart writers, rather than panicking, asked themselves: "Will people still want to buy books?" That's the only question that actually matters. As long as the answer stays "Yes," the rest are details. You cannot decide you're being discriminated against, make excuses for reasons why you aren't succeeding (typically because some version of "the man" is keeping you down), or look for reasons to be bothered. Your business is pleasing readers and selling books. As long as there are readers out there, it is your job to find them. Bitching about how things are unfair solves nothing, so stop bitching and go find readers. If any words in this paragraph bother you, this is probably the wrong book for you. We surround ourselves with positive, dedicated writers who don't make excuses, so you'll see this no-whining sentiment repeated throughout. We don't want you to be a victim, and only victims decide in advance that their success is in anyone's hands other than their own.

CHAPTER THREE:
Terms You Should Know

THROUGHOUT THIS BOOK, WE'RE GOING to use several concepts and terms. We know glossary-style content is boring, but do be sure to glance at what follows so that this stuff will have been introduced to your brain by the time it resurfaces.

Here we go.

1,000 True Fans
This is a simple yet elegant concept, and it could change your life. Some people think publishing — like Hollywood — is built around blockbusters. Be better than that mistake. That doesn't mean you can't ever have a blockbuster, or shouldn't want one, but building your career around trying to get one is foolhardy at best and disastrous at worst.

Most movies fail. It's a fact of Hollywood. Same holds true for books. You shouldn't be looking for blockbusters, you should be thinking about gathering readers. Each time you run a free promotion (for example) you are introducing more people to your work. Some of those people will be your lifetime readers, or "true fans."

The theory of 1,000 true fans states that an artist (not just writers, but musicians, filmmakers, carpenters, whatever) need only acquire 1,000 true fans to make a living at their art.

By no means is this number chiseled in stone. One thousand fans is a concept, not a metric. The point is that a true fan in the context of the reader/writer relationship will want to read (that means buy) anything you write. They will download it on the day it comes out, buy it in print, and tell all their friends. They'll buy the *What Would Boricio Do?* T-shirt from Sean and Dave or the *Unicorn Western* socks from me and Sean (NOTE: Neither of those exists, yet).

True fans don't just give you a great career; they help you to sustain it. But it's *your* job to earn them, and the only way to do that is one reader at a time.

10,000 Hours

In his book *Outliers*, Malcolm Gladwell proposed that in most disciplines, how well people perform has more to do with the time they've spent practicing their craft than any sense of innate talent. The best pianists were those who spent the most time with their fingers tickling ivory. The best hockey players spent the most time on ice. Same for the best computer programmers, academics, whatever. Specifically, Gladwell proposed that in order to achieve mastery, somewhere around 10,000 hours of practice seems to be required. Put in the hours, and you'll be a master. Talent matters, but a 10,000-hour practitioner will almost always outperform a "prodigy" who barely practices.

The 80/20 Rule

The more you pay attention, the more you'll see that it's true: 20 percent of the things you can choose to do in a venture will get you 80 percent of your desired results. Conversely, if you choose poorly, you can spend a ton of extra time doing the 80 percent of activities that do almost nothing, netting you only about 20 percent of the results you *could* be getting. You only have so much time, and you want to be efficient, *so you should always seek to determine if any given action is worth your time.*

Sometimes, entrepreneurs, authors, and author-entrepreneurs think they need to do everything. "Will it increase sales?" they'll ask. And if the answer is, "It may!" or "Probably somewhat," they figure they should do it because every little bit counts, and small amounts add up. That's true, but the decision to do things that may help and couldn't hurt usually stems from a false thought: the belief that you can do it all. You *can't* do it all, so you must choose carefully.

Throughout this book and constantly on our podcast, Sean and I refer to "80-percent activities," meaning those most likely to get you 80 percent of the results, and "20-percent activities," which are those that may work somewhat but aren't ultimately worth the time you must spend to achieve them. Eighty-percent activities are writing more and better books, building a moderate amount of reader engagement (efficiently, not via long e-mails), creating solid calls to action that lead people to your next books from the backs of those they've just finished, completing bundles and product funnels (see below), and so on. For most writers, creating print books and merchandise, or spending inordinate time on social media is 20-percent stuff. You can do those things ... but really only should if you have time after finishing as much 80-percent stuff as you possibly can.

The Long Tail

Essentially, the long tail is a way to describe how the Internet has changed an artist's ability to effectively market themselves in even the smallest niches. Before the Internet, records, books, movies, and other items were geared towards creating hits. Brick and mortar stores had limited shelf space and could only afford to carry the most popular items. All that popular stuff is "the head," or the area corresponding to the big fat lump you'd get if you put "relevance to X" on a graph. The long tail shows us that the big head isn't the graph's only profitable area.

To understand the big head and long tail, think of Google, or any search engine. The first page of results is the fattest part of the big head, because those are the results that most people click on. According to Google, the first result on page one gets over 50 percent of *all traffic.* This dims just with the second and third link. The second page gets fewer hits, and the third page fewer still. By the time you get to the fourth or fifth page, almost no one is clicking. But what the long tail theory says is that in a huge population, "almost no one" — represented by the thin area of the graph that goes on forever, called the long tail — is still significant, and that good money can still be made in it if your marketing is targeted enough to efficiently reach those people.

The same goes for subjects people are interested in, with the long tail being niche areas surrounding a large central topic. Right now, vampire stories are very much in the big head because many people are looking for them. If you write undifferentiated vampire stories, you're competing in the very crowded marketplace aiming for the big head. Vampire erotica, on the other hand, is a bit further onto the tail, and historical vampire erotica is way out there ... but still has ravenous readers. Because the book buying audience is so large, even the smallest niches have large numbers of readers. (If you don't believe us, search for "monster porn.")

The good news for us is that the specificity of their interests means they will *only* buy things that meet them exactly. If you know how to reach readers way out on the long tail, even the smallest sub-niches can be profitable. (NOTE: This is really more FYI than anything and should only be considered after you're done writing. Setting out to write a story in order to specifically hit *any* part of the graph is somewhat creatively bankrupt in our opinion.)

Tactics vs. Strategies

A *tactic* is a specific technique you can use to achieve a desired result. For instance, up until around 2012, using Amazon's KDP (Kindle Direct Publishing) Select program to make your books occasionally free was a highly effective tactic. Up until the middle of 2012, Amazon's algorithms worked such that if a book was downloaded for free *en masse*, it would rank highly on bestseller charts after reverting to paid status, and you would sell many books in the aftermath of your promotion. A lot of writers got used to using this system (which, by the way, required your book to be exclusive to

Amazon, meaning you had all your eggs in Amazon's basket for that particular title), and when Amazon changed their algorithms, many writers were caught with no idea what to do next. They no longer knew how to promote their book because they'd grown reliant on a single tactic.

By contrast, *strategies* are the larger, deeper plans that drive your business. Strategies are things like "write the best books you can," "create reader loyalty and connection," "satisfy customer demand," and "create logical next-step reading experiences and have them ready (and obviously available) for readers when they finish your books." Tactics tend to change quickly, but strategies almost never do. Charles Dickens could have employed all of the strategies above, despite his lack of an iPad. Back in the 19th century, he did just that.

One thing to note is that you will inevitably employ various tactics to most effectively advance your strategies. Tactics are not bad; they just shouldn't be the linchpin of your business. In the above KDP Select example, using Select while it was viable in order to drive sales wasn't a bad idea. Having no other way to drive sales was. Use the tactics at your disposal while you can, but always keep your eyes on the big picture, and never, *ever* forsake your strategies just because a particular tactic seems tempting. And you may well be tempted. We all know that having lots of good reviews on your books helps you out, right? Well, in 2013, author John Locke admitted to paying a company to post positive reviews for his books, and the revelation caused a hubbub in the industry and a huge backlash against Locke. This was a tactics versus strategies problem: The *tactic* of getting good reviews through any means necessary should have been trumped by the *strategy* "be honest and upfront with your readers."

Genre-Hopping

This refers to writing across several genres. When Sean and I announced our intention to do this, our listeners gave us an earful. To this date, the *SPP* audience is not in agreement about whether or not it's wise to write in multiple genres (the counterargument says that doing so dilutes and/or confuses your audience), but Sean and I firmly believe in it — *for us.* We've written westerns, fantasy, science fiction, horror, satire, outright comedy, drama, and more. We write for children under the pen name Guy Incognito. Someday, we'll write a romance, and right now we have two collaborative projects with our erotica author friend Lexi Maxxwell. She writes the sexy parts, and our names aren't on those projects, but we do them because it's fun and awesome. That's the main reason we hop genres, actually: we love *reading* multiple genres, so we want to write in them all.

To be clear, the notion of writing in multiple genres isn't advice. Our company Realm & Sands publishes millions of words a year, and with that much production, we can support readers in multiple genres even if they don't cross. For less prolific writers, sticking to a single genre (and hence one growing fan base) may be — and probably is — far wiser.

Product Funnels

We'll go into this in tons of detail later, but the basic idea is that a product funnel has two primary components: an *introductory product* that is as readily available and consumable as possible, and an *upsell or next step* (ideally bundled at a discounted price).

All of our books are arranged in funnels with very few exceptions. Here's how they break down — again in brief, because we'll go into this extensively later:

For all series of books, our introductory product is the first book in the series. For serials, the intro is the first episode. For longer, single novels, we try to create what we call a "prelude," which is a relatively self-contained story that starts the larger work but can be pulled out to more or less stand on its own, probably with a small cliffhanger at the end. The intro needs to feel more or less complete for what it is, but should ideally leave the reader wanting more. We also have a few short stories that work well as additional intro products. This intro product is always free, and we put it in as many places as we possibly can. (Visit RealmAndSands.com/free to see all of our intro products.)

The intro product, because it's free and we're always trying to send people to it, *funnels* people into our world. Once they finish the intro product, we give them a link to the next book in the series … and, if possible (we usually *make* it possible), to a bundle that will save them money if they buy multiple items at once.

Quick example: *Unicorn Western 1* is free. At the end of that book, readers are presented with an option: They can buy *Unicorn Western 2* for $2.99, or they can buy the *Unicorn Western Full Saga* — which contains all nine *Unicorn Western* books — for $9.99, and save 60 percent.

The best funnels are those where the bundled upsell comprises the series in its entirety. If readers know that they can get the completed story arc in a single 60-percent-off purchase (the completed arc of a story *they know they already like because they just read the first book)* that offer has a strong psychological advantage over piecemeal book sales.

Call to Action

A call to action (often abbreviated as CTA) is a piece of text or a page that you put in the back of a book or story that drives your reader to take a specific action. Most CTAs end with links to somewhere the reader can take that action, either written out in the case of print or clickable for e-books. We usually have several in a given book, but your reader is decreasingly likely to take each subsequent action, so you must put them in order from the most to least important.

Our first CTA is usually for another purchase: either the next book or a bundle of multiple books. After that we'll have a call to join our e-mail list in order to get upcoming books free or at a discount. We often follow with a third CTA that contains either a list of our other books or (preferably) a link to a web page with that list (seeing as we can update the webpage easily but don't want to update all of our books' CTAs). Somewhere in there we usually try adding a request for the reader to leave a review for the book they've just read.

CTAs must be as compellingly worded as possible and contain a very clear reader benefit. Don't just say "join my email list." Give them a reason to do so. For us, people who join our list can get a book ($4.99 or less) for free on joining, hear about upcoming discounts, and get our free, e-mail-only serial story (*Caveman Timecop*). What satisfied Realm & Sands reader wouldn't want to join *that* list?

USP

USP stands for "unique selling proposition." There's a lot of possible verbiage we could add about USPs, but the bottom line is that a USP is what differentiates you from everyone else. How are you unique in a way that makes what you're selling more attractive to your target market? Your USP answers your customer's question, "In a sea of options that seem more or less the same, what compelling reason do I have to buy from *you?*"

What's To Come

This is a BIG book.

When Sean and I started *Write. Publish. Repeat.* back when it was only known as "untitled SPP Book," we assumed we could say what we needed to say in 50,000 words. Then, like a jerk, Sean gave me a huge outline, and the project expanded. Then, as I wrote and realized the project's complexity, it expanded again. At final reckoning, it ended up growing to well over twice its originally planned length.

We tried to get everything we could into these pages. We're going to spend the rest of *Write. Publish. Repeat.* telling you what we do, why we do it, and how a businesslike approach to writing and publishing can make a substantial difference in your writing life. You will not find a formula in this book. Too many writers are looking for an easy path to follow. We are not Google Maps and cannot tell you how to get wherever it is you want to go because every writer is different, and everyone starts at a slightly different place. Read this book and use what works for you. Discard the rest.

We will help you understand the current self-publishing landscape, and we'll cover the truths and myths about what it means to be an indie author now and in the foreseeable future. We're going to tell you how to create books (products) that your readers (buyers) will love, and will eagerly tell their friends all about. We'll show you how to look professional rather than amateurish. We'll explain the steps we use to write our books and write them fast — how to know your world, your characters, and your stories. We'll tell you how to assess your market and define your ideal reader. We'll cover the best tools for writing your draft, and the best practices for editing. We'll talk about covers, titles, formatting, and some of the other stuff that matters to readers — and probably matters to them more than you think. We'll discuss pricing and publishing on multiple platforms. We'll also tell you a little bit about getting your books into print and why it may or may not be a good idea.

A huge section of this book is devoted to marketing: the vehicle that drives your publishing business. We'll talk about gathering and nurturing your tribe (finding your ideal readers and communicating with them). We'll talk about product funnels, calls to action, how to use free books to gain new readers, how to get more reviews (and deal with the bad reviews you will inevitably get), and many smart ways to supercharge your marketing.

Finally, we'll help you to future-proof your writing career. As current as this book is at the time of publication (late 2013), 90 percent of our advice is evergreen and will remain valid for years and years after. The core principles in this book were true when sales was young, and they're not likely to change anytime soon.

Write great stuff, get that great stuff out into the world, connect with your readers, and then do that same thing over and over and over again.

In other words: *Write. Publish. Repeat.*

WRITE. PUBLISH. REPEAT.

PART TWO:
Understanding the Self-Publishing Landscape

CHAPTER FOUR:
The Good News and the Bad News

THERE'S NEVER BEEN A BETTER time to be an indie. Today, basic publishing is as simple as opening your software, crafting your manuscript, clicking through a few settings to compile an e-book, then uploading that e-book to the booksellers' easy-to-use dashboards. (Creating print books is a *bit* more complicated, but not a ton. You can do that, too, also without permission.)

Then, maybe 24 hours later, anyone looking will be able to find your book on those sites and buy it. Congratulations! You're a published author!

Anyone who's read the product description or back cover of this book (or who knows us from our podcast) is probably already waiting for the hammer to fall. You've likely figured that we're not about to bask in the sunshine of your awesome new career and tell you that the hard part is over, or that you'll soon be a bestselling author.

Instead, it's time for some good and bad news.

The Good News

Let's take a moment to delight in the good news, so we can frame this incredible journey before the ice water hits us. Because it really, truly *is* a fantastic time for writers. Sean is a wonderful, prolific writer who loves his craft, but he's said many times that he wouldn't have wanted to be a writer at any other time in history because it was too hard and that too much of a writer's success was based on luck. Dave probably would have slaved away forever, writing dark tales like the true artist he is, and starving to prove it.

I (Johnny) am somewhere between Sean and Dave. I *did* want to be a writer from an early age, and my mother has hilarious evidence to show the world if I cross her. But before the e-book revolution, my writing career went exactly nowhere. Getting published before 2008 or so was an often-humiliating nightmare. You had to schmooze at conferences or pick up this Yellow Pages-sized tome called *Writer's Market* to find the names and addresses (yes, physical addresses) of literary agents. You had to write those agents a letter in a very specific way, pitching yourself and your book. Usually you'd get a form letter in return that said something like, "This isn't what we're looking for" or "I wiped my butt with your stupid letter" or "Bark like a dog for me and maybe I'll reconsider." You'd add that rejection letter to your pile (nobody got away without accumulating a rejection pile), then you'd keep writing and try again.

Pitching an unsolicited novel in those ancient days had about as much chance of success as spitting from high orbit and hitting a shot glass, so you had to establish "credits" before agents would even pretend to listen. Typically, this meant publishing short stories in literary magazines: snooty periodicals that three independent bookstores in the country each carry a single copy of. The "best" literary magazines, though, usually didn't accept unsolicited short stories, and you had to have credits to get into them, so that meant moving down a rung and pitching your story to a mid-range magazine. They mostly didn't accept without credits either, so you pitched to magazines so unsuccessful that they would "pay" you with a free copy of the magazine. If you weren't accepted by those magazines, you might as well have stapled your story to a telephone pole and cited *that* as a credit. The upside of this option was that significantly more people would see your story than if it appeared in any magazine.

If you were very persistent and lucky — and if your writing aligned well with current publishing trends; nothing off-center, please — an agent might ask for a summary of your book and the first three chapters. This was your cue to send those documents off for prompt rejection.

If you got tired of running on the hamster wheel (query low-end magazines so you could query mid-range magazines that might pay as much as $5 so you could query higher-end magazines so you could query agents, who would then reject you), you *could* self-publish. But then wasn't the same as now. Being an indie wasn't cool in the early 2000s. You'd put your book up on a print-on-demand site like Xlibris, print a few copies, then start trying to pawn them off on your relatives. Before print-on-demand, the process was different: You'd spend a ton of money on large print runs then stack the boxes in your garage, where they'd stay until you moved out of your house or had a fire. At the beginning of your 20ᵗʰ century self-publishing venture (called "vanity publishing" for obvious reasons), you might also suffer a fit of optimism, at which point you'd head to the local bookstore to get laughed at by a small balding man.

I did that song and dance. I never ordered print books (though there were lots of predators willing to sell me that service), but I did accumulate a massive stack of rejection letters. Some of those rejection letters were from big-name agents, some were from small-time agents, and plenty were from graduate students who ran literary magazines, which basically meant they had access to a Xerox machine and a stapler. I queried for a few years after finishing my first book, *The Bialy Pimps*, in 1999, and got nowhere just like the rest of the writers I knew. And I *did* know a bunch of writers. None were hopeful, and none had had any real success. All pursued selling their work like a man in a pitch-black room stabbing randomly with a plug, hoping for that one in a billion chance he might end up shoving it into a socket.

Writing was once a desperate game. You did it out of love, because you sure as hell couldn't count on doing it for anything else. You might get lucky and have a rare breakout success, but it was far more likely that even if you got yourself an agent and managed to sell a book to a publisher, you'd probably never earn back your advance. Even if you *did* manage to earn additional royalties, you'd be selling print books — print books that were promoted by the publisher at the publisher's whim. The profit margin on print books is small even for the publisher. The best an author could expect is 15 percent of the hardcover price — the royalty for a highly-successful author of mainstream novels.

I've always been optimistic — and Sean is so optimistic it's like a disease — but both of us figured out relatively quickly that writing books wasn't a smart income plan for most people. If you were a speaker, you could sell books at your gigs. If you were a big name, you could move books. But for the everyday Joe or Jane? *Fuggetaboutit.*

But that's all changed. There's an element of luck to self-publishing in the e-book age, but the much, much larger factor that determines success and failure is *how hard you work and how smart you are about your marketing.* Do you see how amazing that is? Do you see how *liberating* that is? How well you write matters, of course, but back in "the old days," countless tons of fantastic writing never saw the light of day because the sheer amount of "noise" coming across agents' desks drowned it out. Back when your only option was to pitch to traditional publishers, you were also subject to big-game thinking — which basically means that even if a publisher loved your book and thought it might sell moderately well, he or she would pass, because in the volume business of traditional publishing, it's not enough to sell moderately well. They don't want to back anything that won't be a *large* success, and they still don't today.

But today, because self-publishers control every aspect of their careers, *they* can decide if a book is worth publishing. Will every book sell? No, of course not. My first novel finally went indie in 2012. A year later it was *maaaaaybe* selling five or ten copies per month. But it *sells*, whereas it wouldn't have ever had a chance under the old paradigm. Not all books will sell that poorly. All of us have titles that sell much better — like a few-hundred copies per month — and those books would never have survived under the old paradigm, either.

A traditional publisher would never want to touch a few-hundred-copies-per-month book, but you and I can build a full-time income on books like that, doing it over and over.

Tie your books together in intelligent ways, create smart marketing funnels that drive your readers from one book directly into the next, and take control of the connection between you and your readers, rather than abdicating that task to your publisher (who, by the way, would ignore it anyway). Maybe a given book will only make you $200 per month. But what if you had 10 such books and they all fed into each other? What if you had a 100?

Write. Publish. Repeat.

That's all you have to do. Done right — as described in this book — you'll start to see something very interesting:

Success comes from hard work and the accumulation of small numbers. Unlike yesterday, today's prosperity can bloom from continuous intelligent production. For the first time in history, life as a full-time writer has become about simple math.

The Bad News

Maybe you've already cued in on something.

On one level, the idea that your career comes down to simple math — that ten books will earn you more than two and that 100 books will earn you more than ten — is an encouraging thought. It means that repeated hard effort will almost certainly be rewarded. But on another level it's daunting. *It's 10 damned books. It's 100 damned books.*

So yes, the bad news — if you choose to see it that way — is that becoming a successful indie author is hard work. *Very* hard work.

We want to get that out there, up front, in as unambiguous language as possible: *You will have to work your ass off and endure many ups and downs if you want to make a full-time living from your writing.* There are too many people out there telling the world that there's never been a better time for writers, that indie authors can now barge past the old gatekeepers, compose their grand masterpiece, and make it a bestseller. All of that is true (kind of), but the chance that you're going to be the one in a million to hit a home run the first few times you step up to bat is — we're going to be honest — so slim it's practically see-through.

If you have a few books (or only one) and aren't planning to write more, you're as doomed today, during the e-book revolution, as you would have been during the query-and-hope days. In fact, if you're that few-book author, this time might be more cruel to you than the old days because the freedom of self-publishing might give you false hope, and a level of on-the-ground guerrilla competition you wouldn't have had to face before. You'll see success stories like Hugh Howey's, and think that what happened to him might happen to you. Hugh was working in a book store, scribbling in his free time, when his *Wool* novella suddenly exploded in popularity. As I write this, Hugh can count on making six figures a month at a minimum. Not bad, right?

But that's not how things work. When we had Hugh on the podcast, he said he worked for years in total obscurity, cranking out book after book and attracting no real attention. And when we asked about his blockbuster work, he told us that he thought nobody would ever like *Wool*. It was too dark, too bleak, too short ... you name it. But Hugh didn't write *Wool*, put it on the market, and hope. He could ignore it because he was writing his ass off, putting his attention in other books, novellas, and series. He put out a piece of work, set it aside, then got started on the next one. He watched his sales numbers, but wasn't invested, emotionally, in seeing any single title make him famous or rich.

In time, one did. *Wool* took off, seemingly out of the blue. Hugh said he didn't understand one iota why it happened, but *did* know what to do once it had. Because he's smart and "gets" the new age of self-publishing, he started writing sequels to capitalize on *Wool*'s initial popularity — the "I-want-to-know-what-happens-next" factor. He also kept working on his other books and series. When readers were done with *Wool*, they decided they liked Hugh and dug into his archives. And because he kept producing — and had produced all along, since well before *Wool* hit — he had plenty for those happy readers to buy.

What we love about the new world of writing and publishing — and what we'll say repeatedly throughout this book — is that it's a true workman's paradise. There is almost a direct line between "how hard you work (intelligently)" and "how much success you have." Talent is required, yes, as is some luck. But hard work and smart marketing will strap booster rockets to both. Film producer Samuel Goldwyn said, "The harder I work, the luckier I get," and that is absolutely how we all feel about luck, publishing, and life in general. For the most part, you need a spark at some point in your publishing career — a fortuitous discovery of your work, or a *Wool*-like surprise hit. But the more work you produce, the more likely that is to happen.

In other words, *you can outwork luck.*

If you don't like that idea — the notion of producing 10, 50, or a 100 quality and strategically arrayed books before you make more than soda money — then, hey, you can go ahead and hope for lightning. Or you can try to cheat and take shortcuts. Why not, right? Someone is reading this right now thinking, "Oh, hell, this book isn't telling me what I want to hear. I heard there was an e-book gold rush. I don't want to work that hard."

If that's you, stop reading right now. This isn't the book for you.

We'll say it again, this time bolded: **If you want to succeed in indie publishing, be prepared to work your ass off and demonstrate patience.** Writers who aren't willing to do those two things will fail. Period.

Now, with that out of the way, let's go ahead and discuss the quick-success mentality. Because hey, why would you deliberately back away from rapid growth? Among our trio, Dave is the most distrustful, skeptical by a factor of approximately 200,000,000. Sean and I are substantially more optimistic and would likely consider faster routes to success if they had merit. Problem is, they don't.

There are plenty of books and courses out there — some decidedly scammy and, in our opinions, predatory — that will "teach you" ways to hotwire the system. They'll say you can take one book, do some voodoo, and shoot that book to the top of the charts. Problem is that artificial momentum is always short term. If you have a book fly high because you bought a bunch of positive reviews, paid a service to buy bazillions of copies to boost your rankings, or anything else that isn't "a lot of people discovering and loving your book," it will come back to bite you. Not only are Amazon and other e-book retailers actively looking for things like that (Remember indie author John Locke, who took a huge hit in 2013 after admitting to buying reviews, hence setting off a witch hunt?), but even if it works and your book rises on its own, the chances of it continuing to sell are virtually nonexistent. The e-book space is so incredibly crowded today that rankings are seldom "sticky," meaning that a Top-100 book that isn't being sustained by a genuine, organic, ongoing flow of real readers will quickly fall. You might have seen a burst of sales, but now what?

There are other gold rush-type methods out there suggesting you take public domain material, slap a new cover on the front, and start selling that. Do this enough and you'll be making fat stacks of cash from stuff you didn't even have to write, the hucksters say. But that doesn't work either, because the e-book sites are smarter than that. Taken as a whole, Amazon, Kobo, Barnes & Noble, and other stores don't care nearly as much about you, the author, as they do about their customers. They want the best content in their stores, so they're constantly yanking the weeds.

You can't scam your way into long-term success, or hope for it to happen at random. The stories of indies who hit it big are either lightning strikes (which you can't count on) or the result of years of work (like Hugh Howey). Your only real option is to write good stuff, get it to market, then do it again. The simple truth is that it takes hard work to do that, but aren't you a writer? Don't you like writing? All three of us do what we do because we love it. And yes, we need to put food on our tables, but if we wanted a sure paycheck, there are much, much better and faster ways to do it.

The good *and* the bad news is that in the indie world, all of the control is in *your* hands. *You* are responsible for every molecule of your success. Decide now that you won't depend on luck, or blame a lack of it for what happens to you. Yes, we finally got rid of the gatekeepers ... but that also means we lost our ability to pass the buck.

If you're not succeeding, keep working. Keep producing. Do what we suggest in this book. Word by word, you'll get to where you want to be ... with no luck required.

Now, let's get a look around this brave new world that we all feel so unbelievably fortunate, as writers, to be able to explore.

The Discoverability Shift

BEYOND THE INDEPENDENT PUBLISHING ASPECT of modern book selling, there's another major difference between how things once were and the way they are today. Let's illustrate with the following scenario:

Imagine you enter a bookstore. You don't have any particular title in mind; you're simply browsing. You only know you want something to read. Something you'll enjoy. Beyond that, you're not really looking for anything specific. So you wander, and look at the books on the shelves. If you have a genre preference, you head to that section and start looking. Perhaps you're into horror, so you scan the horror books. Maybe you're a romance reader, so you thumb through romance titles.

You're getting closer to finding something to buy, but aren't there yet. You still don't know what you want, and the books in front of you are for the most part a sea of undifferentiated spines and covers. As you picture yourself in front of the shelves in this imaginary bookstore, think about something: How will you make your decision about which book you want to buy and read?

You're likely going to give the most attention to the books that are prominently displayed (on tables at the front of the store or featured on end caps). Beyond that, you'll look most closely at the books that have been placed on the shelf with their front covers showing. But what about those other books? Only a handful will be on display or cover-out, so what about all of those thousands of spines?

You're an intelligent reader, so you know there must be some good ones in there. But man, that's a *ton* of books. You have to pull each one out and look at the covers, then read the descriptions on the back or on the dust jacket. That takes forever, so you don't read *every* description in the store or even in that section. You're most likely to read the descriptions of the books with the most compelling covers, and you're most likely to pull a book out to *see* its cover if its name, visible on the spine, piques your interest.

Do you see the problem? If you're the author of a spine-out book that isn't featured in a front-of-shop display, your chances of being seen are barely there. You need an amazing title to get someone to even pull your book six inches forward and look at the cover, and a hell of a cover to get that same reader to spend a minute on the description. (Don't let anyone tell you that people don't judge a book by its cover. They *absolutely* do.) Even after someone likes your description, you still have another huge hurdle to leap: They must decide if they like your description (and cover, and title) *enough* to spend many hours with you. It's not enough for them to think, "This is interesting." You must hook a reader much, much harder than that.

I had this epiphany in a Barnes & Noble once. B&N stores are enormous. I was standing in the middle of the fiction area, looking for something to read, and I couldn't help but flip between my dual roles as writer and reader. As a reader, I didn't want to bother looking through all of those books. There were way too many, and I had no idea where to start. As a writer, I couldn't help but think that every one of those books had been written by someone like you and me — a person with a story to tell who sat behind a keyboard for hours and hours, pouring his or her soul into that work. Each book that I was too overwhelmed to bother looking at was someone's labor of love. That writer had written and polished and slaved and sacrificed, and I, as a reader, simply didn't care.

Feeling desperate yet? Well, don't. Hang in there. Because now that you have this picture of your book getting lost among a cloud of others, ask yourself what you, as a reader, would do next. If you were me that day in Barnes & Noble, what would you have done to make your decision?

I'll tell you what I did. I got onto a few online social networks and asked my friends for recommendations. But when none of their recommendations sounded quite right, I simply went and looked for books I hadn't read by writers I already knew I liked.

Read that last sentence again, because it's the way out of the hopelessness, and the key to your entire career as an independent author: *I looked for books by writers I already knew I liked.*

I ended up getting *Neverwhere* by Neil Gaiman. Neil isn't short on readers, but on that day, the author whose book I bought could just as easily have been independent author Ed Robertson, whose work I also happen to like. So, what's happened? My "mental book store" has shrunk significantly. Instead of being faced with a forest of undifferentiated books, now I'm really only looking at a much, much smaller subset that happens to include, among others, Ed and Neil.

This is pretty damned important. If means that if a reader already likes you, a bookstore's size is irrelevant. *The reader enters the bookstore looking specifically for you.* You don't have to be on an end cap, or the front table. You don't have to be cover-out on the shelf. The bookstore could hold 60,000,000 titles, and it wouldn't matter because your hard-earned reader is on your team. He'll cut through other books to find yours. He'll cull the stacks; he'll ask a clerk if he has to.

Your goal isn't to find ways to be prominently featured. That'll help your growth, but you can't count on it (especially if your track record hasn't yet earned it), and it's not your primary goal. When you release your first book, all you really need is to get a few people to love it. When you release your second book, you want to let the people who already loved your first book know it's available, because they'll want to buy it, and you want to get a few new people to like your work. Repeat, then repeat again after that.

The Barnes & Noble metaphor is there for a visual, but in reality few of us are (or will ever be) on the shelves of a brick-and-mortar store. We're mostly online, and online the problem I had that day in Barnes & Noble is *much* worse. A new book buyer on Amazon.com won't have a clue where to start, so she'll probably move into a book category and look at the bestsellers. Unless you're a bestseller, you won't have a shot. The only way to stand out is just as we've already said: Build your reader base one reader at a time, then make those people love you so that the next time they're on safari for a quality read, they're searching *with you already front and center in their minds.*

Obviously, this won't happen fast. But if you can tell good stories and tell them often, it's a *sure* thing. Building a loyal, Team You readership doesn't depend on luck or being in the right place at the right time. It doesn't depend on "who you know." It's stable, meaning that a change at one bookseller or another won't instantly destroy your business. Loyal readers buy again and again, and they tell their friends. They champion you. I asked my social networks for suggestions when I was looking for books. Your readers will be working for you when friends ask them for *their* recommendations. Your best strategy is to build fans, and you'll do that a few readers at a time. Your second book will sell better than your first, and your third will sell better than your second. It may take 10 books before you have a launch worth beans, but if you build fans intelligently, that simple accumulation is something you can count on.

I said a few paragraphs back that the sense of being overwhelmed in online bookstores is worse than that in a physical bookstore, and it is. But your discoverability, once you put in the time to earn a positive reputation, will actually be much *better* in online bookstores.

For your book to reach a reader, it must somehow show up — ideally, with some sort of a recommendation behind it rather than simply appearing. Before the proliferation of e-books and the subsequent explosion of online booksellers, there were really only a few very slow, very inefficient ways for that to happen. One of your readers could tell a friend about your book, and maybe hand him a copy. The other would be for a potential reader to see your book on a bookstore shelf, which we've already determined is a tough proposition — and even if that person *does* defy the odds to find your book in a store, he'll be looking at it cold, without any clue if it's any good.

Today, there are many, many more avenues for book discoverability. Even online, booksellers might put your book "on the front table" (Kobo has featured *The Beam* and *Unicorn Western* prominently several times, and Sean and Dave have been Amazon's Deal of the Day for *Yesterday's Gone*, *Z2134*, and *Monstrous*), but you can claw your way in front of readers even without an ounce of help. All of the major booksellers have recommendation engines that will suggest your book to readers. If enough people buy both my book and yours, the website will suggest your book to people who are looking at my book as something they might also like. You'll almost certainly end up in your own books' recommendations, meaning that your space opera might show up as a suggestion to people who bought your western.

Amazon.com currently has the most comprehensive recommendation engine, featuring many different Top 100 lists (bestsellers overall, bestsellers in a genre, best rated overall and in a genre, popularity lists) and will even send e-mails to customers suggesting new titles. Most sites will remember customers in some way, know their purchase history, and put appropriate books in front of them. Imagine you walk back into that Barnes & Noble, and the clerk hands you the best book you could possibly want at the time. That's what the online booksellers are trying to do.

In addition to recommendations and Top 100 lists, there are a bevy of social ways for people to discover your books that didn't used to exist. Social networks weren't around in any meaningful way when I first wrote *The Bialy Pimps*, but today there's Facebook, Twitter, Pinterest, and dozens of others. There's even what we would argue is the most important network for books: Goodreads. Goodreads, in case you don't know, is a social network devoted entirely to reading and sharing book reviews and book discussion. Readers on Goodreads will rate your book, write reviews, and curate lists of their own. If you wrote an excellent post-apocalyptic novel, someone might list it next to Stephen King's *The Stand*. So, what happens when someone finds that list? Well, to some degree they'll learn not only that your book exists, but also that at least one person thought it was worthy of being mentioned alongside *The Stand* — a book that reader may have loved.

Even the bookseller websites are social, meaning that ratings and rankings on those sites do a lot of your selling for you. Enter a physical bookstore and glance at a book, and you'll have no way of knowing if anyone read and liked it. That's a big deal; reading a book takes a long time, and most of us don't invest that time lightly. When you run across Sean and Dave's *Yesterday's Gone* series on Amazon, you can see 4.5 stars shaded, and you can be certain others found it worthy. You can look at its numerical rankings, read reviews, or skim the few quotes that Amazon has pulled and featured, like, "It was a great story, well written, great characters." Directly beneath that, Amazon says, "200 reviewers made a similar statement." Plenty of reviewers say they're going to buy the next book. That's a ton of social proof, and that helps to sell books.

So, while the risk of feeling overwhelmed today is greater, so are the ways your book might get discovered and recommended. At the beginning, you'll only have the "discovered" part of that equation, but that's OK. Impress a few people, you'll gain a few readers, and they'll want to buy your next book. You can build from there.

While you read through this book, keep in mind that it's your job, as an independent publisher, to become one of the go-to authors for your readers. Once upon a time, a writer's job was to write, while the publisher supposedly did the rest. Authors went on book tours, but only the most progressive authors actively engaged with their fans, built themselves a platform where they could speak to those fans, or groomed e-mail lists populated by their fans. For the most part, publicity, marketing, and reader relations were in the publisher's domain, and the publisher did virtually nothing for the vast majority of authors. That made authors helpless, and trained them into a dependency mindset. Perhaps your publisher would get you on that front table in a bookstore and people would find your book, but if they didn't — and if you became one of the millions of spine-out titles that were only given a few months on shelves before getting yanked as failures — there was nothing you could do, because you were destined to become lost in the sea of sameness.

Smart, marketing-savvy writers today can flip that around. Get your readers to head into their next book search already looking for what you might have, and it won't matter how many other people are out there publishing. You'll become a bookstore of one, where customers shop for only your titles.

CHAPTER FIVE:
The List of Truths

THINGS ARE BETTER FOR WRITERS today than they used to be ... but without a plan in place (which we'll show you how to develop; keep reading), they're arguably worse. Discoverability is easier, but because anyone can now publish, there's a lot more noise to get in the way of that discoverability.

(If we were more literary-minded, we might say, *It was the best of times. It was the worst of times.* But we're not. We write about unicorns, gunslingers who shoot pink smoke, and serial killers who make poetry out of profanity.)

But hey, don't let us overstate the negatives. They exist, but are dwarfed by the positives. Today, we can push a button and get worldwide distribution. We can design our own book covers if we possess some artistic talent, control our own marketing, distribution, and pricing from our home offices, and write as much or as little as we want. Indie publishing isn't for everyone, but for some, it's a match made in heaven.

You may or may not be a fit. Let's take a look at some of today's truths that will remain true for the foreseeable future, so you can decide for yourself.

TRUTH #1: Everything from pricing to customer loyalty to promotion is in a willing writer's hands, meaning that you are responsible for your own success.

That's both good news and bad news. If you're not selling well in the U.K., maybe it's because you haven't promoted enough in the U.K. Maybe it's because you should manually adjust your U.K. price rather than letting it adjust based on the U.S. dollar, because although $4.99 USD converts to £3.08 as of this writing, £2.99 is a better price psychologically, and hence might convert better despite the lost nine pence. Who knows? Your flagging U.K. sales could be due to anything. It's *your* job to figure it out.

If you publish traditionally, you won't control your price or your marketing, so you can safely pass the buck on this one. Whether that amounts to "delegating" or "giving up" depends on whether your publisher will 1) notice your flagging U.K. sales, 2) care, and 3) be willing to do anything about it.

If you're an independent publisher, you will have many, many, many more tasks. You have to do everything yourself (or, for some purely mechanical tasks, outsource them). More tasks mean more control, but they also mean … well … more tasks. So you must decide which you'd rather have: control (which, for people like us, means the ability to make things happen when and how we want them to) or a simpler work day.

TRUTH #2: Just when you think you have it all figured out, things will change.

Used to be, if you enrolled your book in Amazon's KDP Select program (trading Amazon 90 days of exclusivity for a five-day window to make your book free), all you had to do was flip the five-day switch and you'd sell a lot of books. Promote that free book in any way possible, then turn the book back to paid status so you could rake in the money flooding in from your new, higher sales rank. But in 2013, Amazon changed how free "sales" counted toward your post-free sales rank, and that particular tactic totally stopped working. Authors who didn't know how to pivot were screwed.

When Sean and Dave started writing serialized e-books, they wrote their faces off to maintain a weekly publishing schedule, and thereby form a habit with their readers. They released a project's six "episodes" over the course of six weeks, with each episode priced at 99 cents. When the "season" was over, they complied the episodes into a single collection and sold it for $5.99. Because the commission percentage on a 99-cent sale is half of that on a $5.99 sale (35 percent versus 70 percent) and they wanted to push the full season instead, they started writing the full season first and releasing the six episodes afterward, again in six sequential weeks. But then they realized they could get more traction if they had several titles ranking highly at once, so they went back to publishing the episodes first. That didn't work especially well, so most recently they've completely abandoned the weekly release schedule and now *only* sell their serialized projects as full-season packages. Each time they switched tactics, they did so for a specific reason based on self-publishing's ever-shifting realities.

We promise: Things will change again. Constantly. If the above back-and-forth feels disorienting, it was to all of us as their strategy evolved live, too. But the moral is not that Sean and Dave have figured out what works. It's that Sean and Dave have figured out what works best *for them, in their specific situation, right now.* You can never think you've "figured out the way" in indie publishing when it comes to individual tactics. What works for you today might not work tomorrow, and what works for me right now might not work for you at all. Staking your business on a handful of tactics that could change at any time (like the authors who banked on KDP Select's old algorithms) is a recipe for impending disaster.

TRUTH #3: It is always smarter to focus on strategies, not tactics.

If you read Truth #2 and felt yourself panicking ("How can I base my business on anything at all if it's always changing?"), don't worry. Because while it's a huge mistake to set your foundation atop specific tactics, the strategies that should underlie them never really change at all.

The KDP Select change punched many people in the gut. A somewhat related change that triggered widespread panic through the indie community was a rule change initiated by Amazon that severely impaired the ability of huge blogs to promote free e-books. Authors reliant on free downloads later translating into paid sales (see above) ran in circles screaming that the sky was falling. To make things worse, Amazon was, at the same time, changing their website to hide their Top 100 Free lists so that free books became much, much less visible to casual browsers.

So what, right? Well, at the time, Sean and I were cranking out a book a week in our new publishing company Realm & Sands. Our standard M.O. was to make our books free for the first three days so that our faithful readers could snap them up, leave reviews (to give us some solid social proof for later buyers' eyes), and seed those books in the customers-who-bought-this-also-bought-this lists of as many shoppers as possible. It also used to mean something to rank well in the free lists, and wait for a wonderful sort of critical mass: People who'd never heard of us would see the book at the top of a free list and download it. Abracadabra, brand-new readers.

That change decimating "free" as a promotional tool thoroughly sucked, but it wasn't devastating because we were only using free giveaways as one of our tools. It was a *tactic* — a specific useful thing in place at the current moment that we knew could help us. The underlying *strategy* (to get books into as many ideal readers' hands as possible in a way that rewarded our faithful regulars and maximized reviews) was unaffected by the change. We simply abandoned the tactic of making the book free for the first few days and asked how else we could implement the same strategy. We asked, "How can we reward our regulars, maximize reviews, and get those books into the right hands?" And the answer became our next tactic.

(In case you're wondering, our follow-up tactic was to price books at 99 cents for the first three days, and these days we tend to discount only to $2.99. Because most of our books as of right now are normally priced $4.99 and up, this was a good loyalty discount and had pretty much the same effect. But in the end, paid strategies worked even better than free promotion because only people willing to open their wallets bought the books. Free-seekers are different from even 99-cent purchasers, and this new tactic led to better reviews and better reader loyalty and engagement.)

You must have rock-solid underlying strategies, and *never stake your business on flash-in-the-pan strategies* — a recurring theme throughout *Write. Publish. Repeat.*

We first published this book at the very end of 2013, but if you're reading this in 2023, 90 percent of what you read here should still be applicable, because strategies are timeless ... whether you're selling ebooks in 2013 or door-to-door vacuums in 1955.

TRUTH #4: Print isn't doomed ... but its function in publishing will change.

My grandmother isn't going to pick up an e-reader or an iPad the next time she wants to read a book. My mother-in-law still gets an armload of books at the library every few weeks. We may be immersed in the world of self-publishing, and in that world, e-books are king, but it's not how everyone reads. That will change over time, but as things stand now, not everyone understands, likes, or is remotely interested in reading on a screen. A large proportion of readers out there still will only read on paper, at least for now.

But while that's true, you as a self-publisher may not really care. You *could* knock yourself out trying to reach those people with print only, but it's probably not worth it. According to the "80/20 Rule," this is firmly in the 20 percent.

You may be worried that you're missing a lot of readers if you ignore print, but consider it from both sides: not just the potential profit, but also what's required of you — both in time and money — to reach that profit. Designing digital book covers can be tricky, but designing print covers is trickier. You have to get your dimensions and resolution exactly right, and know how to correctly output the file. You must format the interior, getting page sizes and margins perfect. And that's if you do it yourself. You can spend a lot of money having someone else do it, and a ton of time trying to meet with bookstore and distributor representatives to get your finished books out there. You may have to buy books in advance, and be prepared to accept returns. And for what? So that, if you're successful in getting your print books out there, they can sit spine-out on a shelf and sell a copy or two per month?

Print, as a primary reading medium, is on its way out. Thinking of print sales as a significant income generator is likely a poor use of your time and is — at best — an attempt to grab a slice of a rapidly diminishing pie. My grandmother and mother-in-law may still read print books, but I seriously doubt my kids will — at least as their primary reading vehicle. Even if print still has a large presence today, that will change significantly over the coming years.

Are we saying that you shouldn't bother with print? Nope, not at all. You're probably reading this book as a digital file, but we offered it in print from day one. *Why?* Because while we feel that print isn't worth most writers' time as an income generator, it can be very worth it for other reasons. We'll go into these in more detail later, but a few are: to hand out as promotional pieces, to reward or satisfy your hardcore fans, to sell at in-person events, for reasons of pride (we both have a shelf lined with our print books), or to provide contrast that makes the e-book version look better, and therefore helps it to sell. Again, we'll go into this later, but briefly: If you have both a Createspace print version and an Amazon Kindle version of your book, the price of your Kindle book will show as a discount from the print book's price — a small sleight of hand that makes your e-book version seem comparatively inexpensive to buyers. It will also anchor your e-book with real page numbers (making it seem longer) and will make your book's buy page more complete (making you look more professional as an author.)

We do believe that one species of print book is doomed: the mass-market paperback. Mass-market paperbacks were created as a way for people to read your book while spending as little money as possible — something that e-books already do better.

TRUTH #5: There are more gatekeepers than ever!

This is where you find somewhere to prop up your book or reader, grab a handful of rotten tomatoes, and hurl them at the copy.

Haven't we been saying from the start that gatekeepers are a thing of the past? Wasn't that *why* we said we liked self-publishing so much — because we, and *only* we, decide what we publish, without asking for permission? It's even the *Self Publishing Podcast's* intro, read each week: "... the podcast that's all about how to get your words out into the world without contending with agents, publishers, or the other gatekeepers in traditional publishing." So, what the hell is this crap about there still being gatekeepers?

Let's clarify. If "gatekeepers" refers to people in positions of authority who have the power to keep your book out of print or e-ink, then correct, there aren't any gatekeepers in self-publishing. And that's awesome.

But if "gatekeepers" refers to people who have the power to dictate how well your book sells, whether it makes sense for you to write a sequel, and whether you get good reviews and solid word-of-mouth promotion, then guess what? There are a ton of them. They're called *readers*.

Some indies seem to think that the "self" in self-publishing makes them an island. *They* are in charge, and *they* can do whatever they want. If they want to put a flying shark on the cover of their historical romance, no one can stop them. If they want to never edit anything and put their computer vomit online in its rawest form, they can. If they want to ignore feedback, act rude, and price their short stories at $20, that's up to them and no one else. But while that all might be true, having an actual career (rather than a time-intensive hobby) requires *actually pleasing readers.*

Self-publishing isn't about writing and doing whatever you want; it's about having a direct pipeline to the people consuming your work. When we talk about "removing gatekeepers," we're talking about eliminating the people who presume to tell you what your readers want without letting you find out for yourself. Author J.A. Konrath has a story about his book *The List.* Joe already had a traditional publisher, to whom he presented *The List.* They said readers wouldn't want it. Joe thought he knew his readers better than they did, and felt certain they'd like it, so he self-published and proved it.

That's what we mean when we talk about getting rid of the gatekeepers, but don't forget that there are still plenty of people "keeping the gates." Please your readers — keep them engaged, respond to their needs, and effectively lead them from each book they finish to something else they might like — and you can build a fantastic indie career. Fail to do this, and you'll find yourself locked out in the cold.

TRUTH #6: Everything has changed ... except for what's important.

Time for the big picture.

Today, we can hit a button and directly reach our readers, without needing a middleman to help us. Today, we have the Internet's power at our disposal. It's a brave new world of publishing, defined by a connection between author and reader, creator and consumer. That's all amazing and fascinating, and we're both incredibly grateful to write at this time in history. (Seriously. The text messages Sean and I send back and forth are as obnoxious as teenage girls yammering about boys: "Can you believe this is our job?" "Life is so awesome!" Until Dave steps in and tells us we're idiots.)

Despite the giddy thrill of the indie revolution, the things that matter most are exactly the same. I used to teach Internet business courses, but stopped pretty quickly because I realized that people seemed to think that when you put "Internet" in front of "business," it magically changed business to something with fairies and pixie dust, and that you could therefore ignore sense while focusing on secret ninja tricks. I wanted to scream, "BUSINESS IS STILL BUSINESS NO MATTER WHERE YOU CONDUCT IT!" And similarly, we both sometimes find ourselves wanting to scream at starry-eyed writers who think that just because book-selling's gone digital, human psychology and the rules of sensible business have done a 180.

Indie authors are in the book-selling *business* … and business is business, no matter where you conduct it. There are still customers and sellers, even if the seller isn't a big bookstore and the customer is shopping on Kobo. Price, packaging, presentation, intelligent upsell offers, and customer service still follow the same guidelines as they always have. Whether we're talking about a traditionally published book or an e-book, a sale still tends to drive people to buy where they might otherwise not. For both e-books and print, an overpriced product still won't sell well, and an underpriced product will confuse customers and lead them to undervalue it.

In 1950, readers read books. In 2013, readers read books. Readers in both times enjoyed well-crafted stories with compelling characters. If a good book ended on a cliffhanger, both readers would want to know what happened next, and were therefore more likely to read the sequel. Both readers would enjoy a chance to get to know a bit about their favorite authors, and engage with them if they could. Both readers would feel appreciated if they got a shot at special deals or reduced pricing. Both readers would feel motivated to buy a box set of three books if the set cost less than the three books purchased individually.

As you read through the rest of this book, we urge you to continually return to these essential (and rather simple) truths. Whenever you hear about some change or another regarding the nitty-gritty details of the indie world (a new bookseller opens; a prominent social media vehicle closes down), ask yourself before being reactionary and shifting your current strategy: *Does this change how readers read or how business is done?*

Remember, tactics change. You can use the currently-available tactics that will best advance your underlying strategy, but you should always think long-term. Never forget that in the end, what matters most is that an author writes great stories to satisfy their readers, and that a businessperson sells quality products to please their customers.

The rest of this book is ultimately about the ways we've found to do those core things better.

CHAPTER SIX:
The List of Myths

NOW THAT WE'VE TALKED A bit about what's true, let's talk about what isn't. Because even if you've self-published something already, we've found that certain myths persist right up to the point where someone sees decent success. And if you're starting to think about self-publishing your first book, your head is likely filled with doubts and questions that are mostly variations on "Sure, I *can* self-publish ... but *should* I?"

The answer, in our humble opinion, is that there's little reason not to. There are advantages to traditional publishing in some situations (we're not purists and won't argue that no one — including newbies — should ever go with a publisher), but there's virtually no way in which self-publishing commits you to something with an inevitable downside. In other words, if the question is "I'm not sure if I should self-publish, so should I do it anyway?" our answer would probably be, "If you don't have another immediate option, then why the hell not?"

Let's look at some of the myths about self-publishing that might be fogging your head.

MYTH #1: If you self-publish, you can't publish traditionally.

We've gotten this question a few times on the podcast, and it usually looks something like this: "I've just finished my book, and figure I have two options: I'm trying to decide if I should self-publish or shop it around to literary agents. Why should I consider self-publishing instead of traditional?"

The root of this question is a fear that the writer has used up what's inside them — often *all* they feel is inside them, because the notion of writing a second book feels daunting — and that they therefore have exactly one shot and don't want to waste it. They see self-publishing versus traditional publishing as a binary decision wherein they can choose one or the other ... but not both. If they use their only chance to pursue self-publishing, they'll never see their book in a bookstore.

Even in 2013, as the first edition of this book is being written, self-publishing still has a distinct stink to it. That scent is fading fast, but it's still here. Traditional publishing is seen as "better" and self-publishing as "Well, at least you did something." Traditional publishing is often referred to as "real publishing," as if it's somehow more genuine or has more inherent value. We get it; if anyone can self-publish but not everyone can traditionally publish, the latter means you've passed another tier of approval. But does that matter? Maybe and maybe not.

The question about whether or not self-publishing or traditional is better for you is addressed many other places in this book, so we'll leave that alone for now and assume you really do *want* a Big Six publishing contract. If that's the case, is it a mistake to self-publish that masterpiece rather than banging on doors until you crack your way into an agent or publisher?

Well, yes and no. There is some truth to the idea that a publisher won't want a book that's already been published ... at all ... anywhere ... including by you. Publishers want fresh meat, so they can shape it how they'd like without worrying about your current readers who may have earlier versions. So if you have *Novel X* and you self-publish, it's possible a publisher won't later be interested in *Novel X* because it's already out there in the world. So, if *Novel X* is all you have in you, and your life won't be complete unless you see *Novel X* in a bookstore, and nothing less is acceptable, then maybe you'd better keep querying and networking and trying to get it to a publisher. If you're a total unknown, and *Novel X* is your first and only book, the odds are very, very heavily stacked against you, but if you want to keep at it, that's your business.

On the other hand, let's say you can write a second novel, called *Novel Y*. If you publish *Novel X* yourself, and if *Novel X* is a big self-published success, then publishers will be *much more interested* in looking at *Novel Y*. You'll be able to tell those publishers, "Look at *Novel X* ... I already have readers and fans who love me!" Publishers always want to know about your "platform," which means "your ability to promote the book without our help." Racking up a few self-publishing successes before pitching traditional publishing is like playing baseball in the minors: Publishers can look at your record and see you have the chops needed to sell in the majors.

But what about *Novel X*? If you self-publish, is it really "doomed" (quotes meant to convey sarcasm) to remain in the indie realm?

If there's one thing that's absolutely true about the rules and conventions surrounding self-publishing, it's that there are no firm rules and conventions yet. If you build your self-publishing career until you have enough cachet to make even old *Novel X* appealing to traditional publishers, is there any reason they might not sign it anyway? *Nope.* Not at all.

There's also a lesser version of this myth that you might have heard, the one that suggests you must choose one or another publishing option not just on a book-by-book basis, but *as an author.* This is not even close to true. We know many so-called hybrid authors who publish traditionally for some books and go indie for others. Sean and Dave have two books with Amazon's 47North imprint, which means that they're hybrid authors, too. Diversifying in this way can be wicked smart under certain circumstances.

MYTH #2: Self-publishing is what you do when you can't publish traditionally.

Without revealing details, Sean and I already more or less have a traditional publishing offer on the table for the coming year. If things go as we're fairly certain they will, it'll be a *really good* offer, too.

Despite this, the track records of the people involved, the likely income, and the fact that *I've wanted to see my book on store shelves since I was a teenager,* my first reaction when we discussed the whole thing was, "Meh, I don't know if it's worth it," same as Sean's.

Now, the offer is like a pre-pre-offer, and in no way certain. But if it goes, it would be the sort of thing most writers dream about. Problem is, self-publishing has ruined us. We like being in control of our work. We like knowing we can run sales without asking people, can cross-promote our books, alter calls to action in the backs, or tweak the cover. We like knowing that when our indie books gain serious traction, we'll get 70 percent of the gross. By contrast, when you have a traditional publishing contract, you usually see something like 15 percent. Sean and I believe so firmly in our ability to score long-term home runs in publishing that we're always looking a decade down the road. Even if we earned a massive advance for a traditional book, it's hard not to see the huge chunk of income we'll lose once that advance is earned back. The more books we retain total control over, the more we'll make in the end.

Taking a traditional deal at this point wouldn't be for the income from that one book. Instead, it would be a "portfolio piece," meaning we'd be able to claim a traditional publishing credit, see that book in stores, and have new connections with which to leverage our indie titles.

Tell us that self-publishing is the thing you do if you can't publish traditionally, and we'll vehemently argue. Dave and Sean already turned down a traditional deal this year, because they *preferred* to do it on their own. The fulfillment of yesterday's dream *today* might be a step down.

The choice between traditional and indie publishing is entirely dependent on you and your goals. If you remove the uncertainty inherent in both options, accepting a traditional publishing deal is like taking a salary job with a secure company. By contrast, self-publishing is like striking out on your own as an entrepreneur. It's no surprise that Sean and I — both entrepreneurial by nature and who think we can do better for ourselves than anyone else can ever do *for us* — always default to the latter, no matter what shiny offers might appear from the former.

MYTH #3: Publishers can do things for you that you can't do yourself.

Okay, there's technically some truth to this one, but there's only a little, and it's irrelevant for most authors.

If your name happens to be Stephen King (and if it is, HEY STEVE, WE'D LOVE TO HAVE YOU ON THE SHOW!), then you can get a significant push from the marketing arm of a large publisher. They'll push the living crap out of your book, Steve. You (Steve) couldn't make all the connections the publisher can make, couldn't get your book into all the nooks and crannies that they can, couldn't take out all the advertising they could. On your own, Steve, you probably couldn't cover the front table at major booksellers and coordinate pre-sales that send you to the top of the charts before the book even comes out. And what about all those foreign sales, Steve? Are you really going to handle all that distribution yourself?

Okay, so that's for Stephen King. If you're not Stephen King, keep reading.

Big publishers are built for scale. They can, in essence, take large things and make them larger. They can handle those 20-percent tasks and do them for you, because when your name is big enough, even 20 percent is too big to ignore. But the average writer will get a marketing budget commensurate with what they expect your books to sell. That means virtually nothing for most of us. There's a certain "chicken versus egg" loop at play. Authors think it's a publisher's job to earn them money, but publishers don't see it that way. In their eyes, you and your book are assets at best and liabilities at worst. You're a stock in their portfolio; you'll either perform, or you won't. They won't market the crap out of you to ensure your success. It's more accurate to say that they will market the crap out of you *if you become successful.*

Book publishers can get your book into big brick and mortar stores. That's true. But unless they expect your book to sell quite well, the publisher won't pay the extra money to get you prominently featured in that store: face-out on the shelf, displayed in the end caps, laid out on the front tables. That positioning isn't earned by merit. With the exception of something like staff picks, a bookstore isn't going to think your book is awesome and set it up front. Chances are, for most authors, you'll be another anonymous spine on the shelf, begging for attention. Your book will then have a few weeks or months to prove itself, and if it doesn't, the bookstore will declare it a failure, pull it from the shelf, and return it to the publisher.

What about publishers helping you reach more readers? Our friend CJ Lyons, a hybrid author with successful books on both sides of the traditional/indie fence, tells a story about meeting with one of her New York publishers. When CJ proposed some unconventional marketing based on her readership's unique characteristics, the rep told her that the publisher didn't know who bought her books. CJ, who possesses a business savvy that few writers do, presented customer demographics she'd mined on her own and said, "Well, I do ... here they are."

The publisher was flabbergasted. When CJ told us this story, my exact words were, "But that's what a publisher is *supposed* to do for you! If they're not doing that, what *are* they doing?" But see, publishers don't actually know what readers want. They know what *distributors* want. Joe and Jane Smith? No clue. Barnes & Noble? Wal-Mart? Publishers know what *those* guys want. Welcome back, gatekeepers.

For most authors, publishers will handle editing, covers, and book packaging. They'll get your book into stores. From publicity to promotion, the rest is up to you.

If that's the case — and if neither Sean's name nor mine is Stephen King — you might wonder why we'd consider traditional publishing at all. It's simple: We both understand exactly what we'd be getting and what we'd be losing. Following that knowledge, we have decided that the former carries a significant enough benefit to outweigh the latter. We wouldn't make our decision based on a single deal. We'd be making it while considering our portfolio as a whole. In other words, it's true that traditional publishers can get us exposure we can't get ourselves — and while that exposure probably wouldn't matter all that much for a single book, we know it'll raise the profile of our entire indie catalogue. We understand that we'll have to do our own promotion. That's fine; we do it anyway.

To put it another way, the question isn't, "Is this a good deal for Project X?" It's, "Is this a good deal for our publishing company, Realm & Sands? Is this a good deal, taken as a whole, for Johnny B. Truant and Sean Platt?"

Yes, technically, traditional publishers can do a few things that indies can't ... but for most writers, those things are irrelevant, especially compared to the loss of control. You can't make assumptions. Sean and Dave found themselves somewhat handicapped by their traditional deal, severed from their usual strategies, and unable to pivot when needed. What they didn't know when they made their deal that they do now: Sean and Dave were better at pleasing their readers than their publisher. This affects everything — not just the number of books sold and the profit per download, but how readers feel about their experience. This influences the quality of your reviews, and how likely those readers are to buy whatever else you have to sell (your traditional publisher will *never* care about leading readers to your other indie titles).

Always weigh all sides of any deal. Know what you're getting *and* what you're giving up.

MYTH #4: Self-publishing is for artists who want to give their art the chance to succeed in a true meritocracy.

Do you think of yourself as an artist? Awesome. Us, too. But if you want to be an artist and *only* an artist, you might want to stick with traditional. To be a successful self-publisher, you must be a businessperson as much as — or maybe more than — an artist.

Further on in this book, you're going to read about marketing programs, product funnels, buyer psychology and psychological triggers, pricing strategy, calls to action, e-mail list management, and a thousand other things that usually want to make Dave (a purer artist than Sean or I) barf all over his keyboard. If you're like Dave, prepare yourself. This is *business*, baby. Pure artists who refuse to sully their hands with business will get trampled like Mufasa under the stampeding gazelles. Guaranteed. If you're a pure creator with no business sense or strategy whatsoever who's made a good living from book income, we'll refund what you paid for this book.

We run into plenty of "pure artist" types in this business, and we love them. Pure artists are awesome. My dad is a pure artist. He literally paints all day. Sean's sister is a pure artist. She's a florist who designs gorgeous weddings using flowers that are too pretty for much of a profit, and an artisan who makes greeting cards by hand that are impossible to scale. But the problem with pure artists, when they enter the realm of self-publishing, is that they seem to feel that the merit of their work should cause it to

93

rise to the top as obviously better than the competition, and that pretty much never happens.

Our friend Lexi Maxxwell, who writes erotica, is hilarious on this point. Lexi's stories aren't just sex tales; they really are amazing stories that just happen to have a lot of fluids exchanged. Sean and I co-write a series with her (uncredited, because erotica has a stupid stigma that we can't tie to Realm & Sands) called *The Future of Sex*, based in the world we created in our sci-fi serial *The Beam*. It's super-intelligent stuff, and yet Lexi is always battling the most ridiculous, poorly written titles for the erotica chart's top spots. She seems to think that the charts should be a meritocracy where the best stuff rises to the top, but that's not how it works. To reach the zenith, you have to do all the right business stuff. You must build your base of true fans, and market to them in all the right ways. You have to create product funnels and write smart calls to action and place them intelligently at the back of your books. Lexi's getting there, but for now, her deeply moving coming-of-age drama *Divorced* keeps falling behind *Butt-Banged by the Hot and Sweaty Gardener Who Looks Like Brad Pitt.*

MYTH #5: Self-promotion and marketing are dirty.

You read the section at the front of this book about our evil ulterior motive, and yet you're still here. Now that you've read 20 or so percent of this book and likely even skimmed ahead, do you hate us, think us unhelpful, see this book as unworthy of your time, or feel that we're scammers simply because we've admitted that one of this book's purposes is to help advance our overall profile as writers? No? Well, what the hell is wrong with you?

Nothing is wrong with you. And dammit, nothing is wrong with *us*. Nothing is wrong with promoting your work, being proud of the stories you tell or the information you articulate, telling people about your work, or encouraging people who already like your work to get more. This book isn't an advertising brochure. It's the most helpful guide we could possibly write, and we hope it has the side benefit of making our other books sell better. If you find yourself resisting the idea of "selling" — which, rest assured, is an absolutely essential talent for an indie author to master — you need to get over it.

Much of the resistance to selling and marketing that people naturally have is the fault of used car salesmen, timeshare companies, and multi-level marketers — fields based on the hard sell. Nothing matters more than nabbing the buyer, and if you must deceive and bully your prospects to get that sale, so be it. *Coffee is for closers,* they say. So close, at all costs.

But life, for most marketers and sellers, isn't *Glengarry Glen Ross.* The world's used car salesmen and high-pressure realtors have left a bad taste in our mouths, because no one likes being *sold to,* but that's not what we're talking about. Being sold to, for most people, is something that happens almost against your will. Like an assault. When you're sold to, the salesman might as well be putting a knife to your throat. But haven't you ever bought anything outside of a high-pressure situation? Have you ever seen something in a store or seen an advertisement, thought you might like that thing, then bought it? That's selling. That's marketing. The seller set the object or service in front of you and accentuated the positives so that you could agree to buy it. Transaction done, and no one had to get knifed.

Have you ever gone to see the sequel of a movie you liked, or ordered dessert when the waiter offered it after your meal? Have you ever Super-Sized your Value Meal? Those are all examples of an upsell — another "dirty" marketing word. Yet you probably don't regret any of those transactions. You might, in fact, have *appreciated the chance to get more of what you already knew you liked, often at a preferred price.* Shocking!

We could beat this to death, but you get the point. In valid, non-sleazy salesmanship and marketing — which is the kind we practice and the kind you're going to learn a bit later — everyone wins. Do you really feel that you "lost" and that the seller "won" whenever you buy something? Do you really feel that duped? No? So, why be hesitant when you're in the seller's position?

In an ethical sales transaction, the buyer and seller should be equally pleased. Each party should feel like thanking the other. Ethical marketing is nothing more than letting people who might like your product know it exists — and, ideally, giving them some sort of deal that makes the offer better for the potential buyer.

If you ever find yourself resisting sales and marketing, read the previous paragraph a few times until you believe it, because it's true. If you refuse to believe it is — if some deep part of your brain continues to insist that all sales and marketing are about manipulation and winning at someone else's expense — then you'll never succeed as an indie author.

MYTH #6: Readers care if a book is self-published.

We hear versions of this myth all the time. We contend that the vast majority of readers never have a clue that a book is self-published unless an author's lack of professionalism makes it obvious. Even if we're wrong, it doesn't matter. Maybe they do *know*, and don't *care*.

There are exceptions, of course, but you don't want those readers anyway. People who would turn a book down solely on the basis of its pedigree and nothing else are like people who would treat a person differently because of the color of her skin. You can't please those people. One of our core tenets (and we'll detail this later) is that you should always cultivate your tribe and not worry at all about those who don't jibe with your style. This is simply one more example.

By and large, people understand that a story is a story. Big-name authors have an advantage over us, of course, because they're proven. But poke around online and you'll find plenty of lesser-known, traditionally published authors who are being lapped (in terms of sales, reader engagement, glowing reviews, etc.) by indies like us. Hook a reader with a good story, and the issue disappears. The great majority of readers care about *authors*, not publishers.

MYTH #7: Self-publishing is a lottery, and you can (or have to) get lucky.

This is one-book thinking.

If you're thinking self-publishing is a lottery (either one you hope to win or one you hesitate to enter because winning seems impossible), please do yourself a favor and look at the title of the book. We called this *Write. Publish. Repeat* for a reason. You must write, publish, then do it all over again.

There are success stories out there like *50 Shades of Gray*, where an author had exactly one title, and that book blew up big time, but those *are* lottery scenarios and in no way typical. E.L. James scrambled to write the rest of the *50 Shades* trilogy after she started making the equivalent of a small nation's GNP each month, but even today every book in her catalog starts with *50 Shades*. E.L. James *did* hit the self-publishing lottery, and never has to write another book if she doesn't want to. But don't let her story discourage you because it seems so unlikely. Don't let her story encourage you, *either*, because you're hoping for the same.

To the gamblers: You're not going to have that one-in-a-million hit, so stop hoping for it and keep writing.

To the skeptics: You don't *need* to have that one-in-a-million hit … because you can keep writing.

In case we haven't made this abundantly clear, *we do not believe in lightning-strike thinking*. You'll read nothing in this book to suggest or imply that you must hit it big to find success as an indie. A surprising hit would be great, and surely boost your catalog. Sean and I have raised a dozen funnels to market, with around 40 individual titles. If one of our titles hits BIG, *everything* sells at least a little more. But the magic is that we don't *need* a big hit. The approach we believe in, use ourselves, advocate, and evangelize is workmanlike. Get one book that makes $200 per month, then create another 20 or 30 like it over time. Two hundred dollars per month is in no way a big hit, but it's good. And achievable. It certainly isn't the lottery.

Any good, persistent, business-minded, prolific writer can succeed if they keep writing and moving forward. For the modern author, that's excellent news.

PART THREE:
Preparing Your Books and Making Readers Love You

CHAPTER SEVEN:
How to Avoid Looking Like an Amateur

REMEMBER HOW WE SAID THAT readers don't care if a book is self-published, and that most readers don't so much as *know* that a book is self-published most of the time?

That's only partially true. Or rather, it's *conditionally* true. Readers (those gatekeepers we said were still around, there to determine if you succeed or fail) don't care or know that a book is self-published ... *if* its lack of a "proper" pedigree isn't leaping from the screen and punching them. Many self-published books *do* look like total crap, and readers don't like books that look like crap — indie or not. It's the "looking like crap" they don't like, and one thing traditional publishing seldom gets wrong is appearance. I've seen some traditionally published books with covers I hate, but those have definitely always been a case of "I hate that cover" rather than "Holy crap, they clearly had a hobo draw that cover with a crayon." Traditional books aren't immune to horrible covers, but are more or less immune to *unprofessional* covers. The same goes for shoddy product descriptions, poor editing, and other hallmarks of rank amateurs.

From top to bottom, with few exceptions, everything about traditionally published titles will *look* professional. Indie titles, on the other hand, *don't* always look professional. Thanks to this, lines are now blurred. Too many self-published authors aren't as professional as they should be, and that makes some people use "unprofessional" and "self-published" as synonyms.

Other things that "self-published" means to people who've seen some seriously crappy, unprofessional work from the indie community: anemically edited, poorly presented, badly formatted, full of typos, meandering, uninteresting, and full of flat characters. You know ... things that any self-respecting author, independent or not, should do everything to avoid.

Before we get to the rest of this section, you'll want to keep two things in mind:

First, if you do everything you can to put your best face forward to potential readers, your books will become more or less indistinguishable from those with a Big Six pedigree. This is what we meant by readers not knowing you're self-published. Unless you scroll down to look at the imprint name in a book's listing, how could you possibly tell them apart?

And second, if you *don't* do everything you can to look professional, readers will run screaming from your book with cries of "Self-published books are crap!" no matter how wonderful the story may be.

We don't want that. You don't want it for your book, we don't want it for you, and we as a community of indies don't want poorly presented books out there making the rest of us look bad. But there's good news: It's not a hard problem to solve. All you have to do is to pay attention and have as much pride in your presentation as you put into your story.

Giving your readers the best possible first impression is essential. If you look professional, readers will go into your book anticipating a professional reading experience. They will be mentally pre-programmed to expect the very best from you, and will therefore be more likely to overlook little things that might otherwise have bothered them.

If, on the other hand, readers buy your book in spite of it looking completely amateurish, they will go into it anticipating a shoddy, half-assed reading experience. *These* jaded readers will be mentally pre-programmed to expect the *worst* from you, because who else but a total slob would post a terrible cover, fail to capitalize and punctuate properly in their sales page synopsis, and price at less than a dollar with no clear and obvious reason (like a limited time sale) for doing so? "Real" books and "real" publishers would never do that, so you *must* be a hack. As they read your book, their minds will be on the lookout for every little error. They'll be overly critical of your characters and plot twists from page one, and much more likely to leave a poor review — having subconsciously decided *before they even opened the book* that they didn't like you or your writing.

Hopefully we've convinced you that creating a professional appearance is much, much more important than something you do "by the way" once the hard work of writing is finished.

What follows is a brief list of the best ways we know to avoiding looking like an amateur, therefore giving your book the best chance of impressing the people who crack it open.

The following section touches on a few things you can do to avoid looking like an amateur. All are elaborated on later, but all are also essential enough to your success that they deserve mention here.

WAY TO AVOID LOOKING LIKE AN AMATEUR #1: Have a Professional-Looking Cover.

Here's some news that will raise the hackles of many a serious *artiste*: People *do* judge books by their covers. You may not want to hear that, but it's true. You may have the most awesome story ever told, and it might deserve to kick Hemingway and Steinbeck in the nuts and run off with their girlfriends, but nobody will ever read it if you have a terrible cover.

We as a species are hard-wired to avoid overstimulation. The human mind is always looking for ways to eliminate stimuli and pay less attention. You might think that the purpose of the brain is to help you focus, but what it does even better is the *opposite* of focusing: ignoring everything it possibly can, then reluctantly paying attention to whatever remains.

When a human brain finds an excuse to dismiss something, it gets excited and does a little brain dance. Think of your potential reader's brain as having a to-do list, but instead of having tasks on that list, it has things in the world it's supposed to devote brainpower to. Readers' brains, like the rest of us, love to cross things off their to-do lists, and a crappy cover lets them cross *you* off. *The book beneath that crappy cover has to suck,* your potential reader's brain says. *Let's move on. There's no reason to investigate this one further.*

And hey, that's just a normally wired brain. Once you add the overstimulation of modern society, cell phones, and the Internet, the urge to pass your book rather than taking the time to consider it only grows stronger. That's why a good (or at least a professional) cover is essential: to make sure your potential readers' brains don't have an excuse to dismiss you out of hand. And if you *really* nail it, your cover can be an outright attractor. It won't just skip over the mental dump pile; it'll actually stand out in that reader's mind and demand their attention.

WAY TO AVOID LOOKING LIKE AN AMATEUR #2: Edit Meticulously.

There's a state we call "flow" that you want your readers to experience when consuming your work. Flow is a Zen-like state where the reader is reading … but almost unaware that they're doing so. Instead of seeing words, they're seeing your characters and what they're up to. They're feeling excited, or nervous, or sad, or happy, as if they were there. I once almost closed a book and decided not to read further after being freaked out by the intro (*House of Leaves*) and felt my spirit sink when I realized a disturbing truth (*Catch-22*). That's flow. Your story stops being words for your reader and becomes a world instead.

The worst thing you can do is to kick a reader out of flow by reminding them about the words they're reading. There are many ways to do this (an unintended WTF moment is never good), but the most obvious — and easiest to address — have to do with the words themselves. If you use an incorrect word, that will stop a reader. If you omit or misspell a word, that'll do it, too. If you have a sentence that's too long and convoluted to make sense, the reader will be forced to back up and untangle its meaning. You may correctly argue that the reader will be able to figure it out, but that's not the point. You don't want readers to work for answers, unless they're big-picture mysteries in the larger plot. Pauses shatter flow.

No matter how good you think you are at spotting typos, confusing sentences, unclear story lines, and other things that may break reader flow, you simply won't be able to see them all. Looking at the big picture, your reader may not understand certain things about the story as you understand it, and hence you may not have thought to fully articulate their thoughts. Looking at the micro level, you're going to miss typos because your brain, which is familiar with how the text *should* read, will fill in what's missing or incorrect.

Your reader won't miss them, though, and if you have too many, your work will look sloppy at best, and disrespectful to the reader at worst.

WAY TO AVOID LOOKING LIKE AN AMATEUR #3: Double-Check Everything.

I'm amazed at how many times people will output their manuscript, plop it online, and never really look through it fully and hence miss something stupid obvious.

I've seen manuscripts where the title will appear twice in a chapter: CHAPTER ONE / CHAPTER ONE: THE QUICKENING. I've seen manuscripts with the wrong cover image, incorrect pages, or links in the back that don't work or that go to the wrong place.

Having compiled hundreds of e-books, we understand why this happens. If you produce a lot of content (as we suggest) and distribute it across many platforms, then you'll have many permutations. There's book #3 for Amazon with the Amazon CTAs in .mobi format that you compile from the "books 1-3" bundle file, then the Smashwords version of book #2 in .epub format with the *has-to-be-exactly-this-way* Smashwords version of the copyright page that you compile from the same file. Each file has different covers, different pages in the front and back, and so on. There's a lot to get right ... or wrong.

But *that is exactly why you must double check everything*. This isn't a remotely difficult step, but it's annoying and tedious. It can take forever if you keep screwing up small things, but would you rather get them wrong? Because I'll tell you ... if someone is reading *The Beam* Episode 3 and the CTA asks them how they enjoyed *The Beam*'s Complete First Season and there's a request to review Episode 1, that looks bad. Like we're either stupid or don't care about our readers.

Before publishing *any* file, you should open it using a suitable reader and leaf through everything leading up to the story, a few pages of the story itself, and everything after the story. Check the cover image, the table of contents (to ensure that you actually did include the entire story; if you fail on that one you're going to look like a jerk). Click on your links and make sure they go where they should. Or, for print books, *remove* all links and replace them with text equivalents. I've seen plenty of print books with back-matter CTAs that say, "To see all of my books, click here" but don't then write out the link. No matter how many times I press my finger to the pages of those print books, for some reason I'm never taken to a website.

I've found that the easiest way to do this step is to store (and output) your project files in a cloud storage space like Dropbox, then install several reader programs and Dropbox (or whatever) on a mobile device like a tablet. You can navigate to each of the book files in Dropbox, choose to open them in the appropriate program (the Kindle reader for Kindle files, something like the Kobo, Nook, or iBooks app for all .epub versions), then go through them that way. Or for print books, carefully go through the proof.

Don't skip this step, or phone it in. Pay attention, look for and/or click on everything. It's easy to screw up, and you'll look like an amateur if you do.

CHAPTER EIGHT:
Creating Professional Products Part 1: Pre-Production

WRITING IS AN ART, AND publishing a business.

We've said that a few times already, and we'll keep on saying it because it's a core principle understood by successful indies, and the source from which just about everything else naturally flows. You can be a pure artist ("just a writer") if you publish traditionally, but you'll never make it that way as an indie author unless you're partnered with some smart, business-minded people.

Your writing should start out as pure, inspired play. Stories should excite and compel you (if they don't, how do you expect them to compel your readers?), and in our opinion you should always obey the story and go where it wants to go. We don't bring business into our creation process at all. As you'll see later, we believe in listening to the story and our muses so strongly that we're publishing heretics who refuse to stick to a single genre. But once the creative part is behind us, we *always* put on our business hats. At that point, our art is our product, and that's how we treat it. You have to remember that readers are customers, and part of your business as an indie author is reader acquisition. If that sounds cold, you can give it another name. We prefer precision.

The next four chapters are about our process for creating the very best, most professional reading experiences we know how to create. As you read, keep in mind what we said earlier: When you're an independent publisher, there are no gatekeepers between you and readers, but all that means is that your *readers* have now occupied the gatekeeper position. You no longer have to impress agents and publishers with query letters and pitches, but now you must impress *readers* enough to keep them buying and talking about you.

To do that, the only real tools you have at your disposal are your books (products) themselves.

Knowing Your Market

This bears repetition: *You can't please everyone.*

That's OK. Ideal, actually. You don't want to be a writer who's mildly appealing to a lot of people. It's better to be a writer who is absolutely *loved* by a smaller number. Remember the idea of 1,000 true fans? If you have 1,000 people who truly love you, you'll have an extraordinary career. Those 1,000 people will buy everything you produce, push your books up the charts, tell their friends, buy print versions of your books *even after paying for the e-book versions,* will collect merchandise if you create it, and so on. They will become your biggest evangelists.

The *best* way to create those true fans: Turn your back on a certain section of the market who will never fit that criteria.

That might be a shocking way to put it, but the less shocking and equally accurate way to say it is that in order to appeal strongly to your best readers, you must be and remain authentic. This is hard, because it means that you must stand firm even when people disagree with you.

For instance, when Sean and I decided to publish *The Beam* (a dead-serious political sci-fi serial) immediately following *Unicorn Western* (a deep but paradoxically light-hearted epic fantasy/western mash-up), people told us how stupid we were for moving away from what our readers already liked and knew us for. Then, apparently intent on making our critics' arguments louder, we followed *The Beam* with an even more diverse array of "pilot" products: a horror series called *Cursed*, a philosophical "meaning of life" serial called *Robot Proletariat*, an extraordinarily violent revenge thriller called *Namaste*, and three "sitcoms" that were all filled with unbelievably stupid, immature humor: *Greens*, *Space Shuttle*, and *Everybody Gets Divorced*. Sean already had a ton of horror under his belt through his Collective Inkwell work with Dave, and I had done horror, humor, and coming-of-age drama on my own.

When we first described our scattershot product catalog, it led to one of the biggest debates our podcast has seen, with tons of listeners weighing in. Most said we were idiots, that we should stick to a single genre so as not to confuse readers. They said we'd lose readers if we did what we were planning to do. But our reply was that no matter *what* we did, we'd lose readers. All we were doing by standing firm was choosing to be authentic to our multiple-interest selves, thus attracting readers who "got" what type of art we were most interested in making, and shedding those who insisted that a writer stick to a single genre like the dead skin they would be. What our naysayers failed to see was that if we'd listened to them and stayed in one genre, we'd have attracted single-genre readers and lost those who preferred variety. Worse, we would have been stuck there. We wanted to be known as storytellers, not authors of a particular genre.

Both scenarios would result in gaining some readers and losing others. The difference was that the latter (single-genre) option would have left us frustrated and denying our most authentic passions and interests.

Are we saying you should write in multiple genres? Nope, not at all. Dave only writes horror, dark fantasy, and sci-fi — basically, fiction to slit your wrists and crap your pants to. That's great for Dave, and it's authentic to his passions and interests. Sean and I are like monkeys, unable to stay in one tree. Moving around is authentic to our passions and interests.

The more authentic you are — and the more vehemently you hold to that authenticity — the more true fans you will eventually accumulate. We know we're turning some people off. But we're really *turning on the right people for us.*

You'll get a halo of readers outside your true fans, of course, but making a conscious decision about who you're writing for is really important. In fiction, it's about voice, attitude, and themes. It's about fearlessness and honesty. In nonfiction, it can be some of those same things, but it can also be more quantifiable and objective. For instance, this book is for self-published authors. A how-to book on sales would be for salespeople. Obvious, right?

But regardless of whether you're writing fiction or nonfiction, we'd urge you to go beyond the obvious. Be specific about your target market. Drill down as far as you possibly can. Try to imagine your ideal reader — a concept that we're shamelessly stealing from Stephen King in *On Writing*. There's one person you're writing for, and that person represents your perfect reader. You'll capture readers who don't fit your ideal archetype, but writing with them in mind will help you to focus. Your ideal reader will help you make the decisions you need to make when writing. When I wrote the essay "The Universe Doesn't Give a Flying Fuck About You," my ideal reader didn't mind 1) swearing, 2) the writer getting in his face, and 3) harsh realities that most people don't want to think about (such as the fact that we're all going to die, and time is running out). So, when I asked myself if I could or should say something in that essay, I just thought of my ideal reader. Would *he* be cool with it? If yes, then I did it. If not, I didn't. I never considered what everyone would think … just that one imaginary guy.

Back to the nonfiction example of this book. It's for writers who want to self-publish, yes. But there's more to our ideal reader than that. Take a look back at the section toward the beginning, where we detailed exactly who this book is and isn't for. You'll notice that we clearly detail who will benefit most, and actively discourage certain other types of people from reading. That section is part of our ideal reader's résumé. But there's more to it. This book is written in a certain style, and decisions about that style were made based on our ideal reader. Would our reader mind the familiar, first-person way this book is written? Would he or she mind if we included Lexi Maxxwell, who writes erotica and has some rather saucy titles? Would our ideal reader mind if we asked rhetorical questions like this one?

One more thing that may seem trivial but isn't at all: We're shameless about mentioning our own books as we explain our businesses. That matters. We want the type of reader who doesn't mind us doing that, because a reader who has a problem with it 1) thinks promotion is somehow wrong and 2) thinks it would be better for us to make things up than speak from our experience. Think about that for a minute. If you're a reader who would rather we make things up so as not to "dirty" our book by mentioning our in-house titles — if you want vague examples rather than the tangible experience that got us where we are — then you're probably not suited to successful self-publishing.

Put all of that together, and you'll start to get a clear picture of the kind of writer and person we wrote this book for. We'll get a lot of people who aren't 100 percent in the sweet spot (I'm talking to you, guy who hates our rhetorical questions), but we had to make a choice and stick to it. We didn't worry about that guy who doesn't like our rhetorical questions. He could deal, couldn't he?

Ideal readers aside, if you're writing nonfiction, make sure you're also qualified to write about your topic. Make sure you've read at least a few of the titles in your market, to get a feel for what they're like, what that specific market expects, and what your competition covers versus what it considers obvious and not worth explaining. This part should be simple if you're actually interested in your topic, which you *should* be. If you hate boating but decide to write a boat book because boat books are hot, you're sort of skirting that line where you might be a disingenuous douchebag. To stay on the right side of that line, if you *must* write a book about boats despite your hatred of the topic, then at least spend some time riding in boats, working on boats, reading about boats, and learning what boat owners think and expect. The same goes for fiction. If you want to write romance for no other reason than that romance is popular, at least read a few romance novels to get an idea for the conventions, tropes, and expectations of readers. If you were pitching a book to a traditional publisher, that publisher would want you to pick out a few comparable books in your niche and explain how yours compares. Just because you're self-published doesn't mean that this isn't an excellent idea. It *is*, so do yourself a favor and tackle it anyway.

In summary, we spent a fair number of words explaining the idea of knowing your market, but really it can be boiled down to a few:

Know your stuff, or *learn* it.

Respect your audience and give them what they want, need, and expect.

Decide what you stand for and don't waver.

The better you know the people you're writing for and the existing market you're writing in, the better what you deliver will fill a need ... and hence sell books.

who is
my dear
reader

Knowing Your Story

As I mentioned in the introductory section, I wrote a book called *The Bialy Pimps* in 1999, then wrote my second novel, *Fat Vampire,* in 2012. During the 13 intervening years, I tried many novels, many times. Over and over, my characters would get into a room and stare at each other. I wouldn't know what to do with the story. Many projects died horrible, half-finished deaths, including one that got me through NaNoWriMo. If you know NaNoWriMo, then you'll immediately see that I did it all wrong. National Novel Writing Month is in November, and the idea is to write 50,000 words in 30 days. I did, but I forgot the second part of NaNoWriMo's directive, which was "… so that at the end of the month, you'll have a finished novel." I had 50,000 words where nothing happened.

When I got to *Fat Vampire*, something clicked, and I haven't had trouble finishing a project since. And I've written *many* projects since.

What clicked was the realization that *I had to have a story.* Sounds simple, right? Maybe painfully simple? It should have been. Instead it was simply painful. It took me a long time to realize that what I had were *situations*, not stories. I'd say, "What if this crazy thing happened?" So, using my words, I'd make it happen. Then everyone would stand around and shrug and say, "Okay, that happened. Now what?"

Some of you more accomplished writers are rolling your eyes, but I know from hearing from plenty of folks that many, many writers can't finish a project. Some of this, I'd wager, is due to fear or resistance (and on that note, we'd strongly suggest you read Steven Pressfield's excellent book _The War of Art)_ but sometimes it's due to having a setup rather than a story. You don't necessarily need to know every detail of your story before word one, but if you're having trouble finishing, it might be a good idea to sit down and see if you can start with your situation and ask "Then what?" until you reach something that feels like the satisfying end of a decent adventure.

I think the reason _Fat Vampire_ finally shook me loose was that I already knew the story. _Everyone_ knows the vampire story. Someone gets bitten, they turn, they discover amazing new abilities — or, in the case of my hero, Reginald, they discover that their new abilities are more or less absent. That in itself introduced some obvious "what nexts" to follow, most of which were the reason the whole _Fat Vampire_ idea ever came up in the first place. He'd have to try to hunt, then inevitably fail. He'd have to try running like a vampire and get winded. But in order to get Reginald winded, I had to explain some alternate vampire physiology, seeing as vampire hearts don't normally beat. The situation itself kept me asking "How did that happen?" and "How could that work?" and "What then?" so often that all I had to do was to keep answering questions to find the rest of my story. I had to explain how he'd feed if he couldn't catch victims. I had to explain what abilities he'd find if he didn't have physical abilities (answer: All of Reginald's amazing vampire abilities are mental). That led me forward until his unavoidable clash with a rather nasty Vampire Council. By then I was already through most of the book. Only at the very end did I get a bit stuck — but this time, rather than getting mired in _what_ had to happen, I got stuck on *how* it went down. It took some thinking, and then I was done.

If you ever get stuck, ask yourself what happens next, then next, then next. Don't get an idea for a situation; develop the arc for your story. Pretty much every story goes like this: Someone is complacent, they face a challenge, the challenge nearly beats them, they find a way to conquer the challenge, then emerge changed at the other end. There are variations and anti-stories of course, but those are time-tested standards. Make sure you have at least a basic idea of your elements *before* starting if you have even the slightest doubts about your ability to reach the end.

Knowing Your Characters

You haven't lived until you've been writing a scene you thought you were in control of, and something happened you never saw coming.

Almost every writer who's been at it for a while has had that experience. It's delightful; it's surprising; it gives you an odd feeling of confidence because the story almost seems to be breathing on its own. If you allow it, it happens because your characters are taking over.

Our contention is that good storytelling is good because the characters — not the author — are in charge. Bad storytelling is often a case of the author shoving his or her big nose into the narrative. You can see when this happens as a reader, and it'll clang in your ear like a sour note. Author interference is what makes you shake your head and say, "Why would X character do that?" What follows often feels artificial and contrived.

(Note: If you're wondering how you can steer your story if you're not allowed to force things to happen, keep reading. We cover that in the "Preparing Your Beats or Outline" section to follow.)

Dynamic characters shake things up. They cause chaos. They act autonomously without permission. This is very, very good, because it means that readers will be less likely to predict what's coming. If you as the author don't know what exactly will happen, how can a reader?

Some writers create full character profiles, complete with a character's entire physical appearance, their background and education, their likes and dislikes, significant events in their childhood, and so on.

We don't usually go that far, but do make brief sketches that give us some idea of who our characters are.

Here are a two of the character sketches Sean gave me before we started writing *The Beam*:

Nicolai Costa: A teenager from a ridiculously wealthy Roman family. Nicolai's parents, brothers, and sisters were all murdered in the riots of '27. Nicolai disguises himself as one of the rabble (not hard at the time) and makes an epic journey across Eurasia with only the clothes on his back, a small pouch of food, and a crossbow, to escape the famine. Surviving bandits, floods, and hurricanes, he arrives at America's border in 2034, starving. Desperate for food, he pushes his way to front of the queue. He is refused entry but articulates his way in anyway, using the same skill set that kept him alive throughout his journey to America. He is the last person allowed across the border. At the border, Nicolai is interviewed by Isaac Ryan, who is struck by his quiet intellect and superb articulation. A friendship is formed, and as Isaac moves forward in his political career, Nicolai becomes his speechwriter and right-hand man, helping him to quickly rise through the ranks of the Directorate. I would cast Johnny Depp.

Kai Dreyfus: Not much is known about Kai, including her age. Though she looks to be in her early 20s, she pours a tremendous amount of time and attention into looking and staying that way. It's possible she's as old as 60. She is one of Doc's best clients, though she rarely pays with credits. Kai is a high-class escort, servicing only the elite. She is also an occasional assassin. She would be amazing at what she does anyway, but with her add-ons, many tailor made, Kai's never had a client who didn't feel she was worth every credit. Escorts are one of the few jobs that can straddle both sides of the parties, and Kai services both Enterprise and Directorate clients. Kai is fascinated by the Wild East and dreams of traveling the world. She's a collector of experiences, and secrets. With clients spanning the highest levels of power, Kai is the keeper of many, though her only true love is held for Nicolai. I would totally cast Mila Kunis.

I haven't looked at these in a while because by now I know Nicolai and Kai as if they were old friends, but it's interesting to look back now. Let's take a look at a few things of note.

First, you might have chuckled at the casting at the end of each description. Sean and I do that a lot. When he doesn't give me an idea, I often pick someone and leave a note so we'll be on the same page. We don't do it for every character, but it's amazing how many have a real-life doppelgänger. Having someone to compare the character to works well for a few reasons. For one, we don't need to remember their physical attributes (like the color of their eyes) because we can always look to the real person. And second, it gives us a shorthand to understand something about their personalities.

Our characters quickly outgrow their models, and Nicolai and Kai were nothing like Johnny Depp or Mila Kunis by the end of our story. (For one, Mila had the wrong feel for me, so I changed her to Natalie Portman.) But this is like pre-starting a tree in a pot before moving it to a permanent home outside: All you need is a jump-start. After that, once in situations, they'll grow on their own.

Second, it's interesting to see how the characters changed and how they didn't. Kai does love Nicolai, but she also has a very, very wily edge that Sean didn't indicate. She's also funny, incredibly intelligent, and intensely loyal. Nicolai is a closet artist. The Directorate, which is the party Nicolai works for in *The Beam*, is a 9-5 group, more left-brained than right. But that told me things, too, so throughout Season 1, I knew Nicolai's desire to play piano and paint would be at odds with his position working for Directorate official Isaac Ryan.

You can do this or not, but do allow your characters to have multiple dimensions. In real life, no one can be described with a one-sentence tagline. Kai is not just "the hooker with the heart of gold," and Nicolai is not just "the rich kid from the East." That'd be stuffing them in a box and sitting on the lid. They both have desires that conflict with each other, and although both would probably be considered "good" characters in the story, they sometimes do bad things. They're human, like the rest of us, and even good guys are never perfect. (On the flip side, letting your "bad" characters have redeeming moments will also make them much more believable.)

Profiles aren't intended for publication. They exist for the writer and only the writer, so that the writer can know the character as if he or she were a real person, which helps them to predict how a character would react to a given situation. This makes the act of writing very natural. It starts to feel as if you're an observer to the scene, and that instead of creating it, you're recording what happens as it unspools before you.

Knowing Your World

Some worlds are self-explanatory. If your characters live in our everyday world, there's probably not a lot of time required to understand it yourself. The same may or may not be true if your characters spend significant time in parts of our real world that aren't "everyday" to everyone, such as behind the scenes at a carnival. On one hand, the carnival world still has gravity like ours and the same political systems and history, but on the other hand there may be conventions unique to that world that you, as the author, must understand. But even if that's true, you probably don't need comprehensive notes. You probably just need some firsthand experience (visit a carnival to see life behind the scenes) or research.

Other worlds, by contrast, are unique and require as much exploration and understanding on the part of the writer as the characters who live inside it. As with character sketches, any work you do to explain or understand the world will probably never see publication, but it's still worth doing. You may never even *mention* parts of the world in your story, but it's still ideal for you to understand them.

The world of *Unicorn Western* grows increasingly complex the more we write inside it (as of this writing, we have at least three large novels comprising *Unicorn Apocalypse* to complete), but our best example is, again, *The Beam*. The world of *The Beam* is absolutely enormous. It's *so* enormous, in fact, that we've invited several other indie authors to write their own non-intersecting stories inside it.

Before I started writing *The Beam*, Sean gave me a 21-page document that explained everything that happened between 2013, when we wrote Season 1, and 2097, when the story begins. When I got the document, I panicked. It was so much information. Here's an abridged sample:

> 2026: Unforeseen catastrophe slams the planet. A year of devastating weather triggers extreme droughts that ravage nearly a third of the globe, mostly throughout Eurasia, Africa, and the Middle East. The melting of Siberian permafrost vents massive amounts of methane into the air. The unprecedented technological advances of the previous decade mean nothing as quickly decaying environmental conditions lead to a substantial population die-off, with millions of deaths in the first few years ballooning to billions over the coming decade. Entire regions of the world, previously populated, are quickly abandoned and surrendered to ruin. Once-mighty rivers run bone dry, and wildfires swallow thousands of square miles. Desalination technology is able to save some countries, but for the most part fails to meet demand. Efforts to reverse climate change on a global scale are insufficient.

2031: While landlocked and arid areas of the world are dying of drought, many of the world's cities lie partially submerged due to rising sea levels. With over 10 percent of the world's population living on coastlines, hundreds of millions are forced to migrate. Despite attempts to build flood defenses, main global arteries such as New York, London, Hong Kong, Shanghai, and Sydney are affected. Those worst-hit countries are plunged into anarchy. There is widespread damage to buildings and infrastructure. Vast uninhabitable wastelands blanket the equatorial regions, as desperate streams of refugees flee from city to city, fighting over scraps.

2036: A gradual stagnation of the white population, simultaneous growth of Hispanics, and a globally unique economic boom in Canada all pave the way to a North American Union slowly taking shape. The same soaring global temperatures that ravaged much of the world cleared access to a treasure trove of natural resources, previously buried in the frozen north. North American citizens are now flocking to Canada's cheap, wide, green lands. With Europe in Chaos, the Middle East and Africa mostly wasteland, Asia unifying itself beneath a single umbrella, and South America in ruins, the USA initiates early talks with Canada and Mexico. The three presidents step down, a temporary constitution is drafted, and the NAU is formed.

2042: The first version of The BEAM is complete and is launched by the companies West and Quark, slightly ahead of schedule, unifying the AI from emerging technology with the aging information superhighway. The BEAM is not global, and is accessible only to NAU citizens. Once The BEAM is live, it becomes clear that the Singularity has been achieved, making AI growth now exponential. Heavy research into nanotechnology is started.

And hell, the above is just a tiny sliver of the NAU's chronology — there was the rest of the world (flooded and in chaos) to think about, too!

It was a ton of information, and at first I almost tried to memorize it. But the world document didn't exist for me to narrate; it existed as background. It was something I had to understand as part of our story's collective psyche. Our characters never discussed that the NAU was cut off; they simply lived in a world where it was. But this also gave me a lot of things to riddle out, and doing so made the story that much better because we were both constantly finding ways to understand it. For instance, I wasn't buying the fact that we were going to have exponential AI growth and intelligent nanobots by 2042, but we wanted them anyway. That meant finding a way to explain why there would be an unprecedented period of mysterious exponential growth, so in Season 1 we did.

The entire process was like a volley. Sean batted the timeline at me, and I batted back my interpretation in the manuscript. We sifted and sorted elements in the draft, then incorporated them in a revised world document. As an example, I adhered to Sean's indication that the "first version of The Beam" went live in 2042, but I also knew that the full version of The Beam didn't show up until 2063. Something that existed for 21 years would have to have its own identity, so I named that first version Crossbrace. It was always a give and take, but all of it helped us see our world as real and treat our characters as real people.

We were always going to keep the timeline to ourselves as background, but all of that history was too fun to ignore. As a sort of Beam 1.5 we decided to write a fiction-posed-as-nonfiction (future history) called *Plugged: How Hyperconnectivity and The Beam Changed the Way We Think*. Writing *Plugged* allowed us to explore this timeline from a 2097 perspective, looking back at these events as relevant to the evolution of human thinking, and that was fun to do. It also forced us, yet again, to further clarify our world. As long as the world document stayed in the background, it was enough to know that North America was covered with "some sort of protective net" and that Crossbrace and The Beam debuted 21 years apart. Once we dragged that chronology into the fore and used it to explain changes in human thought, however, we had to work out the details. What exactly is the protective "lattice," and how does it work? How was The Beam different from Crossbrace, how was Crossbrace different from the Internet, and why were the changes evolutionary for the people inside the NAU lattice?

Sean has said he would have been happy to write *Plugged* even if we sold zero copies. I agree. We not only feel that the narrative is fantastic, but it helped us to understand our own world more than we otherwise would have. The richer our understanding, the better our story. The better our story, the happier our readers. The happier our readers, the more likely they are to want to stay with us forever.

Force yourself to make fantasy worlds real, and you may find ways to articulate them as if they were.

Preparing Your Beats (for Fiction)

Among fiction writers, there are two main groups: "plotters" and "pantsers." Plotters like to create plots for their novels in advance. Pantsers like to fly by the seat of their pants, never knowing what comes next until it happens on the page. The way we work — me and Sean and me alone — is somewhere in the middle. I used to be a pure pantser, and today I blame it for my inability to finish a second novel. Conversely, as far as I'm concerned, our current use of story beats are *the* reason we're both able to move so fast.

Story beats are kind of like an outline without being an outline. They're sort of like CliffsNotes, written in advance, by someone who is barely paying attention. The reason I say that last is because story beats, for us, are merely a starting point. The beats are the plotting part of our mid-range writing style, but the story always, *always* grows beyond the beats, and that process is very "pantsing-like."

The process looks like this: Working together, we come up with a vague idea for a story. For *Unicorn Western,* that vague idea was born on our *Better Off Undead* podcast. Sean wanted to write a western with Dave; Dave grumbled that westerns took too much research. Sean and I both balked that you don't need research; you need a gunslinger, horses, a love interest, and a man in a black hat. Dave continued to bluster, saying that we didn't even know what color smoke came out of guns in those days. He said we'd screw it up, and end up with unicorns.

I said that was a great idea. If we put a unicorn in the story, we could point to that unicorn whenever someone suggested that the story seemed unrealistic. Sean then laughingly proposed that we write a straight-up western, but instead of riding a horse, the gunslinger could ride a unicorn.

That was it. That was the vague idea. We chatted it out a little — deciding what the gunslinger and his unicorn might do — but basically that's all it took to get *Unicorn Western* started.

So, after we have our basic idea, Sean will write story beats. He breaks them down by chapter, and we always decide in advance how long the book should be, so we therefore know how long the chapters should be. In the case of *Unicorn Western*, Sean gave me 12 short paragraphs that I was supposed to grow into chapters of 2,000 to 2,500 words each.

Here are a few, keenly noting that Sean is more or less incapable of writing story beats without repeatedly using the word "fuck" and/or mentioning weed:

> Chapter 5: Clint is now all angry and grizzled and fuck everyone, so he decides to go up on the Mesa, and use Edward's magic to look across the plains and see what he can see. As he's leaving town, he's approached by Theodore (mention him earlier), an orphan kid who does odd jobs for everyone. Teddy wants to go with Clint, but Clint tells him he can't. He's too young and will get himself killed. Teddy insists, and reminds Clint that he was looking for reinforcements. Two is almost worse than one since it's more like a tagalong. He either needs a lot of people, or he needs to be by himself. The kid sticks up for himself, and after a short and funny argument wins Clint's approval. He finally agrees to let him go. He has his own horse, but he's so poor that his horse is the cowboy equivalent of a Pinto. Edward

acts like a cock about it. They ride out of Solace together. Clint feels guilty during the ride, wanting to go back to Mai. He thinks about his haunted past, and how lonely he's always been. How maybe all of his habits are wrong. Maybe the best thing he could do would be to return to Solace, sweep Mai onto the back of Edward, then ride through the night on their first day toward The Realm. Not far from the Mesa, they run into trouble. A band of outlaws is stopping by a stew pool, wells of water scattered throughout The Sprawl. The water inside stew pools is replenishing for mind and body. One might say magical.

Chapter 6: The kid wants to charge them, and knows the Marshal could do it. Clint tells him he's a fucktard and too young to know it. The kid argues that Clint's too old, and that his instincts are dull. Clint smacks him down, articulating why he's the king of the motherfucking desert. Way Clint sees it, no one's in The Sprawl by accident, and it makes a lot more sense to see what they're up to than to kill them outright. The kid argues that they need the element of surprise. Clint checkmates his shit because the element of surprise isn't dick when you ride with a unicorn. Clint tells some story about the kid that shows he's an impulsive fuckup, then they agree to circle around and use Edward's magic to see what they can find out.

I adhered fairly closely to the beats for the first *Unicorn Western* book (the finished story does follow the word frame above), but that changed dramatically by the time we reached later books in the series. I started deviating all over the place, going down rabbit holes that appeared during writing, chasing ideas that Sean couldn't have seen coming because he wasn't the one discovering the increasingly complex draft as he went. Still, beats are *always* worth doing for us. We always sort of follow them, at least at the beginning, and they give us a framework to work within. They also allow us to discuss in the middle of stories, because we both know what's going on — more or less, anyway.

Unicorn Western was our first project together, so our beats have evolved. Sean understands that I deviate and that some of our best gems are discovered outside the beats (that was certainly true of the larger *Unicorn Western* saga), and many times I ask him for thinner beats because I can never get to them all if they're comprehensive.

This also varies by project. For instance, here are three chapters' worth of beats for the pilot of our sitcom *Everybody Gets Divorced:*

> Scene 3: Alex and Andrea's proposal plan explained.
>
> Scene 4: Alex and Andrea's proposal plan executed.
>
> Scene 5: Alex and Andrea's proposal plan horribly backfires.

Neither of us had any idea whatsoever what Alex and Andrea's plan would be. We only knew who Alex and Andrea were (smart, friendly, mischievous twins whose best intentions always collapsed into something horrible) and what the plan had to accomplish (a suitably "romantic enough" way for our hero, Archer, to propose to his girlfriend, Hannah). The rest had to come from the blue, during the first draft.

Stephen King says in *On Writing* that he thinks plotting is clumsy and anathema to creation. Overall, we tend to agree. Some books — often fast-paced thrillers — suffer from a mechanical style of progression, where everything is really convenient because it has to be lest the structure crumbles. But we also think, for us at least, that having *some* idea of where the story will eventually go is absolutely required to avoid a meandering narrative. Stories should be tight and focused, even if they're quiet pieces without serious action. Beats will help that. We don't think Stephen King would object to the idea of beats (not that we need to impress him) because they're not rigid. You think you're going *here*, but if you end up *there? Ain't no thang.*

We write our beats with the idea that we're *predicting* what will happen rather than *requiring* it to. Sometimes we guess right, and sometimes we guess wrong.

If you guess wrong but still feel that something *must* happen, this is where the "pantsing" part takes over, and you deviate from beats on the fly. Here's the rule: *You're allowed to manipulate the environment, but not the character.*

Let's say that you need your character Mary to reach Chicago for some reason vital to your story. In your beats, Mary was planning to leave her daughter with a friend before heading off to Chicago. But during writing, you realized something about Mary: She's very, very attached to her daughter. Like, overly attached. She's a helicopter mom. Also, during the course of your story — and you totally didn't see this coming — the daughter's become sick. Now Mary is worried in addition to being overly protective.

Mary can't just leave, though that's what a hack writer would have her do regardless. Someone who didn't truly understand or obey her characters would say, "Well, Mary has to go to Chicago, so I'm going to write her boarding a plane anyway." Boom, just like that, your story lost veracity.

A smarter, more skilled writer will realize that while she can't manipulate Mary, she *can* manipulate Mary's world. Here are a few options that, if you handle them correctly, would all feel more "real to character" than Mary simply leaving her sick daughter behind: Someone could kidnap the daughter and take her to Chicago; something could arise to make Mary believe that the only way to help/save her daughter is to leave her and go to Chicago; the best hospital for the treatment of the daughter's condition could turn out to be in Chicago. In all cases, you change things in Mary's world to see if you can nudge her in the direction you want (or need) her to go, but in the end, you can only nudge. *Mary must go on her own.*

If you choose to use story beats in your writing, remember that they are guideposts, not rigid plot elements. If your characters start to deviate, you must be prepared to adjust your beats and keep massaging as you go until you reach a satisfying conclusion to your story.

I think that rigidity is what Stephen King doesn't like about plot, and we agree with him on this one: An inflexible structure forces characters into a predetermined framework rather than letting them be what they want to be and prevents them from finding their own organic (and often better) ways. Working with flexible beats that can change on the fly can be a very nice happy medium, wherein you have that organic character feel while also having an idea where your story is headed. Plus, it satisfies

Stephen King, which is important because he's the sage and all.

Preparing Your Outline (for Nonfiction)

Immediately before starting on the book you're reading right now, we wrote *Plugged*, our fiction-disguised-as-nonfiction project written by fictional author William Gibson in the year 2097. *Plugged* tells the future history detailing the 84 years between the year we wrote *The Beam's* first season and the year our story takes place. While it was fictional, it was written like one of Malcolm Gladwell's books, as a kind of casual narrative covering the years leading up to the "current" state of technology and connectivity in 2097. Our goal was to give *Beam* fans more about the world, but we also wanted to talk about the changes that technology might soon make (and is already making) to the way humans think and interact. So yes, it was a work of imagination and speculation. But it was also written as if that world truly existed, and it contained a lot of true facts about today's world — stuff that really existed — right up to the day we wrote it. (For instance, did you know a guy named Dennis Hope laid claim to the moon years ago and has been selling it off acre by acre without any real permission?)

We finished *Plugged*, and moved into *Write. Publish. Repeat.* What we learned from the first translated neatly into the next, and both were quite different from fiction.

134

We believe that great nonfiction still tells a story (*Plugged* certainly does, and *Write. Publish. Repeat.* tells, in part, the story of how a few writers built their self-publishing success, in sufficient detail that readers can follow and learn), but the process is very different. Rather than writing story beats, it's best to think in terms of an outline.

To create your outline, ask yourself what your readers need and want to know most. List those points, then ask what big topics you could cover under each of them to explain those points. Keep drilling down, always looking for the best possible examples, until you get to brass tacks. Then, as with story beats, be flexible as you write, adding more where necessary.

Here's a snippet from our original outline for this book:

> PART 2 - Preparing Your Product (How to Make Readers Love You)
> ESSAY: How to Avoid the Self-Publishing Stink (better title later)
> - You have to please the gatekeepers. You want to make a great/amazing book. You know you have it in you.
> But if it looks self-published, it will tank. This is a fact.
> - Most readers don't care if something is self-published, but that doesn't mean they want it screaming at them. If it's "obviously self-published" in a bad way, a reader's presuppositions are set in advance and they will GO IN looking for your book to suck, for typos, etc. Nobody notices typos in traditional titles, but they sure as hell are in there.
> There are things you can do to avoid this:
> - Clean production
> - Clear writing and editing
> - Solid layout

- Titles, product descriptions, layout, cover
- Intelligent pricing
- If you wouldn't buy it, neither will your reader.
- People DO judge a book by its cover, and countless other intangibles. You owe it to yourself and your reader to make sure they're in place.

Pre-Production
- Understand that writing is a business. If you're an indie author, that means you must be in the business of buying, and selling, books.
- If gatekeepers are readers, then quality is everything. You must make the best product that you possibly can.

Knowing your market
Who is your ideal reader?
- This makes your book easier to write, and easier to sell later.
- Knowing your story
- Knowing your characters
- Preparing your beats
- The difference between preparing fiction and nonfiction

By contrast, you'll see that our outline for *Plugged* is a little different:

Chapter One: Covers the earliest events. Gibson argues that the world of 2097 started on July 21, 2019 when the first lunar base and telescope were established to prepare for eventual and permanent human habitation. This bonded the world in a way that wasn't possible before, and wouldn't have been possible before the Internet. This is the first bridging chapter, so I'm thinking it needs a lot of stuff to instantly familiarize the reader. Talk about Twitter and FB and how all the early social networks and blogging started to connect us in new ways. For the supposed reader of this book (in 2097) this would read like history. To most, a world before Twitter is horse and buggy.

1. The company who designed the moon base is led by a Richard Branson-type maverick — Clive Spooner. Spooner consulted with an Apple style company for usability and stuff like that. What made this project so revolutionary was that it really was "for the people," all along. (It was a "team effort." He wanted people to rally, like a country's soccer team or Russia vs. The U.S. in the space race ... everyone can rally, and he can use that momentum to make it work better and faster. Looking at open source ... everyone can participate, nothing is secret, etc.) You didn't have to be on the moon to experience it.

2. Tell the story of the team that "appified" the experience. Spooner commissioned a dream development team — the best the world had ever seen — to create an "experience." The LunarLife app was HUGE. It enabled people to see all the designs (nothing was secret), play games, participate, and most importantly, access the telescope. Here is this private enterprise that is made totally public, and enjoyed around the world. It connected people in a new and beautiful way that seemed to buoy the planet with unexpected hope.

Your first instinct may be to conclude that the *Plugged* outline is more story beats-like because it's fiction, but that's not it at all. The entire outline is like the above, with a major idea per chapter followed by a few points — and, where needed, subpoints. Like the *Write. Publish. Repeat.* outline. The reason it seems more narrative is because it's a narrative style. This book is more mechanical, more detail-oriented, more how-to. But remember our model: The outlines Malcolm Gladwell uses for his books might look very much like the one above because he tells his nonfiction through stories.

Which style of nonfiction you write will determine how you outline, but the structure is always the same: major points with examples and explanations underneath, nested as deeply as seems necessary to deliver the information you want to teach.

Regardless, organization is key for this type of writing. If you know your topic, you may find that you can write nonfiction as fast as anyone can write fiction — but only once you know where to actually put it in the draft. So for instance, when I wrote the rough draft for the book you're reading right now, I recreated Sean's outline (with my on-the-fly modifications — doesn't that sound familiar if you read the "Story Beats" section?) in the writing program we use. Only once I had a place for every individual point (like this place to write about nonfiction outlining) could I move quickly. Until then, it felt like one big, undifferentiated soup, with no clear place to begin, go, or end.

The other major difference for nonfiction is research. You may need to look things up to support your points (I did a shocking amount of research for *Plugged*, despite its being fiction), but lucky you: You have the Internet. If you're making a persuasive point, you'll want to back it up with opinions beyond your own. If you're teaching how-to, make sure you know your stuff, and that what you aren't 110 percent sure of, you look up and verify.

If you read the preceding section, you'll know you can also plop a unicorn into your work and eschew research entirely. That way, if anyone asks what you were thinking in recommending non-galvanized nails to build an outdoor deck, you can point to the unicorn and say, "There's a unicorn in this story. Did you think you could just trust everything else?"

CHAPTER NINE:
Creating Professional Products Part 2: Writing

WE'RE NOT GOING TO WRITE a comprehensive writing guide in this chapter, because there are a ton of great books already out there about the craft and practice of writing. If you want a great book on writing, our favorite (not too surprising, if you've read this far) is Stephen King's *On Writing.* King's book is half instruction manual for writers, half engaging memoir. We love King because he stands as a fantastic example of how to deliver a lifetime of consistency and quality. A few other nonnegotiable titles for serious (career) writers: The *Elements of Style* by William Strunk, Jr., and E.B. White; *Zen in the Art of Writing: Releasing the Creative Genius Within You* by Ray Bradbury; *Eats, Shoots & Leaves: The Zero Tolerance Approach to Punctuation* by Lynne Truss; *The Hero with a Thousand Faces* by Joseph Campbell.

You can read those later if you haven't already. For now, let's get started.

Decide On Your Workflow

As I write this, my 9-year-old son, Austin, has just announced that he is going to write a book. Because I know my son, I can predict how this will go. He will try to write an opus from the get-go rather than starting with something shorter, and he will insist that it be perfect in the first draft. Because first-draft perfection is more or less impossible, he'll get frustrated. I'll then try to convince him that with a few adjustments, writing can be less frustrating. I doubt I can convince him to do it any way other than the way he's going to do it, and if he decides to keep writing, we can trade tips once he's put in some hours. But you aren't my son — and if you aren't Sean's daughter Haley, who is on her fourth or fifth book and remains insistent on doing things the hard way — you're more likely to take our advice.

We both suggest a three-pass strategy for writing:

First draft: Write for yourself with the door closed. *Say it.*

Second draft: Revise for readers with the door open. *Say what you mean.*

Third draft: Polish. *Say it well.*

Both Austin and Haley will try to write a publication-quality third draft on their first pass. Please never do this. Don't even try. The first draft is your "vomit onto the keyboard" draft, wherein your task is to simply keep moving and outrun your doubts. Try not to pause for thought (you're thinking already, whether you realize it or not). Just *go.* Tell your story. Don't worry about getting

Ralph's phrasing precisely right when he's talking to June; have him blurt it instead. If there is action in the scene, just say what's going on. Don't try to choreograph everything perfectly at the expense of not getting it out.

The best way to get blocked as a writer is to start second-guessing yourself, and the best way to do that is to pause and think too much about what you're writing. Everyone has an overly-developed internal critic, and if you give that critic a quiet moment to speak, he *will* crap all over whatever you're writing. Don't let him. Bulldoze forward. Vomit those words onto that keyboard. *Get the story out of you, because once it's out, you can manipulate, tweak, and make it better.* If it never gets out, you'll have nothing to shape. Keep your metaphorical door closed: Don't let anyone see your first draft until it's finished, so they won't be able to influence the story as it's forming.

Every writer is different. For some reason, my first drafts come out very clean, with certain sections (especially near the end of a story) often needing only a light polish. Sean's are far messier, often requiring extensive rewriting and reorganizing. But in both cases, the story is out, which is where it needs to be.

You can then "open the door" for the second draft, and have some early readers give you their thoughts if you'd like to. But as to mechanics, there's a bit of debate among writers over how to handle the second draft, so we advise you to experiment and see what works best for you. Most writers and instructors will tell you to rewrite that draft until it flows well (the dictum for the second draft, as stated above, is "Say what you mean" as opposed to the first draft's simple imperative, "Say it"), but others disagree. Dean Wesley Smith, who's appeared on our show, is a bit of a heretic in that he advises not editing your first draft beyond fixing typos — or, if it needs more extensive work, simply trashing it and telling the entire story again from the beginning. Dean's method (inspired by science-fiction icon Robert Heinlein) is based on the idea that a writer's creative instincts are damaged when that harsh, critical voice inside is allowed free rein. We agree in some cases but disagree in others. It depends on the writer, so experiment to find your sweet spot. Sean usually spends longer on his second draft than he does on the first.

Once you have your draft flowing like you want (once it "says what you meant" instead of simply "saying it"), we recommend a third draft where you polish it up, fine-tuning points and really making your story's language and clarity sparkle.

When we work collaboratively, we employ one of two processes. For most works (like this one), I write the first draft after Sean hands me the beats, then he handles the second and third before it's sent to our editor. But for our biggest, cornerstone projects (currently *The Beam* and *Unicorn Western*), we employ a fourth draft. After Sean does drafts two and three, it comes back to me for a final polish to really make it shine. Our two skill sets are different and perfectly complementary, and each of us catches things the other misses. So, going Sean-Johnny-Sean-Sean-Johnny on our most important projects results in a next-level result.

Decide on your flow in advance if you can. If you added Austin and Haley's current ages together they still couldn't legally drink, but you're old enough to know better. If you know you'll get two or three passes after you're "done," you're more likely to loosen up enough to get that first story out. Without that permission, you might mire yourself in self-criticism in a quest to get it perfect from the start.

Write Fast

We strongly believe you should write your first drafts as fast as you can.

Now, note that we said "as *you* can." Emphasis on *you*. Sean and I are both kind of stupidly fast, but we're not going to give you our word counts here (and intend to stop doing it on the podcast, though the cows have already kind of left the barn on that one) because we don't want you comparing yourself. We've gotten feedback that says that while our speeds are inspiring, they're also kind of discouraging because others who aren't as fast feel inferior — and that, our friends, is the last way we want you to feel. Everyone has different skill sets and strengths as a writer, and ours happens to be first draft speed, enhanced by 30 hours or so per week of practice writing those first drafts. Sean pays for speed on his first drafts with time spent on the second.

So, don't worry about us, and don't worry about what "fast" means. Worry about learning to move your own fingers (or speak, or however you write) as fast as *you* can, and trying to improve that speed as you go. We're actually anal enough to suggest tracking your words-per-hour rate over time to see if it increases. Sean has been tracking his word counts for the last year and a half because he sees it as a formula to continuously improve.

We know how this sounds. People tend to equate speed with rushing, and equate rushing with shoddy work. My grandfather told me that any job worth doing is worth taking the time to do right. The whole idea that fast and good are mutually exclusive is embedded deeply in the modern world's psyche, especially among creative people. It's the pesky Puritan Work Ethic rearing its obnoxious head. If someone wants to prove how good and honorable a pursuit is, one of the most common things they'll do is to explain how long they slaved over it.

We disagree. Vehemently. In our opinions, slow is the domain of the internal critic, whereas fast is the domain of pure creativity. When you go slow, you're allowing yourself to focus on phrasing and grammar and possibly even theme. The first draft is an absolutely horrible time to focus on any of those things, and giving your critical mind quiet space to ask whether you're doing good work or hack work is a mistake.

Keep telling the story and telling the story. Don't stop to think. Vomit onto that keyboard. Keep things moving. Don't worry about getting it right. Go faster. Faster. *Faster.*

Writing fast helps you to capture your most natural voice. Done well, it also leaves you with copy that's easy to edit. Manipulating your thoughts into elegant prose takes a long time. Capturing unedited thoughts as they fly through your mind, however, can yield clean, concise copy, with clarity and voice — as is the case with Johnny. *(Johnny's note: Sean added that flattering sentence, but for some reason I can't bring myself to remove it.)*

Imagine you're having a conversation with someone you love. You probably wouldn't use big words to try and impress them or stop to think of the best way to say things, right? That's the same immediacy you want to bag in your rough draft. The important thing is to get your copy down as quickly and naturally as possible. You'll use your editing phase to trim run-on sentences, unnecessary words, or anything else that might dilute your delivery.

Sean and I, being data nerds and consummate improvement-minded people, actually time ourselves when we write. I have a $10 timer from the kitchen section at Target, and most mornings I set it for three hours and watch it count down. At the same time, I have a window in my writing software that shows me my live word count for the session. I glance at both from time to time as I write, and if I'm not hitting the target I want, I try to go faster. And at the end of the session, I record that time, always striving for a high number.

Now, please understand what we're saying here. Writing slow, especially on certain projects, is not bad. With certain projects it's an absolute requirement. When I wrote the first draft of *The Beam*'s first season, my lack of knowledge about the world Sean had built caused me to write at least 25 percent slower than usual. *Plugged* was monumentally slow (almost half speed) because despite my intentions, I kept having to stop and think about which points I should explore next and look something up online or in Sean's timeline. So, don't think you're doing something wrong if you're moving slowly, and don't beat yourself up. *Never* compare yourself to anyone other than yourself.

Try to move as fast as you can, but remember that in the end it's not about finished words in a certain period of time. It's about getting that critic out of the way and immersing yourself in a flow of pure creativity. Do that, and you're doing well.

Be Consistent and Have a Plan

For most writers, it's more important to write regularly than to write a lot in any given session. Sean writes every day. At the time of this writing, he's written for five months straight for *at least* an hour each day. He writes more during the week than he does on the weekends, but to him, it's the habit that's most important. It's exercise. As a result, his brain is conditioned to put new words on the page with a minimum of effort. By contrast, I write every weekday. Because I take Saturday and Sunday off, Monday is always my hardest writing day. Why? Because I'm out of flow, and it takes me time to get out of weekend mode and rediscover my rhythm.

Two days isn't a big break and doesn't hurt me much. I feel that the reset, increased sleep, and family time I get on the weekends is a fair trade-off, but for most writers, significant binge-versus-rest phases are a mistake. Some people can pull it off; most people do better through habituation and writing regularly.

Of the three of us on the podcast, Dave is the only one who reports any real trouble "getting in the mood to write." Other phrases people use for getting in the mood include "waiting for inspiration" and "finding the groove." Sean and I argue that Dave would have an easier time if he had a regular writing schedule, which he very much doesn't. How can you find the groove if it's always moving? If you're having trouble sleeping at night, one of the suggestions the brainiacs give is to always get up and go to bed at the same time, and to follow the same rituals and routines in preparation for sleep. If you do things repeatedly and in the same way, your brain will eventually form automatic habits. Pavlov got his dogs to salivate by ringing the dinner bell, and the same goes for writing. If you always go through the same routine before sitting down to write, you're training your brain to anticipate some forthcoming words ... and hence to "salivate" subconsciously before you sit.

Sean and I both write first thing in the morning. I get out of bed at 5:45am, start the coffee, then spend the few minutes of brew time checking out where I am in my current project. I adjust my monitor, take the little wrist elevator off my keyboard because I write with it flat on my lap, and close distracting windows. When my coffee's ready right around 6 a.m., I get a cup, sit down, start my timer, and write for three hours straight. Real life doesn't intrude until after that.

Having a schedule is part of a good plan. Other parts include knowing what you'll be writing for the day in advance (I open my current project and arrange the windows, notes, beats, and pertinent details to remember the night before, like some people lay out their next day's clothes), having goals, and maybe even a deadline.

We have deadlines for all of our work. It's rare that I deliver a draft to Sean later than he's expecting, and the fact that I respect that structure keeps me on task. Correspondingly, I have word-count goals that I want to hit each day and hour along the way to those deadlines.

Now, we want to add a few words about this "have a plan" thing before we continue, because we're sure that some of the more right-brained among you are either furious or confused by our insistence that our art conforms to something as anti-creative as a *schedule* and *deadlines*.

If there's ever a serious discrepancy between the project's natural length and our guess at the corresponding deadline, we always obey the book rather than our deadline. This happened with *The Beam*. We originally planned for the first season to be around 85,000 words, but it ended up at twice that length. As the first-draft writer who was already feeling slow and bogged-down in the complex sci-fi world, I was *thrilled* when Sean suggested doubling the word count ... and yes, that sentence is thick with sarcasm. But he was right, and I knew it; the story wouldn't fit into 85,000 words. It was demanding fuller expression and more time, so we gave it both. Similarly, *Write. Publish. Repeat.* was originally conceived as a 50,000-word project. It didn't take long to see that that was impossible. There's simply too much to say. Again, we ended up at more than double our projections.

Those instances of expanding projects and deadlines are rare, though, because for most projects, the deadline *is part of our art.* Austin Kleon said that, "The way to get over creative block is to put constraints on yourself. It seems contradictory, but when it comes to creative work, limitations mean freedom." We agree. If you decide that you're going to paint a portrait using acrylics, you've locked yourself down, haven't you? Specifically, you've restricted your art to the medium of acrylic paints. Nobody ever thinks that doing so is a problem, but for some reason people *do* tend to think it's a problem with word-count restrictions. But really, how is "I'm going to write a story about X of 50,000 words" any different from "I'm going to paint a portrait with acrylics and fit it on this canvas"? Both are art within a defined set of boundaries, and we'd argue that knowing your parameters beforehand makes your work *better*, because it must be disciplined and not sprawl simply for the sake of sprawling.

We write everything with an idea in mind about how long it should be, and we usually more or less hit that word count. If nothing else, we suggest you try it as an exercise, and see what you end up with.

Use the Right Tools

Our opinions about writing software may change, and this isn't exactly evergreen advice, but as of late 2013, all three of us would recommend Scrivener as our go-to writing software. Our second choices are likely all different, and so far behind Scrivener as not to matter at all.

I wrote *The Bialy Pimps* in Microsoft Word. It was a nightmare. I wrote every chapter as a separate Word document because I was terrified of keeping all of my eggs in one basket. Word was (and remains) notoriously flaky and would crash spontaneously, causing massive losses. Word would also do strange things from time to time, like you'd hit a button and every apostrophe would turn into a bullet point or something. (That didn't happen, but things just as odd and unfixable did.)

Thanks to the duct-tape way I was organizing my files, version control was a nightmare. Each time I made revisions, I had to create yet *another* copy of each chapter and carefully sequester the old versions from the ones I was editing. This also meant I couldn't globally find-and-replace; at one point I decided to change the name of the deli where the story takes place as well as the names of all of the characters, and had to keep a list on my desk of everything that should change because I had to open every one of the 20 chapters and find-and-replace it in all of them.

Rearranging scenes and managing my scrap files was super-difficult. At one point, I rearranged a few chapters and had to go through and re-number every one of them. I also had subchapters within the chapters, and I often screwed *those* up as I edited; I'd have two subsection 3's and no subsection 4. Or my formatting would be different among them; I'd have a single blank line above new sections in one chapter but forget that and have two blank lines above new sections in later chapters.

When I decided to make an e-book out of those files, that was a nightmare, too. Word (as I've said many times on air to Sean's delight) thinks it's smarter than you. It inserts crap markup code behind the scenes in your manuscript that screws up the e-book file. It's proprietary Word HTML, which makes zero sense because Word isn't an HTML program. It's nearly impossible to strip out and make sense of, and that's assuming you've made it that far without punching a hole in your computer when Word changes a bunch of stuff as you type that you meant one way but brainiac Word assumed you were doing wrong.

It was so incredibly difficult to make a coherent, functional e-book file out of my Word document, in fact, that I painstakingly took *The Bialy Pimps* apart and put it into Scrivener. The process was obnoxious but made things so much easier in the end. Sean only started writing five years ago, hated Word two minutes into using it, and has really *only* used Scrivener, except for managing files back from the editor, and he uses Mac's Pages for that.

Remember how I described my setup in Word? Well, here's a screen shot showing a section of how the same book came together in Scrivener:

Folders and documents. Nothing else. I created high-level folders for each "book" (major section) within the novel (there were three) then folders beneath for the chapters. Inside the chapters are the individual subchapter documents, which is where all of the text is. The documents were in one file, and if I wanted to rearrange them, I could simply drag them around in the order I wanted. Numbering of the subchapters is automatic, same for the chapters. Formatting is handled on output ("compile" in Scrivener language), so it's consistent across everything.

I didn't set up *The Bialy Pimps* totally correctly in Scrivener because it was my first time using the software, but I was close. Everything got easier. Scrivener's compiled documents are clean, free of that crap code inserted by Word. Adding new pages (like a new call to action at the end) is simple. The process became painless.

This won't be a comprehensive Scrivener tutorial (for that, we recommend Gwen Hernandez's *Scrivener for Dummies*), but in brief, here are a few things we love about Scrivener — which double as reasons why, for now at least, we'll use nothing else:

It Never Loses Anything

Scrivener is a paranoid person's wet dream. It rapid-saves your draft every few seconds, and you can hard-save to the backup copy (kept in a separate location from your active file) whenever you want. It also hard-saves to the backup automatically whenever you close a file. We keep all of our Scrivener files in a shared Dropbox folder, and Sean has the "Pack Rat" Dropbox plan, meaning it has prior versions of all files going back to the dinosaurs. As long as he keeps giving them money each month, they promise he can keep them until the robots are here.

When you delete something in Scrivener, it goes into the trash. I've never emptied mine, meaning there's yet another layer of protection to retrieve old stuff.

I won't guarantee that you'll never lose any of your work if you use Scrivener, but I can't imagine how you could unless you were actually trying to.

You Don't Worry About Formatting. You Just Write Words.

Remember how I said I didn't set up *The Bialy Pimps* correctly? Look back at that screen shot and you'll see that I put *BOOK ONE* in the name of the *Book One* document title. That's not the right way to do it, but I was overthinking things. When you use Scrivener, you should create text documents in the "Binder" on the left, think about what you'd like to title them, then type words in those documents. Most of our files are simpler than that earlier screenshot; they usually have no folders and are simply a collection of named text files. If you have multiple subchapters inside chapters, you can group documents inside folders. If those chapters are formed into parts, you can make a second level of folders. Don't think about formatting; just think, "I want to group these into this" and pretend you're organizing a filing cabinet. Name things as you want them. Only at the "compiling" stage should you consider the font and size of chapter titles.

When I worked in Word, I spent a lot of time thinking about the look of my book's chapter titles, spacing, format of subheads, etc. In Scrivener, nothing should go in those bottom-line text documents other than the actual text of your story. It's a pure story vehicle, with all the other crap lifted out of your way until the very end.

You Can Organize, Sift, Sort, Filter, or Shuffle However You'd Like

The beauty of text-only writing documents is that you can drag and drop them however you'd like, and the program will handle re-numbering, repagination, and everything else. You can use "corkboard mode" where it'll show you all of your scenes as if they were on index cards tacked to a corkboard, and you can drag them around to your liking. You can tag and label chapters with metadata that the reader will never see, so you can remember which chapters are for which characters or storylines.

Writing for multiple publishing platforms? Yeah, that's us, too. And it's tricky, because we want the Amazon version to have one call to action at the end with a link to the next product on Amazon, but we also want to compile a Kobo version with a Kobo-specific CTA. Smashwords requires a different copyright page. And of course print has its own set of requirements. Scrivener makes it simple to handle all of them, because you can create "collections" that are standard groups of documents: In other words, you don't have to remember which documents go to the Kobo version. You just compile the Kobo collection you've set up, and it's all filtered correctly for you.

What if you're writing a series? It's really handy to have all of the books in one file, so you can search for names and dates, and keep notes together. Collections are great for that, too. Just shove everything together, and use different ways to sort, filter, and compile work for you when you reach the end and are finally ready to ship your products where they need to go.

It Has Places For All of Your Stuff

Want your story beats handy? You can slip a document into the "research" folder in your project file for quick reference, then pop it open in a separate window if you like to work that way. When I was working on *Plugged*, I needed frequent access to the master timeline Sean had given to me for *The Beam*. I had it as a PDF, but it was simple to drag that into the research folder. Ditto anything else you find and need while you write.

There are character profile sheets and sheets for tracking places, but we've never used them. There are templates for various ways of writing. Want to keep notes on your story's world, like the heroine's eye color or the name of someone's favorite restaurant? Stuff them into your project notes. Anything and everything you could want has a place in your project's single Scrivener file.

It Tracks Your Progress and Goals
Check this out. It's off to the side of what I'm writing right now:

You can totally customize project targets to your goals. Choose which days of the week you write, set work windows, change deadlines, and so on.

In addition, you get a live word count per document, in the whole manuscript, whatever. There's even a geeky "project statistics" pane you can use if you're that anal.

It's Fantastic For Collaboration

One of the features Sean and I use most often is comments. Basically, I'll highlight a section, hit Option+Shift+8, and it'll open a comment where I can indicate what I need Sean to know about that section. Because I'm the first-draft writer, I often assign Sean to double-check details I'm unsure of, suggest stuff we'll want to touch on later, or explain why I'm writing a certain thing so that he can 1) tell me if it doesn't work or 2) leave it alone rather than changing it arbitrarily, because he'll see my intention.

When I'm done with the file, I'll close it, and Sean will open it. As he revises, he'll often leave comments back to me or answer questions I've asked in comments.

Because we keep our Scrivener files in shared Dropbox folders, we work with the same file, and the app is smart enough to keep us from working on the same file at the same time and possibly overwriting each other. If one of us tries to open a file and it's already open elsewhere, it'll let us know and stop us.

Sean and I have always worked in Scrivener from the start. He and Dave traded their work in Pages for a long time, until Dave was comfortable that they wouldn't lose everything accidentally (after we'd been working on our projects for a few months). Their collaboration has been more fluid since.

It's Nonspecifically Awesome

There are a thousand other cool things about Scrivener that we won't go into because everyone uses the program differently, and we haven't touched a lot of what it does. But let's just say it's beyond awesome, it's inexpensive, and we think every writer should use it.

If you'd like to check Scrivener out, you can try it before you buy it because they'll give you a nice, long, full-function trial period. You can get direct links to that trial on our *Self Publishing Podcast* tools page: SelfPublishingPodcast.com/tools.

Shut Out the World

It's tempting to make yourself available to others when you write. You might even say something to your spouse like, "I'm going to write ... just let me know if you need me."

We suggest you don't. Close your door instead. Lock it if you have to. Close your window and don't have anything in your office that you know will distract you. For a while, I had an electronic dartboard in my office. I don't have it now, because I'd find reasons to stand up and throw a few darts.

To write well, efficiently, and fast, you must be able to shut out the world. You don't want to see or hear anything that might possibly knock you from your story world — or from narrating if you write nonfiction. Writing is a "flow" activity, and you'll lose a lot more than the five minutes you spend answering your wife or husband's question about Grandma Beulah's surprise party. You'll lose all the time it takes you to get back up to speed and "in the zone," too.

The best thing you can do for your writing is to tell those around you that you will be available for them before and after your writing time to the best of your ability — but that while you are in the room with your door closed, *you are not to be disturbed.* My kids come in to hug me in the mornings when they wake up and my son usually grabs my iPad to play games, but they know not to come back in unless the house is on fire. I've told Austin to leave my iPad in the living room when he's done with it, because if he comes back in, I lose my focus. I never stay in for more than an hour in the morning anyway; I come out to refill my coffee and use the bathroom. That's when I greet Robin with a kiss: at a time I'm getting up anyway.

It may sound hard-line or even rude (or selfish; we writers are always worried about seeming selfish) but it's really just about respecting the craft. Are you ignoring your family and friends? Only for a few hours. And wouldn't you do that at any other job, because the boss required it? If you want to get the work done fast so you can be available sooner, give yourself the respect of treating your writing like a job rather than a hobby, and don't open the door unless you have to.

I also taught myself to write while wearing headphones. Not earbuds; *headphones.* Big, poufy, stereophonic, over-the-ear headphones. I used to think I couldn't write while listening to music, but taught myself to do it, and my writing got faster because I'm that much more fully in my own world. Sean is jealous. I'm listening to Green Day right now, and my current favorite writing music is Eminem. I listen to it loud. The world could be ending outside and I'd never know, and that's just how I want it.

Lastly, wean yourself off of the Internet during your writing time. Don't let yourself "just check e-mail quickly" or "just check Facebook for a moment." Also, don't have a ringing phone in your office.

In short, cut yourself off as fully as you possibly can when you write. The world can be without you for a few hours, and your writing will vastly benefit from the seclusion and the increased focus that comes with it.

CHAPTER TEN:
Creating Professional Products Part 3: Editing

IT'S REALLY HARD TO BE objective about your own work, and it's really hard to catch mistakes once your eye has read a given section a few times. You'll become blind to typos, because your mind will fill them in. But here's an ugly truth about typos and other small editing mistakes: *They exist in traditional books, too.* You don't see them often because in part there aren't many, and because your mind is predisposed not to see them. The minds of *your* readers — especially if you've tipped your indie hat — may not be so kind. If a reader knows you're self-published, her mind will be in tune with your typos; she won't fly by. It's essential that you make as few mistakes as possible if you expect to win that reader.

Everyone needs an editor if they expect to look professional. You'll learn your strengths and weaknesses in time, and how much editing your work needs will depend on you and your individual limits. Regardless, work should never publish without someone other than you reading it.

If you're a *Self Publishing Podcast* listener, you might be thinking right now that I'm being a hypocrite because I (and again, all "I's" are Johnny) have said before that I don't hire an editor for titles I write without a partner. But you're missing semantics in the idea of "I don't hire an editor." Do I *hire* one? No. But do I *have* one? Yes, but I pay her in sex.

I should mention at this point that my wife is my editor.

Or perhaps more accurately, she's a very good *proofreader* and *beta reader*. Those are different things, and both are different from what most people consider to be an editor. Above, I said that you'll learn your own strengths and weaknesses, and I happen to produce fairly clean drafts. When you take the 80/20 Rule into account, I feel I can get away without a comprehensive content edit — but I still need another set of eyes on my work, and I always get them.

Let's go through the different kinds of editing you may need, as well as how likely you are to need them as an indie. We'll start with the most comprehensive (and expensive) types, then move to the lightest and least expensive.

Developmental Editing

A developmental editor will, as the title implies, help you to *develop* the flow and content of your story or nonfiction book. An editor of this type is like a minor collaborator, except that you pay him upfront instead of splitting profits. Developmental edits are usually quite expensive and cover your story at the largest levels: How cohesive and coherent is your plot? How clear are your characters' motivations? Have you explained yourself fully and answered readers' questions? Developmental editors may suggest major changes to the direction of a book in addition to smaller refinements that will make your plot and characters (or nonfiction prose and explanatory power) sing.

Relationships with developmental editors usually start early, sometimes before the book has even been started. Most independent authors won't ever work with a developmental editor (in part because they're so expensive), but those who write collaboratively with other writers may find that they essentially get a developmental edit from their partners. If you plan to remain an indie, you may not need to worry about this kind of editing. We'd argue that while developmental edits can be very useful, the 80/20 Rule says that as an indie, the potential benefit probably does not offset the expense.

Line Editing

A line editor's job is to make your prose sound as good as possible. They'll suggest changes to the structure of sentences, removing or revising redundant text, rephrasing where needed, word substitutions, and grammar or typo fixes. But look at the second word in the preceding sentence: A line editor will *suggest* things for you to change, not change them for you. You could hire an editor for your work and then ignore 100 percent of their suggested edits if you wanted to. Don't do that, though. It's possible that you'll get one crap edit and that the editor won't know his butt from a hole in the ground, but if you habitually hire editors and ignore their advice, you're being the worst kind of arrogant: the kind that needs the validation of feeling that you know better than someone else. You're also wasting a lot of money.

Good line editors know when to use semicolons versus commas, and they will spot when pronouns have unclear antecedents. They'll spot unintended sentence fragments, tell you when you're being verbose, and flag my favorite grammar gaffe of all time: improper use of the word "literally." (I once heard a deejay report that at a recent rockin' but non-fatal concert, "they literally turned the stadium upside-down." Imagine the repair bill!)

Our bottom-line suggestion is that independent authors hire a line editor. The expense may suck, but it's better than looking like an indie punk to your readers.

Proofreading

This is the level of editing I start with for my solo work. Follow in my footsteps with caution. After nearly two decades of getting to know myself and my writing style, I feel confident that given the way I work, I can sufficiently developmentally edit and line-edit my own work. This has evoked debate on the podcast, and people usually seem to think I'm at least a little arrogant for working this way. But it's not about being arrogant; it's about putting my time and money where it's best spent. So, at least for now,

I self-edit and polish the crap out of my work, then send it directly to proofreading.

A proofreader's job is to catch mistakes. Proofreaders don't suggest remotely extensive changes, won't usually explain *why* they're suggesting changes, and don't reword sentences. They're there to spot when you've left out a word, when you've forgotten a period or apostrophe, when you've used an incorrect homonym (their/they're/there, too/to/two), and when you've misspelled something.

This is half of what my wife, Robin, does for me. She reads everything I write on my own, and a lot of what Sean and I write together. Not every friend or spouse would make a good proofreader, but Robin does. As right-brained crazy as I am, she's just as left-brained anal. Because she is so analytical, she catches stuff that I don't. Every once in a while, typos slip past, but not often.

Use caution if you want to do something like I've done with Robin, as this is definitely a case of "do as I say, not as I do." Robin happens to be a fast, thorough, and engaged reader, and does genuinely like my many books. There's a significant danger, if you tried to pull something like this off in your life, of causing problems. Plenty of people would see your need for a proofreader as an imposition and resent being asked to read significant amounts of work as a favor to you. They might also see it as work, because reading as a proofreader feels different than reading for enjoyment. (If there's time, Robin actually likes to read my stuff twice: once for pleasure and once for typos.)

Our best first-stop advice would be to hire a line editor for your work, because a line editor will also catch what a proofreader would. Failing that, our advice would be to hire (and pay) a proofreader for a lighter mistake-catching edit. We don't recommend imposing on a spouse or friend as I have. If you do it anyway, you'd better be certain you can deliver a damned clean manuscript, and you'd better be certain they're well-suited to the work and genuinely don't mind (or actively enjoy) doing it.

You've been warned.

Beta Readers

The other thing Robin does for me — and this *is* something you can ask your family and friends to do, if they like your work — is to act as a first reader. This is a great enhancement in our relationship, because despite the occasional uncertainties she's had in the past about the finances of being an independent writer, Robin is my biggest cheerleader. She's proud of me, and heavily invested in several of my story lines, often asking questions like, "When is the next *Beam* coming out?"

If you have people like this in your life, engaging them as beta readers can be a great win-win. They get a first look at your new stuff, and you get feedback on *how* they enjoyed it: what they liked and why. Sean reads most of what he writes or polishes out loud to his wife Cindy. This helps him to catch typos and awkward phrasing, and it's also something they love to do as a couple.

Here are some tips for working with beta readers:

Solicit Honest Opinions

We're all adult enough here to understand that no matter how many times you tell your spouse, "Be totally honest with me about my book," they're not going to tell you it's crap unless they hate you. With that caveat, do keep encouraging your beta readers to be as honest with you as possible, reminding them that your success and growth depends on accurate feedback. They probably won't tell you your book sucks, but a good rule of thumb when receiving feedback from people who like and love you, in order to get a more accurate impression, is to double the negative things they say, then halve the positive. (Dave's formula: Multiply negative by 10 and subtract all the positive).

Ask Specific Questions

Beta readers will generally answer specific queries honestly but hedge on more general ones. Instead of asking a giant question like, "Did you like it?" ask about situations, character motivations, narrative chain, believability of certain moments, and what things surprised them (something *better* have surprised them!). The more you drill down, the more honest and objective your readers are likely to be — and you, then, will be able to extrapolate the overall reader experience. For example, your husband might say that he didn't find what happened in the confrontation scene totally believable, but if that scene is the linchpin of the entire plot, failure in your delivery will lead to a poor reader experience whether your husband will admit it or not.

Listen to Everything

These people have taken their valuable time to give your work feedback, so listen to what they say. Don't ignore the opinions you don't like because you're awesome and they don't understand your staggering artistic genius. Listen with an open mind, then be as objective as you can in deciding what to change and what to leave alone.

But even beyond that, your first readers might offer you some nifty little ideas for future work in the series if you pay attention.

Robin suggested a major plot twist that happened in *Fat Vampire 6.* She did it totally offhandedly, but I thought it was a great tidbit and ran with it. Your readers, if they're engaged — and it's your job to *make* them engaged — will offer all sorts of idea and theories and desires for your story's future. Listen to them all, and you might find some gems. Even better, keep in mind what your beta readers are: *readers.* If they have specific hopes for the story, they're probably not the only ones among your larger readership. Satisfy your beta readers first. The rest will follow.

We actually *solicited requests* from a beta reader once, just for kicks. Our friend Kyeli absolutely loves the *Unicorn Western* books, so before writing the final book in the core part of the series, we asked Kyeli what random thing she'd like to see in *Unicorn Western 9.* She thought for a moment and said, "I'd like to see a prophetic owl." So, we wrote them in — not one, but *two* prophetic owls.

Don't Listen to Everything

When you send your work to beta readers, you want opinions and feedback, but you can't be like a mote of dust in a sunbeam, tossed helplessly about by those opinions. Stand firm as the creator, and listen without feeling compelled to change the manuscript every time someone offers a thought.

The best way to consider beta reader feedback is in aggregate. It might not matter that Tom didn't like X while Sally loved it, because in aggregate those two opinions cancel each other out. In general, you can usually choose to ignore matters of opinion if only one out of a handful of readers felt it should change and if you want it to remain as is, but if you find that three or four people felt the same way, or are saying the exact same thing, that's a trend, and you should definitely listen.

Be Appreciative

Regardless of whether early readers loved or hated your book, they took the time to read and offer feedback. Respect the time and affection for you and your work that went into their willingness to act as your beta readers. Smile, say thank you, and maybe do something nice for them from time to time if you use them repeatedly.

Best Practices for Editing

We've had a lot of editing work done and have worked with several editors (some better than others), so we thought we'd use a few words here to give you some of our best tips on how to work with editors and how to maximally benefit from edits received.

Learn to Revise Your Own Work

You should always run your work past an editor, but you will get better editing suggestions if your draft is as clean as possible before you send it off. If your draft is full of errors, your editor will be overwhelmed by noting them and won't be able to ease into the story and catch deeper, more subtle issues that could really make your manuscript shine. So, it's to your advantage to self-edit as thoroughly as possible. This is a learned skill that will continue to improve, so long as you do the hard work of paying attention.

When I do this, I read through my manuscript inside of Scrivener, stopping to smooth out sentences that clang in my ear. This is a habituation thing, and you'll learn it through practice, but in general anything that makes you hesitate will do the same for a reader. Reading should feel effortless, so make your sentences easy to absorb. This doesn't mean dumbing down your language. Sean and I write some pretty complex stuff, especially with *The Beam* and the non-Lexi parts in *The Future of Sex*, and the stuff Sean does with Boricio in the *Yesterday's Gone* series is ridiculous. But complicated construction should still be pleasant for the reader. We both love listening to Eminem, and appreciate his gnarled and knotted, intelligently crafted rhythms and rhyme schemes. They are incredibly complicated, but easy on the ear if his music is your kind of thing.

By the time you start your edit, the story's end should be clear in your mind, so focus on removing any of the loose ends you undoubtedly wrote when you weren't 100 percent sure how everything would eventually turn out, while simultaneously adding bits here and there that steer the story more faithfully toward your conclusion.

Tighten your prose as much as possible. When in doubt, cut passages that seem to over-explain something or that are redundant. (Scrivener gives you the ability to take a "snapshot" of a scene before you start editing it so that you'll always have the earlier version. There's no reason not to hack sections out; they'll still be in the snapshot if you decide you want them back.) Personally, I tend to write a lot of nonsensical fluff when I'm in a thoughtful, non-action-oriented scene. My dialogue, action, and narrative scenes (where characters are actually doing something) tend to be tight, but I'm sloppy when characters are musing. When I edit those scenes, I'll remove entire paragraphs because I realize I'm just restating something I've already said. Strunk and White's writing dictum is "Omit needless words," and we agree. Sir Arthur Quiller-Couch said "Murder your darlings" (remove sections you might love if they don't serve the story). We agree with that, too. Cut when in doubt. Your second draft should usually be around 10 percent smaller than your first, and taking out that 10 percent will invigorate your prose, guaranteed.

The more you do this, the better you'll get. You'll learn to read with a reader's ear, and start to notice things like unclear pronouns (you can only say "he" a few times before you should really say the character's name again) and sentences that just sort of hang without due explanation. Keep practicing, and logging your 10,000 hours. If you're paying attention, each one will make you better than the one before.

You should be constantly improving the quality of your copy. Once you start to catch most of what the editor would normally catch before it leaves your desk, the editor will be able to do his or her job that much better, and really bring out the very best in what you send off.

Find an Editor That Understands You and Your Work

That doesn't mean "look among your friends for an editor," but it does mean to put in the time to find and develop a relationship with an editor rather than considering him or her to be a disposable person you hire for one-off deals. Spend a lot of time seeking out the best editor you can find (and afford), basing your decision on referrals, track record, testimonials, or recommendations from writer friends. Try out a few editors and have them all edit something small as a trial. Some editors will suggest changes that will make you roll your eyes and say, "OH MY GOD, DID YOU EVEN READ THIS?" because the changes would invalidate the point of an exchange or section.

Find someone you jibe with, who gets what you're trying to do with your writing, and who understands your product catalogue as a whole rather than just an individual work. Then, as you work with the editor, think of the relationship like dating. At first, it'll be a little awkward as your writing and the editor's editing style get to know one another. In time, the edits will become more aligned with the work, as the editor gets a feel for your voice and style.

Our editor, Jason Whited (hi, Jason!), used to work with Dave at a newspaper (in an undisclosed location). He understands our sense of humor and writing conventions. He can spot places where we've made a mistake or a misstep versus places where we're doing something that's technically "wrong" on purpose, as a device. Every manuscript we get back from Jason is a bit purer (catching more mistakes while not flagging things that he understands we're doing for a reason), and we agree with his edits more and more.

In a way, working with a line editor should be like working with a collaborator, and that will happen naturally if your editor understands both you and your work. The writer/editor exchange shouldn't be linear and unchanging. It should evolve and improve, so you start to think and work like a team.

Always Edit for Flow

You want your reader in a state of "flow" when they read your work, so whether you're self-editing or reviewing suggestions from your editor, make your decisions based on what best serves that flow.

Once, our editor suggested removing some jargon I'd written for one of our characters. I didn't agree with the edit; the character was a jargony kind of guy who used big words to convey his superiority over others. But Sean did agree, and he axed it. This was totally fine, because although I would have left it, the character had used other big words in the same passage, hence keeping the spirit of his obnoxiousness intact. Moreover, Sean axed the jargon for the best of reasons. "I think it might make a reader pause," he said. And we both know how important it is to never jar the reader, making her suddenly aware that she is, in fact, *reading* rather than *experiencing*.

For the same reason, we've suggested that writers whose primary audience is American use American spellings even if the writer is British or Canadian. You might sit down for a cup of *yoghurt* in Canada, but an American is going to WTF all over that spelling, and it'll slap him right out of flow. You might accurately head to the *centre* of town in England, but the U.K. spelling will clang on an American's ear and eye. I'm not trying to be ethnocentric here; if I were writing a book for Brits, I'd use British spellings. It's all about maintaining that flow state, for whoever your primary readership is likely to be.

One exception before we move on: We once had a British podcast listener argue for his use of the British slang word "chav" in his book, despite the fact that most readers would likely be American. We absolutely encouraged him to use the word and *not* change it, because it was being used in dialogue by a British character. Dialogue is different than narration. The narrator's voice shouldn't clash with the likely reader's voice, but dialogue is the sole business of the character speaking. If the character was British and was the kind of guy who would call someone a "chav," then he should absolutely, 100 percent use that word, and the writer could make its meaning (which Americans and others wouldn't automatically know) clear from context.

Practice the 80/20 Rule

Some traditionally minded people will tell you that you need all kinds of editors to generate a respectable manuscript. They'll suggest hiring a developmental editor to help you with the story, one or two line editors to help you get the wording right, several proofreaders to check for errors, and dozens of beta readers.

We think this is overkill for indies.

Is that kind of comprehensive editing ideal? Sure, maybe. For a publishing house, it might make sense. For large-budget books that have to be just perfect in order to earn maximal profit, it might make sense. But for your average independent self-published author, it's way too much. It will cost a fortune to buy all of that editing, and few self-publishers will ever earn that money back.

We suggest you employ the 80/20 Rule. Get *good* editing, but don't worry about *perfect* editing. Get a good line editor, hone your own ability to self-edit, get a few beta readers, and call it a day. Do an 80-percent job using 20 percent of the potential cost and time so that you'll still have the remaining 80 percent of time and money and can use it to create and publish more books.

Don't Over-Edit

As mentioned earlier, writer and publishing authority Dean Wesley Smith advocates not rewriting your work. Dean follows "Heinlein's Rules," which include "You must refrain from rewriting, except to editorial order."

Okay, Dean fans, pay attention to what I just wrote twice: *rewriting*, not *editing*. So for one, let's be clear that even Dean agrees that you can't just sloppily hand off a manuscript that might be filled with errors.

But still, most of what writers have been taught to do in the editing process — and, honestly, most of what we've talked about so far in this book — is closer to rewriting than Dean's definition of editing. This is a sticky issue, and we simultaneously agree and disagree with Dean about it. The line is very, very fine, and you'll only find it with practice.

Let's start with what we — Sean and Johnny — believe.

Most writers have an idea in their heads of what seems to be the "correct" way to write. This is often school-taught stuff — or, in some literarily superior cases, school-*shamed* stuff. If you don't write "properly," you're a hack. You're not doing it right, etc.

But we feel that "correct versus incorrect" is separate from "voice." It is possible to be very technically incorrect while still being correct as far as your book is concerned, and the difference goes to your voice as a writer. Consider this passage from Chuck Palahniuk's *Fight Club*:

> The only woman here at Remaining Men Together, the testicular cancer support group, this woman smokes her cigarette under the burden of a stranger, and her eyes come together with mine.
>
> Faker.
>
> Faker.

177

Faker.

Short matte black hair, big eyes the way they are in Japanese animation, skim milk thin, buttermilk sallow in her dress with a wallpaper pattern of dark roses, this woman was also in my tuberculosis support group Friday night. She was in my melanoma round table Wednesday night. Monday night she was in my Firm Believers leukemia rap group. The part down the center of her hair is a crooked lightning bolt of white scalp.

There are editors who would crap their pants reading that. The "rules" that Chuck violates on a regular basis number in the dozens, but in the end it's just his voice.

Here's another — one of my favorites from Bret Easton Ellis's *American Psycho*:

"Come on," I yell, taking her hand.

She puts her drink down on the bar and follows me through the deserted club, up the stairs toward the rest rooms. There's really no reason why we couldn't do it downstairs but that seems tacky and so we do most of it in one of the men's room stalls. Back outside the men's room I sit on a couch and smoke one of her cigarettes while she goes downstairs to get us drinks.

She comes back apologizing for her behavior earlier this evening. "I mean I loved Barcadia, the food was outstanding and that mango sorbet, ohmygod I was in heaven. Listen, it's okay that we didn't go to Dorsia. We can always go some other night and I know that you probably tried to get us in but it's just so hot right now. But, oh yeah, I really loved the food at Barcadia. How long has it been open? I think it's been three, four months. I read a great review in New York or maybe it was

Gourmet ... But anyway, do you want to come with me to this band tomorrow night, or maybe we can go to Dorsia and then see Wallace's band or maybe go to Dorsia after, but maybe it's not even open that late. Patrick, I'm serious: you should really see them. Avatar is such a great lead singer and I actually thought I was in love with him once—well, actually I was in lust, not love. I really liked Wallace then but he was into this whole investment banking thing and he couldn't handle the routine and he broke down, it was the acid not the cocaine that did it. I mean I know but so when that all fell apart I knew that it would be, like, best to just hang out and not deal with

J&B I am thinking. Glass of J&B in my right hand I am thinking. Hand I am thinking. Charivari. Shirt from Charivari. Fusilli I am thinking. Jami Gertz I am thinking. I would like to fuck Jami Gertz I am thinking. Porsche 911. A sharpei I am thinking. I would like to own a sharpei. I am twenty-six years old I am thinking. I will be twenty-seven next year. A Valium. I would like a Valium. No, two Valium I am thinking. Cellular phone I am thinking.

After reading that, the editor nauseated by Chuck Palahniuk's passage would probably send him flowers. The absurdity of the above passage is off the hook, but here's the thing: *The narrator is a psychopath.*

Similarly, in the first passage, the narrator is a man who's become totally numb to life. You're supposed to hear his narrative as deadpan, devoid of emotion, almost stream of consciousness.

So, why does this matter? Well, if you believe all the crap that was beaten into you about "proper" writing in school and by snooty literary types, you might go into editing and remove everything about your work that makes it unique and special. I'm one of the few people who likes the *Fight Club* book better than the movie. Why? Because of Chuck's voice. The story is great, but it's the voice that makes it a home run for me. Sean argues that David Fincher captured Palahniuk's voice perfectly, but whatever.

I think that this is what Dean is getting at with Heinlein's Rules. Every writer is different (Dean says that a lot, too), but when most of us "rewrite" (a comprehensive, second-draft edit), there's a serious danger of over-editing and stripping out voice as you try and gut the clutter. Dean says to let it stay, the idea being that the creative, semi-subconscious part of your mind that was in charge when you wrote the first draft knows better than the critical asshole who so often shows up during revision.

We're somewhere in the middle. We advise you to pay attention to your voice and be careful, but to trim the fat as best you can without going overboard and making your work sound like an encyclopedia — yet one more reason to find an editor who understands you and your work.

Study Your Edits and Improve Your Craft

When you get suggested edits back from your editor, it'll be up to you to decide which to accept. You should probably, all other things being equal, accept more than you decline. (If not, why do you keep hiring this editor?)

As you go through your edits, pay attention. A good editor will explain his suggestions, and a smart writer will read those explanations and learn. You'll also see where you most often have issues in your earlier drafts, such as me when I write thoughtful, explanatory passages.

Since I'm writing this and can therefore embarrass Sean, I'll point out two things that I told him he used to do — but that he's since fixed, because he's smart and always improves whatever he does.

First, he used to confuse dialogue attributions with actions. This is what he used to do:

"Let's ride," Clint climbed up onto Edward.

That's an error, not a matter of voice. It should be either a dialogue attribution (and be worded as such) or a stand-alone action (and be punctuated as such.)

Both of these are correct:

"Let's ride," said Clint.
"Let's ride." Clint climbed up onto Edward.

Another thing Sean used to get wrong — as almost everyone does — was the use of semicolons. You should be able to split a sentence apart at a semicolon and both sentences should still make sense. People tend to use them like commas, the clauses around which don't have to stand on their own.

Correct (if not exactly thrilling): Tom stood up; he turned around.
Incorrect: Tom stood up; and turned around.

After I pointed this out, Sean then fell in love with semicolons, and for a while every other sentence, when the draft came back to me on certain projects, carried a semicolon. But then we swung back toward the middle, and now Sean never makes either of the above errors. It's fantastic. It saves him revision effort and me (or Jason) time when polishing.

NOTE: For those interested in learning more about Sean's shortcomings, contact David Wright. Ask him about Sean's early action scenes.

CHAPTER ELEVEN:
Creating Professional Products Part 4: Post-Production

YOU HAVE YOUR MANUSCRIPT WRITTEN, tidied, edited, polished, and ready for the prom. Your beta readers loved what you wrote, and you're ready to sell it to the world. That's awesome; you're most of the way there.

You may be tempted at this point to think that you've already done your 80-percent work on this particular book. Hell, if you listen to us, you might think that we'd agree, because we're always talking about how important it is to write the next book, and how that need supplants most other things.

Well, that's unfortunately not true. What follows in this chapter matters a *lot*, so be sure to read it all. Your book needs to present itself professionally enough that readers will be intrigued enough to give it a shot (at best) or at least not mentally lump it in with other "self-published crap" (at least). And while there are 80-percent and 20-percent activities in everything below, omitting or half-assing what follows as a whole will sink you before your first stroke.

What follows are the things we think you should pay attention to.

Covers

Covers aren't a simple topic, but we've put them first because in almost all cases, your book's cover is the first thing a potential reader will see. The cover is your chance to catch a browser's eye and pull her in so your title and product description can do the hard work of convincing her to buy — or at least download a sample of your book. If you're paying attention, you'll notice that this makes your cover the single most important marketing asset your book has. It is very much worth the time, effort, and cost to get it right.

The cardinal rule in creating book covers is this: *Unless you are totally and completely certain you can do a good job, don't even try.* Seriously. Don't think, "I'm sure I can do an OK job." Don't think, "The book's contents matter more, so whatever." Don't think, "I have a list of people who already love me, and I'm sure what I can do will be *good enough* for them."

"Good enough" isn't good enough. Instead of loving you enough to see past your crappy cover, those people who already love you will be shocked that someone they love made something so crappy.

Accordingly, the vast majority of indie authors should hire a cover designer. Dave has a graphics background and an excellent artistic eye and hence does many of our covers, but we hire out our most important ones. The *Unicorn Western* cover, created by Erin Mehlos, flat-out makes the book, and we can't imagine the series without it:

That cover does it all. It says exactly what the series is (yes, it really is about a gunslinger who rides a unicorn), it conveys the tone (somewhat gonzo but with the potential for epic awesomeness), and looks badass. People see that cover and can't resist clicking further with a sense of positive expectancy. That's what you want.

You can probably get a good cover designed for a few hundred dollars, and believe us — assuming you chose your designer wisely, it will be the best money you've ever spent promoting your book. Go with someone recommended by your author friends, and if you don't have any author friends or if they can't help you, look at the covers of books published by other indies until you find some that really stand out. (Hint: You will often find the best covers on the best-selling indie books. That's not a coincidence.)

But what if you still, despite everything we've just said, insist on creating your own cover? What if you truly want to take the chance of dooming your book with something that nobody likes? Well, then let me pass the mic to Dave so he can give a few thoughts on creating good covers on a shoestring:

So, you're going to do your own cover, eh?

Johnny and Sean really couldn't talk you out of it?

OK, if you insist. I'm going to give you a few pointers to help you not fall on your face. This is by no means an exhaustive list, as I'm not a cover designer by trade. I'm not even a graphic designer. I was a cartoonist, which is an entirely different art form, but I do well enough that a lot of people say they love our covers. I'm also a huge fan of great book covers, so I suppose some of that has rubbed off on me enough that I don't embarrass us (much like years and years of serialized TV have helped Sean and I write what we write).

If you're going to make your own cover, it's essential that you know your limitations. I know mine: I'm not a Photoshop guru and can't manipulate images especially well, so I don't even try. Though I had no vested interest in their stupid unicorn story, that wasn't the reason I didn't make the cover. When I can't find the right image(s) or think the book needs something beyond what I can do, I (we) go to the professionals. You should, too.

If your eye is sharp, or you have some artistic (visual) background and want to design your cover, here are some tips that will help you make the best one possible.

The Image
I'll assume up front that you have a passing familiarity with a photo manipulation program like Photoshop or the free Gimp. If not, you should *definitely* outsource your cover design. Your book cover is not the place to experiment and learn.

You can find a royalty-free photo at places like Shutterstock.com or some of the other stock image photo sites online. But keep something in mind: you don't *own* the image. You are just paying to use it. The original copyright belongs to either the photographer or the website that sold you the image.

Pay attention to usage rights. Most places allow you to use images for e-book and print books under a basic license, but if you want to create posters, shirts, mugs, or other art using the stock images, you may need to pay more for an extended license.

Choose a photo that either symbolizes what your book is about or conveys the mood in shorthand. Some of the best, most iconic book covers are about establishing mood, not spelling out what the book is about in obvious images. Think of Stephanie Meyer's *Twilight.*

Yes, I know there are all sorts of truly artistic covers out there that I could have used for my example, but I wanted to go with something that's reached an iconic status that easily comes to mind, rather than try and impress you with some obscure variant special edition book cover nobody's ever seen. Besides, that book moved millions of copies. The cover had something to do with it.

The *Twilight* publisher could have easily put some hunky teen with vampire teeth on the cover along with a pretty girl and a werewolf. The book might have found an audience. But I think that cover would've limited their audience greatly. The cover they did use (prior to the movie, anyway) of a girl's pale hands set against a dark background holding a red apple is so perfect at establishing mood. It's an image that piques your curiosity, that spells the end of innocence, and the shadows in both the apple and the girl's hands hints at something dark lurking. *Perfect!*

Sean told me a story about how he almost bought that book before the first movie came out. He hadn't even heard of it. He was just in Barnes & Noble and couldn't help but pick it up.

So, think about your story. What would be a good symbol for your cover? Which image would either establish mood or pique the curiosity of people passing it in a bookstore or viewing a thumbnail online?

One rookie mistake I see a lot — and I mean *a lot* — is framing a photo in some sort of colored border. Either the cover artist didn't have a large enough photo or couldn't crop it without losing something of value, so they stuck it in a box.

That looks like *crap!* Don't do it!

The photo should, unless you have some damned creative way to work around it, take up the whole cover.

Some creative ways you can use less of a photo include a box or colored band up top with the book's title. I've seen this used to good effect from time to time. We've done it ourselves with *Yesterday's Gone: Episode 1*. But be careful to make this look like a style choice, rather than the result of a bad photo.

The Typeface

You want your book's title to stand out and be easily readable in the image thumbnail, which is how most people are likely to first see it on a website. That means picking an easy-to-read typeface — often erroneously referred to as "fonts" for a reason that would bore you — that's large enough to... well... *read*. Find the typeface that best suits your cover, but isn't too cute, weird, or hard to read.

A terrific free source of high-quality fonts can be found at www.fontsquirrel.com. Sometimes, though, you'll find that the best typeface will cost you. A good source for not-terribly-expensive fonts is myfont.com.

(Fair warning: Typefaces can get expensive. The one we use on most of our Collective Inkwell titles is Gotham Ultra, which cost more than I ever spent on a typeface, but it was well worth the investment as it's a nice big, chunky, easy-to-read typeface.)

Please, for the love of God, avoid any typeface that you wouldn't see on a bestselling book cover. Yes, I know you can find a typeface made of dragons or panda bears, but THAT DOESN'T MEAN YOU SHOULD USE THEM!

Thanks, Dave! We love all your shouting. But we must say goodbye, lest you turn into the Hulk.

Titles

After your potential customer has been hooked by your cover, the next thing they'll usually notice is your title. You want the title to perk your reader's ears (or eyes) for long enough to earn a serious look at your product description — the last remaining bit of gauntlet they need to run before they decide to buy. You'll handle your title differently depending on whether your book is fiction or nonfiction. Because we're fiction guys, we'll start there.

Fiction titles should evoke a pleasantly intriguing reaction. Together with your cover, you want your title to give your potential reader a feeling for what the book is about, what its tone is like, and what kind of a reading experience they're in for.

In our opinion, a lot of this comes down to feeling and musicality. You want to evoke a "feel," and that's hard to put a finger on — but with practice, you'll know it when you see or hear it. For instance, our comedy *Everyone Gets Divorced* has a somewhat playful title that implies a light (rather than heavy and depressing) take on divorce. By contrast, *The Beam* and *Namaste*, two of our dead-serious titles, have stark, almost ominous-sounding titles. One of our two collaborative series with Lexi Maxxwell has a very clear title: *The Future of Sex.*

Any question a to exactly what that one's about? When you pair the titles with their respective covers, you get a very good idea of what kind of a book you're looking at. If you're the kind of reader who's right for that book, hopefully they attract you as well.

The oddest title I have is *The Bialy Pimps*. Nobody knows what a bialy is (except for Seth Godin, who told me I'd made the mistake of putting a bagel instead of a bialy on the book's cover), but it almost doesn't matter. Everyone knows what pimps are, and when you put a strange word like "bialy" in front of "pimps" as if describing a certain *kind* of pimp, that's usually enough to get the target audience to at least take a look. In this case, it's curiosity evoked by the title that does the work ... and when you see that the cover is a bagel (not a bialy!) wearing rhinestone-studded shutter shades, that curiosity only gets higher.

The title of *The Bialy Pimps* is cute and makes people wonder, and it works with the plot. (The book is as silly as the title and cover; it's about an uprising at a rogue bagel deli ... which, by the way, also serves *bialys*, which are bagels' baked and no-holed cousins.) Still, it could come off as too obtuse, so I added a tagline — an extra descriptor following the title that gives readers a bit more context and curiosity. The tagline for *The Bialy Pimps* is "A Tale of Fame and Baked Goods."

Not everyone agrees on what makes a good title. Dave strongly disagrees with some of ours, but we're only willing to give him credit for being right about one of them because we're jerks like that.

Here's that story of the one we think he got right:

We had a series that was originally titled *Chupacabra Outlaw*, but a few months after finishing the pilot, we changed it to *Cursed*. We don't think *Chupacabra Outlaw* was a bad title per se (though Dave does); it was more that the project we'd conceived turned out to be very different once it was actually on the page. We started out to write something light: a sort of campy werewolf story with chupacabras as the monster of choice. But instead, we ended up with a story that was very dark and sparse that wasn't campy at all. It became a merciless, brooding sort of horror story that was totally wrong for its original title. That new story dictated a new title — but if *Cursed* had turned out as we'd thought it would, we would have stuck with its original name.

Now for an example of a title Dave hates, but that we'll defend to the end of time: *Unicorn Western*. The 9-book series is a sprawling, complex fantasy epic, and although Dave has come around on the series itself, he thinks the name is turning readers off and hampering its growth. We disagree. We could have named it as a western (*Guns of the Fast Hand*, perhaps) or as a fantasy (like *Realm and Sands*, which is the name we chose for our publishing company), but it's not truly a western or a fantasy. It's its own thing. People who went into *Unicorn Western* expecting a western would be annoyed ("a unicorn? That's not right!"), and people who went in expecting an epic fantasy would be annoyed ("a gunslinger riding an asshole of a mount? What the hell?"). Instead, the odd name *Unicorn Western* makes a promise that is more than fulfilled by Clint with his guns and Edward with his surly demeanor and rainbow-colored blood. You go in knowing what you're getting — and by the end, you're rooting for those two misfit heroes to save all of the worlds. Maybe a western-sounding or a fantasy-sounding title would work better in the short-term, but we're not short-term thinkers. For the readers we want long-term, "Unicorn Western" is just right.

So that's fiction. By contrast, nonfiction titles are totally different, and a lot of your nonfiction marketing work can be accomplished by simply choosing the right title (and, optionally, subtitle) for your book. That means selecting a title/subtitle combination that clearly tells people what the book is about and conveys an obvious benefit. Think of your title like this: you want potential buyers to read your title and think, "Wow, that's *exactly* the answer to my problem!"

To get the most out of title selection, it's probably smart to do some basic keyword research in order to align your book's name as closely as possible with what people are actually out there searching for. A "keyword" or "keyword phrase" is something that a person enters into a search engine when they're looking for information, and a bit of research can increase the chances of your book coming up in those people's searches. Google is the world's largest search engine, but Amazon isn't far behind, and a good title gives you a better shot of coming up in searches on both. (The difference between Google and Amazon, by the way, is that most Amazon searchers already have their wallets out and are looking to buy — and that's very good news for you if your title comes up first.)

Keyword research can be invaluable for nonfiction authors and is unlike anything writers, marketers, and entrepreneurs have had available until the last few years. Amazingly, you can get this information with just a few keystrokes. How exactly to do it is outside of the scope of this book, but you can … wait for it … *search around* to find out how to do it. The depth of keyword research we're talking about here can be done for free, so don't spend money on this step. In the past, an equivalent of this kind of market research would have required deep buckets of money for shallow results. Not anymore, though.

Sean's first nonfiction book was called *Writing Online*. He played with many titles, but then realized that clarity should come before cleverness in the case of a nonfiction title. He knew how the game worked and had been making money as an SEO ninja (writing search-engine-optimized copy), so when he finished the book, he did some basic keyword research using Google's free keyword tool and found that more than 50,000 people per month were searching the exact term "writing online." Simply titling his book accordingly made for a bunch of free marketing, putting it right in front of the people who wanted it most.

So to sum up the "titles" discussion, we'll put it this way: For fiction, use your ear. For nonfiction, use your brain (and keyword tools) to get inside the minds of people asking questions that your book can answer. But either way, a title's purpose is to make your book's benefit clear to those who are an ideal fit for it.

Formatting

A detailed tutorial on formatting your book is probably unnecessary in the context of this book (at best) and convoluted (at worst), so we're mostly going to pass the buck.

If you're using Scrivener as your primary writing software — which you should be; go back and read the section on using the right tools — then formatting is all handled in the "Compile" process. That's good news for you as you write, because you can and should be making documents and filling them with text without worrying about chapter headings, subheads, and the rest.

Here are a few of the very, very, *very* basics:

File Types

The two main file types you'll want for e-books are .mobi files (for Amazon Kindle) and .epub (for everyone else). You'll choose the file type option from the bottom of the Compile menu.

You can also compile as a PDF, and I compile to Microsoft Word (Yes! Loathed Word!) as a step in creating print books. The rest we mostly ignore.

Section Headings

Again if you're using Scrivener to write (and dammit, you should be; you're worth it), you'll turn those plain text documents (which should be named with the titles of your chapters, subchapters, or whatever) into formatted text complete with chapter, section, and subsection headings using the "Formatting" section of the "Compile" pane.

You can choose whether the section is topped by *Chapter One* (or *Chapter 1*, or something else) here, and can choose whether or not the name you gave that chapter is included or not. For instance, in the *Unicorn Western* file, the first text document is titled "The Hitching," but "The Hitching" doesn't actually appear in the text document itself. Our compile formatting settings are such that when Scrivener spits out the e-book, it puts two blank lines at the top of each page, then "CHAPTER ONE" in all caps, and "The Hitching" on the next line. It gives us another blank line, then the text file's contents.

Cover and Table of Contents
I sweated this before I discovered Scrivener. There are third-party programs out there that you can run your Word (or whatever) document through to create an e-book file complete with an included cover and table of contents, but Scrivener does it all for you. There's a "Cover" section just as there's the "Formatting" section just mentioned. Simply pull the cover image into the Scrivener file somewhere and choose it in this section. This is typically a file with dimensions around 800x600 pixels, and is actually bundled into your e-book file. This is not the same version of the cover as you'll upload for display on the e-book sites. It's much smaller.

Scrivener also automatically generates and includes your book's table of contents, based on the documents you choose for compiling.

For More Information

That's it for this so-short-why-did-we-bother section. But really, you don't want to hear us go on and on about formatting details when we have so many better things to talk about. We recommend picking up Gwen Hernandez's book *Scrivener for Dummies* for a ton more information on how to format and compile your books if you can't figure out some aspect of compiling.

Anything else we say here will only confuse us as much as you, and keep us from discussing Dave and unicorns.

Product Descriptions

The title and cover of a book make a promise to readers, and the story inside the book keeps it. Your product description's job is to reinforce that promise.

Your product description mostly comprises teaser/description copy about your book's plot (fiction) or benefit and contents (nonfiction), but we usually also suggest adding a customer review or two once you have some. Quotes from satisfied readers act as social proof, and show that other people loved your book ... and that therefore, your prospective reader may, too.

When writing your description, you want to keep in mind what the reader is looking for. Nonfiction readers are looking for a solution to a specific problem, so anticipate their pain and use the description to promise the solution (assuming your book delivers), then give some idea of the book's contents. Fiction readers are looking for an experience and a hook that will draw their interest without spoiling anything. We recommend looking to old movie trailers as a way to do this.

As an example, here's our product description for *Namaste*:

> **Peace Comes From Within. Death Comes From Without.**
> *An unlikely tale of vengeance*
>
> Amit is a Zen monk. A member of the elite order of the Sri, his every waking moment is spent training his body and mind to the peak of human ability — and beyond. But the order is pacifist, a repository for deadly weapons with their safeties permanently set to "on."
>
> Until everything is taken from him, and Amit decides that turning the other cheek is no longer an option.
>
> Now, every ounce of his training will be put to the test. His epic quest for revenge will see wrongs righted — or see Amit forgotten in an unmarked grave.

Your title and cover tell the reader what sort of story they can expect, and we used the bold line at the top of the description to put a fine point on the main hook. Read those top two lines, and you pretty much know what the book is going to be like. If *Namaste* is the right kind of book for you as a reader, you're already sold.

Pricing

We talk a lot about pricing — in many different forms and from many different angles — throughout this book. For now, we want you to understand a few things about pricing.

What It's Worth to the Customer Matters

No one needs convincing of this one. If a customer looks at your book and your price and decides that the former isn't worth the latter, you've lost a sale.

What It's Worth to You Matters, Too

Few people consider this alternative point, though — or if they do, others yell at them and tell them they're being self-centered and/or unrealistic.

We contend that *what a book is worth to you matters,* no matter what anyone says, because you have to know if it's worth your time to write another.

Think about this like you'd think about crowdfunding platforms like Kickstarter. When you start a Kickstarter campaign, you decide how much money you need to raise to effectively fund your venture. The price you set tells the world, "I'm not willing to do this for less than this price." That's neither arrogant nor spiteful; it simply is what it is. If the world likes your plan, they'll fund it, you'll get paid, and you can do your project. But if the world doesn't want to pay you that much (because it isn't worth it to the world), then you don't do it. You shouldn't be mad about that, because you wouldn't have wanted to do it for less.

We suggest you add some of this thought into writing your books. A lot of people argued with us when we priced the full first season of *The Beam* at $9.99. They said it was an unreasonable price, and that indies shouldn't price that high. We had many counterarguments. We'll detail one here: *The Beam* was very hard to write and took twice the length of anything else in the lab, regardless of word count, so if it turned out that we *couldn't* charge $10, we weren't going to do it again.

See the difference? The argument isn't, "We're damned well going to charge $10 and you can take it or leave it, suckers!" This was our Kickstarter. If people bought it at $10 and showed us that it was worthwhile for us to spend the extra time to write a *Season Two* (because that time would be rewarded with a bigger price tag), we'd go ahead. If it failed, we wouldn't. Because there are other, faster projects we could write in that time if all we could charge for that word count turned out to be $5.

NOTE: When we talk about our earnings on projects like this, we are talking about what we make on individual sales, not total revenue. We are comfortable selling fewer copies of *The Beam* at a higher per unit profit, *because* it is our premium product. This is one of the advantages to having an expansive (and constantly growing) catalogue. Not all writers share these same values, and that's okay. You should never let other people (us or anyone) tell you what's best for you.

Price Isn't Always About Profit

Writers who don't truly understand marketing (and the placing of individual products within a larger product catalog) often think in terms of profit maximization. In this way of thinking, there are three forces at play: customer price tolerance, corresponding sales volume, and net profit per unit sold.

In other words, profit-minded people are always asking, "What's the price and sales sweet spot that earns me maximum income?" You can raise the price until your sales numbers slow enough to make the price hike not worth it. Conversely, reducing price is worth doing if the increased number of sales you get from using that cheaper price makes for a higher net profit.

We've said it many times already, and will continue to say it because it's the essential message of this book: Multiple products in the marketplace give you more to play with and make experimentation simpler. You want three things: conversion, readership, and attention. It can be quite valuable to set a price that maximizes eyes on your work, even if doing so is costing you profits.

Our friend Ed Robertson is a great writer and author of the *Breakers* series. He also happens to be a smart marketer and brilliant tactician. He knows as much about the way Amazon works as anyone we know. Ed's *Breakers* novels (as of this writing, there are four) tend to sell normally somewhere between $2.99 and $4.99. In September 2013, he created a box set containing books 1-3 in the series, priced it at 99 cents, and promoted it heavily.

Soon after he did this (shortly after releasing *Reapers*, the 4th book in the series), the series' established popularity combined with the cheap bundled deal shot him up to around #250 on Amazon, where he stayed for *months*. That kind of "stickiness" on the charts is unheard of on Amazon; most high-ranking books usually slide down in time.

Now, Ed's losing money on that box set, almost for certain. Amazon's price structure is such that he needs to sell six times as many books at 99 cents to see the same amount of money as he'd get at $2.99.

But what else happened? *Reapers* shot up to around #1,000-1,500 (also quite high) and *also* stayed there. People were picking up the box set, seeing that *Reapers* was also discounted ($2.99 instead of $3.99) and bought that one, too. As of this writing, books ranked at #1,000 on the Amazon.com charts tend to sell around 100 copies per day.

If Ed had only thought about making money on the box set, it's almost certain that he'd be making less overall ... and even *that* bigger-picture profit isn't the whole story. While Ed is riding high, he's gaining readers. His mailing list is growing larger. Ed's not done with the *Breakers* series yet, and will surely cash in when the next book comes out and when many more people know who he is, and are already salivating for what's coming next.

Over-Pricing Will Hamper Book Sales

Kind of obvious, right? Without a good reason for a high tag, pricing too high relative to other books in your market will usually result in lower sales.

We know this is obvious, but it's also a counterpoint to the next section, which is the *startling truth (!!!)* that ...

Under-Pricing May Also Hamper Book Sales (And Can Make You Look Bad)

When the Kindle marketplace was new, it was common for writers to price their books at 99 cents and see huge sales volumes. That happened because the market wasn't yet crowded, and fewer people understood e-books, so it worked.

Today, the market is used to e-books — and because of that, 99 cents finally looks like the e-book ghetto price that it is. People now understand that a book is a book: something they don't mind paying for. So, when they see an absurdly low price outside of a sale (a full-length novel for 99 cents, a 10-book set with a regular price of $3.99), they wonder what's wrong with it.

If you're having a sale, fine. Note the sale's existence in the product description and include the normal price. But if your everyday, normal price is too low, people will ask why it isn't higher and likely assume it isn't a quality book. They'll go in expecting a 99-cent experience, and even if they buy will be predisposed to finding fault and leaving a poor review.

(And yes, Ed Robertson from the previous section does indicate that his three-book bundle is at a special price.)

Bundles Should be Priced Like Bundles

Bundles are powerful. You're giving people an easy "yes," because they can pick up multiple books at a discount.

This assumes you price them correctly. Unless you're including bonus content (*excellent* bonus content), the price of a bundle should always be lower than the price of the individual volumes. I like a discount of 33 percent or more over buying all of the books individually. Sean is even more aggressive and likes the idea of a "bucket offer," or an offer that's so good it's almost impossible for someone even remotely interested to say no to — meaning a bundle that amounts to about 60 percent off. The *Unicorn Western Saga* is a bucket offer. Individually, the nine books at $2.99 each would be just shy of $27. The full saga (more than a quarter million words) is $9.99. Ten bucks might be a lot for a book (too much for an indie, so say some) but if you read the first one for free, enjoy it, know from reviews that it only gets better as the books progress, and know that you can buy the next 25 hours of reading at a steep discount, you're likely to buy.

Whatever you decide, make sure to include the value pricing in your product description: *"Save 66% over buying all of the books individually!"*

E-Publishing on Multiple platforms

As we mentioned earlier, there was a time when Amazon's KDP Select program offered so much benefit to indie authors that it was worth forgoing other platforms in order to give Amazon the exclusivity Select required. Those days are over for us, and might be for you. If not yet, probably soon. As of right now, late 2013, Select has tried to breathe some last-minute life into the program by starting a program called Kindle Countdown Deals.

This new program gives authors the ability to set time-bound promotions, while retaining their 70 percent royalty rate without the book having to be priced $2.99 or more. Because these deals will be on a live countdown board promoted by Amazon, it should increase your discoverability – especially if you're in a niche category where it's easy to rank.

But you still have to surrender 90 days of exclusivity to Amazon, and as we told Lexi when she was (strongly) considering moving her massive catalogue back to exclusivity, Select is a bit like an abusive boyfriend who promises he won't hit you again if you'll just come back one last time. But because this is a new and "could be good; could suck" program, she's split the difference and is experimenting with a few titles, as are all of us (Realm & Sands, Collective Inkwell, and as Guy Incognito).

The primary benefit of KDP Select — the ability to make your books free for limited periods of time in order to gain exposure and readers — can still be mimicked outside of Select via price-matching, and we'll discuss that in more depth when we get to marketing. Permafree (making your title permanently free) is less flexible than using Select, but we don't care because we want "permafree" titles to be permanently free, and we don't want to (and don't have to) grant any exclusivity in order to do it.

With that said, we'd like to cover a bit about publishing on the various platforms because our philosophy is usually to go wide and be everywhere. This is in no way meant to be a comprehensive how-to guide. This isn't the right venue, and things constantly change. You can follow the specific instructions on each site for more detail, or search Google to find tutorials.

Amazon

Amazon.com is still the big dog. They were the first platform to give self-publishers the ability to reach their audiences directly via e-publishing, and for that we'll always be grateful. Amazon, more than any other company, has changed all three of our lives. They also have the largest buying audience by far, and no one can touch them ... yet. For that reason, if you self-publish e-books, Amazon should be your first stop. If you're strictly adhering to the 80/20 Rule, you could probably publish on Amazon and nowhere else, but we don't recommend it. Different readers shop in different places, and "going wide" isn't that hard. But we'll get to that in a minute.

As we've mentioned a few times, Amazon has a program called KDP Select where if you grant Amazon 90 days of exclusivity and agree not to publish any more than 10 percent of an enrolled work anywhere else (including your own website) during that time, they'll give you two primary benefits. For one, you'll be able to choose any five days during your Select period in which you can make your book free. This will get new eyes on your books, and remember, part of your job is reader acquisition. But the way Select used to work was that a good free run would translate to increased paid sales after your book was done being free. This is no longer the case. If you want your book free because you have later books in the series to sell, this is best done with price-matching (covered in marketing later). Select's second benefit is that Amazon Prime members can borrow your book, and you'll get paid for those borrows (around $2 per borrow as of October 2013). If you're not in Select, readers won't be able to borrow your book. In our experience, the ability to sell your book on other platforms is worth more profit than you'll earn from those borrows.

Publishing on Amazon isn't hard; you'll need a .mobi file (which Scrivener compiles for you), a cover image of somewhere around 1,800x2,500 pixels, and a description for your book. Amazon's dashboard currently sucks giant, hairy donkey balls, but unless you're an oddity, you'll sell more on Amazon than anywhere, so you'll deal with it, and probably thank them for changing your life.

Amazon's primary marketplace is the American Amazon.com site, but the Amazon.co.uk site, which serves (you guessed it) the U.K., is also significant. Sales in other markets, for those who write in English, tend to be small and almost insignificant.

Kobo

Kobo is currently our (conditionally) favorite bookseller. The only thing that stops them from being our unconditional favorite is their size. Our Kobo sales are significant, but still pale in comparison to Amazon. Amazon is gigantic, and Kobo, which is still small, simply can't compete.

That said, we love, love, *love* Kobo. The company "gets" us indies in a way that Amazon doesn't. Their dashboard is beautiful and extremely usable: a gift to self-publishers. Their self-publishing team (called "Kobo Writing Life") is highly responsive. We contact Amazon and get crickets. Kobo is always helpful.

Kobo is our #2 (we sell as many copies of *The Beam* and *Unicorn Western* on Kobo as we do on Amazon), and Kobo sales alone make the idea of granting Amazon exclusive rights to sell our work absurd. We strongly suggest you try them out. They feel like a partner, not some sort of a boss.

Recently, Sean and I had an issue with *Unicorn Western*. Amazon was doing something weird and price matching the Kindle edition of the *Full Saga* with the first paperback, meaning it was lowered from $10 to just over $3. This issue took over three weeks to resolve, and was handled through a few very canned-sounding e-mails, spaced days apart. We get it. Totally. This isn't bitching about Amazon. We're grateful we had a place for a mistake to be made, but the difference between the two companies matters to you: *Kobo can't grow without you. Amazon can.* And it shows.

Barnes & Noble (Nook)

Barnes & Noble's Nook marketplace is, for us, a distant third to Amazon and Kobo. There are plenty of writers who sell very well on Nook, but we aren't two of them. According to our buddy Ed Robertson, who knows such things, B&N's bookstore is like a less usable version of Amazon — meaning it's driven largely by computer algorithms rather than being hand-tended, which is, to a certain degree, what happens more on Kobo and Apple. All the sellers have both curated and auto-populated sections, but B&N seems to be driven by the latter.

It's worth noting that B&N, like all of the stores other than Amazon, is hard to gain traction in via advertising because it doesn't have a robust and popular affiliate program like Amazon's. For this reason, advertisers are less willing to send traffic. As of this writing, the only truly reliable way to reach Nook readers and hence gain non-organic traction is via the list advertiser BookBub. If you can get listed on BookBub — something that is harder and harder to do as time passes — you will have a much better chance of gaining traction at B&N. Sean and Dave ran a BookBub promotion for *Yesterday's Gone Season One* for 99 cents and sold more at B&N in a day than they did in the year before the promotion.

Apple

In case you haven't guessed, we're doing these in order of importance to us. Results vary from person to person, and some indie authors absolutely *kill it* on Apple, but for us (and most writers) it's a distant fourth to Amazon, Kobo, and Nook. You may do better than us. Hell, we hope you do. Please, let us know how you did it — we'd love to have you on the show.

Apple is currently an extreme pain in the ass to get your books into, so for this reason — and because we've sold approximately 10 copies total there this year — we don't bother to publish directly to them. Instead, we publish through aggregators like Smashwords or Draft2Digital, which we'll look at next.

Smashwords

Smashwords is a nice service that can sometimes be a pain in the ass in practice. Smashwords — like Draft2Digital, which follows — is an aggregator, which basically means that they take your book and distribute it to other stores for you. They can distribute to Barnes & Noble, Kobo, and Amazon, as well as Apple, Sony, and many others. We recommend uploading to Kobo, Amazon, and B&N directly. Aggregators are slow to respond and will force you into using a generic call to action rather than one specific to each platform, so hit the big dogs separately and keep more control.

Smashwords also tends to be *very* picky and somewhat flaky. We've uploaded files to Smashwords, been rejected for "premium distribution" (which is where they send it to other retailers outside Smashwords itself), then later uploaded the exact same file and been accepted. It can be frustrating, but we tend to keep trying. Others pull out their hair and surrender.

Despite the difficulties, we use Smashwords for three things: One, they represent another marketplace in itself at smashwords.com, and we'll sometimes get a sale there. (Erotica authors like our buddy Lexi tend to do better than non-erotica authors on Smashwords, on average, in our experience.) Two, we use them to distribute "all in one fell swoop" to minor stores like Sony and middle-range players like Apple, which can be a pain to enter. And three, we use them to get our books free in Barnes & Noble. As of this writing, Smashwords is the only aggregator that can get your book into Barnes & Noble at a price of $0.00, and that matters for price-matching, which again we'll come back to later.

Smashwords will also let you do pre-sales at Apple and B&N, but we haven't tried them because they seem thoroughly 20 percent and not worth the management. In our publishing company, it's simply another avenue, to cover all of our bases.

Draft2Digital

Just like Smashwords, Draft2Digital is a digital publishing aggregator that provides a single portal where you can publish your title directly to other retailers. Draft2Digital is much more polished than Smashwords — friendlier and easier to use. For most authors we absolutely recommend managing the dashboards that fit in the 80 percent of your revenue pile yourself, and only using the aggregators for minor players. However, if you're the sort of author who wants the simplest solution with the fewest moving parts, then using a single aggregator *might* make sense. If that's true for you, we would recommend Draft2Digital over Smashwords.

(NOTE: We aim to give evergreen advice throughout this book, but what we just said is so "not evergreen" that it's already brown. Smashwords could come along tomorrow and blow us all away with an amazing new dashboard that makes Kobo's slick interface look like Myspace.)

Many authors have learned to use the self-publishing tools available at sites like Kindle Direct Publishing, Barnes & Noble's NOOK Press, and Kobo's Writing Life. While some publishers love that level of control, we know there are many authors with no desire to format an e-book or manage more than one account.

Draft2Digital will give you a single place to publish, manage, and track your project's performance across the spectrum of e-book retailers. Draft2Digital also promises that they'll add new venues as they open. It is easy and costs nothing (except your control).

Getting Your Books Into Print

Getting your books into print can be frustratingly tricky — and for most self-published authors, not really worth your time. We'll cover some uses for print in the marketing section of this book, but for now you should know that very few indies see significant profits from print — or even enough to justify the time spent on production. For every $5,000-$10,000 of e-book commissions we see, we have *maybe* $100 in print.

That said, there are reasons to get your books in print, and you may want to do it as long as you know your reasons and have realistic expectations. We both have shelves filled with our print books, and we're not too proud to admit that sometimes we put books into print *just* to stick them on those shelves. You could also pass books to friends, or use print books as an advanced form of business card or promotion. We can get print copies of the first *Unicorn Western* book for around three bucks each, go to conferences, and hand a crap-ton of them out. Some of that generates word of mouth, and a few people will read to the end and buy the *Full Saga*. Still others will act as informal advertising, as people see them reading those odd paperbacks in coffee shops. Some people will form a deeper bond with the story. They're more likely to tell their friends.

But the cool thing is that with the widespread popularity of print-on-demand — where you no longer need to order 10,000 books at once and pile mountains of boxes in your garage — print becomes a real possibility for self-publishers. You can order a single copy; your readers can order one; you can change your book's interior on the fly and have it available instantly if you discover a typo. It's awesome.

Let's talk — again, briefly, because you can learn more elsewhere — about the print options we suggest smart indies consider.

CreateSpace

CreateSpace, owned by Amazon, should probably be your first stop if you're considering print. Print is always a pain in the ass, but CreateSpace's process greatly reduces that pain.

CreateSpace, as of this writing, only prints paperbacks. You'll create an interior PDF file (using Word is probably easiest) and a cover PDF file, then upload them. You can choose from a variety of options. We prefer the 5.25" x 8" trim size for almost everything or 6" x 9" for books too enormous to be practical in the smaller size. We also strongly suggest you choose the matte cover and cream-colored paper. The white paper looks like it was spit from your printer.

Upload your files, select your options, and then, after a series of proofing steps, put your book up for sale. People will be able to buy it either from CreateSpace's dedicated store or (more likely) from Amazon.com.

If you choose to enroll the digital version of your book in Amazon's MatchBook program, people who buy your print book can get the e-book version for free or at a discount. We suggest making the match free. You want happy readers; that's way more important than immediate sales. If someone buys the print version of one of our books, we *want* them to have the digital file — and don't think they should have to pay for it. The feeling they have after bonding with our work is far more important.

CreateSpace's paperbacks are pretty good, and it's nice to hold your own book in your hand. You won't get into your local bookstore via CreateSpace, but you'll be in print, and that's kind of cool.

Lightning Source

If print is a 20-percent activity for self-published authors, using Lightning Source as your print-on-demand publisher is a 20-percent activity for even that small subsection of indies who bother with print.

Lightning Source's books are, in our opinion, simply *better* than CreateSpace's. Their paperbacks (called "perfect bound") are tighter and feel more professional. In addition, Lightning Source offers the option to print hardback books. Again, this is firmly a 20-percent thing, if not 5 percent or less, but your most hardcore fans may want collector's edition hardbacks, and you may want them on your shelf. Consider it only if you understand exactly what you're getting into.

The 6" x 9" print size works a bit better as a hardback than as a paperback, but you'll have many choices. You can also choose your binding type. "Casebound" books are hardbacks that have the cover applied directly to the hard binding. "Clothbound" books have removable dust jackets over (you guessed it) cloth covers. And so on.

Lightning Source books also come at a premium — currently over $100 per title just to set up, plus proof costs and possible change fees. So, only go into this option if you're sure it's worth it for whatever you're doing. Sean and I will be doing this for many of our titles next year, but *only because we want to.* This is *not* good advice for most indies.

Brick and Mortar Book Stores

Your chances of ending up in the local bookstore are slimmer than Sean after that thing he does each year where he won't have any sugar for a month, but if you use Lightning Source for your print distribution and use the standard bookseller discount, a buyer could possibly walk into a bookstore and order your book via the seller's Ingram catalogue system. You might also be able to arrange for bookstores to order books for signings or stock your title as a "local author" offering this way.

If your print books are only available via CreateSpace, bookstores won't order your books. You might be able to order a bunch yourself, cart them into a small independent bookstore, and persuade them to let you have an event, but it's not exactly a high-percentage thing.

Fortunately, most indies don't need to bother. Print and getting into bookstores is very, very firmly in the 20 percent for most of us.

Odds and Ends

This is the part where we'll discuss in scattershot form some of the many details that don't seem to fit anywhere else. Prepare yourself for an onslaught of hodgepodge!

Legal Considerations

You want to know about copyright, libel, and whatnot? Awesome. We're not the guys to tell you because we're not lawyers.

Very briefly, though — and this is the part where we repeat that we're not lawyers and aren't offering legal advice or counsel, yada yada don't sue us — "copyright" is something that your book has the minute you create it — once you put it into a "fixed and tangible form," which includes its first life as a digital file. You don't typically need to file any paperwork or anything in order to protect yourself.

There are, however, benefits to *registering* your copyright — one being the right to reimbursement of legal expenses if you win a case against someone deemed to have violated your copyright. There's a small cost involved. Is it worth it? Only you can determine that.

Incidentally, perhaps this would be a good place to refer you to our podcast episode featuring lawyer M. Scott Boone where he discusses legal considerations for writers. (It was episode 73, if you'd like to search the Self Publishing Podcast archives.) We talk about parody, libel, infringement, establishment of other legal entities, and so on in that episode, for your scholarly enjoyment.

ISBNs

If you own the ISBN (International Standard Book Numbers) your book is published under, you will be listed as the publisher of record for that book. If you use a free ISBN, someone else is.

In practice, this means almost nothing. Sean owns thousands of ISBNs from MyIdentifiers.com, but we don't use them for our e-books. We let whatever platform we're publishing on supply the ISBN if one is required, and we're not the official publisher of record, and we don't care because it matters less than the contents of Dave's decoy wallet.

We have ISBNs for print. You can get free ISBNs from CreateSpace for your print books, and that actually does mean something. Specifically, it means you can't go out and publish that same format (paperback, hardback, whatever) somewhere other than CreateSpace. There are instances where we would want to offer paperbacks via both CreateSpace and Lightning Source (CreateSpace because those books are available via Amazon.com and Lightning Source because the books are higher quality and we want to order them ourselves to hand out or sell), and if you don't use your own ISBN, you can't do that.

This is another one of those "less than 20-percent" issues for the vast majority of self-published writers, so it's very likely that you can ignore all of this. If you anticipate publishing in several places, you'll want to get and use your own ISBNs. If not, don't worry about it.

NOTE: You will need a separate ISBN for each format — i.e., paperback books and hardback books must have different ISBNs even if they're versions of the same book.

Conveying Value for Collections and Box Sets

If you're offering a collection of your books, it's worth doing a few extra things to convey that collection's value. Don't, and you run the risk of buyers seeing your collection as just another book. If your price tag is a bit high (because hey, it's a collection!), you need to justify that. We'd do that in three ways, which we'll exemplify using our *Season One* collection of *The Beam* (which retails for $9.99) as an example.

WAY #1: Via the product image. If you just use a normal, flat image for the collection's cover, there will be nothing to differentiate it from other books on the market, and therefore prospective buyers will *see* it as a single book. You want them to see it — and hence mentally price it — as the value-added collection it is. For this reason, we recommend creating a 3-D product image. Here's the image we used for *The Beam,* created using a program called 3D Box Shot. It shows the six "episodes" in our "full season" as six individual books in a box set:

WAY #2: Via the book's title. The title was originally called *The Beam: Season One*, but when we realized the need to justify the $10 price tag, we changed it to *The Beam: The Complete First Season Collection (Books 1-6)*.

WAY #3: Via the product description. Now that you've established how much value there is in your collection through the image and a clear title that conveys value, ram it home in the product description. Accordingly, here's the opening line of our *Season One* collection, which appears on Amazon in big, bold, orange type: *This collection contains the complete first season of the epic sci-fi saga,* The Beam *— all SIX debut-season episodes. Save 45% versus buying the individual episodes!*

Details Matter!

We started this section by talking about the difference between professional and unprofessional presentations. You don't want to be unprofessional for sure, and getting you out of the self-imposed self-publishing ghetto has been the primary goal of this chapter. Pay attention to everything in it, and you'll look like a pro.

But before we leave this part of the book, we'd like to reiterate: *Details matter.* This is one area where the 80/20 Rule can be deceiving. You can go to 80 percent on your product descriptions, and that'll do you fine. But if you go the extra mile and really polish your presentation — technically stepping over the 80/20 Rule's line — you can stand out and look awesome. Doing so can have a small but cumulative effect.

Here are a few things you can pay attention to, given the time or inclination. Some are easy, and some are harder. Only you can decide which are worth doing. *All* make small differences that can add up:

Initial caps, clear descriptions, reader quotes, and following conventions in your product descriptions. This is an easy one and costs nothing. Initial caps means capitalizing all of the major words in your book's title and subtitle; *The Complete First Season Collection* looks better than *the complete first season collection* in a title. Hone your descriptions until they can cut glass. Include a few reader review quotes in your product descriptions. And look at the bestselling books in your genre in order to mimic what they do with their descriptions.

Using HTML markup in product descriptions. Remember how we said that in the description of *The Beam*, the first line was big and bold? We're not going to teach HTML here, but if you understand HTML basics, you can get that orange on Amazon.com by enclosing text in <h2> tags. A smaller but still noticeable black, bold font will result from enclosing text in <h3> tags. You can also use simple bold and italics by using <b> and <i> tags. These are good examples of small things making big differences.

If you have a print version, making sure it's linked to your e-book version. If you do, your e-book's price will show as if it's been discounted from the price of your CreateSpace print book. So our $9.99 *Beam* e-book? That looks a lot cheaper when you see that it's "marked down from" $19.99, which is the cost of the print book. Amazon will also match the page count of your e-book against the print book's page count, which usually makes the e-book appear longer than it would otherwise. Having a print version available also makes you look a little more professional.

Audiobook versions, etc. Sean and I haven't done this yet, but we will next year. He and Dave already have (*Z2134, Monstrous,* and *Yesterday's Gone* are all on audiobook, with *WhiteSpace* coming next year). If you have an Audible.com audiobook version of your book, it'll show on your product page as yet another version. This is a tiny thing and certainly isn't worth doing for this reason alone, but if you *do* have one, your page will look that much more pro. Same goes for any other versions you make available.

PART FOUR:
Marketing Your Work

How to Market Like a Lover

BECAUSE WE LEARN FROM OUR erotica author friend and collaborator Lexi Maxxwell almost as much as she says she's learned from us, we asked her to write an intro to our marketing section. All three of us are jealous of Lexi's relationship with her audience. We have more readers, but her fan engagement is remarkable. She loves them, and they love her right back.

Lexi has a strong marketing background. She was a well-paid copywriter who jumped into publishing with both feet. She's fearless and funny; she's very creative; she's a helluva story teller. Lexi's stories are so wrong that they are thoroughly right. While juggling her job at a marketing firm, she wrote really dumb one-offs like, *Call of Booty: Modern Whorefare* (YES, THAT IS AN ACTUAL TITLE). But then, something happened (it was totally because she started listening to our podcast), and Lexi decided she wanted to write great stories. She dove in full time, and tried to pace our ridiculous schedule.

Lexi deserves to be here. She started by learning from us, but has since become one of our best teachers. We had some of our most fun and fruitful storytelling sessions for *The Future of Sex*, and probably more undiluted fun writing *Adult Video* than we did with any other project this year. Lexi is vulgar and slutty and totally darling. Here she is to tell you "How to market like a lover."

I tell dirty stories for a living, and love what I do.

I used to write great copy, and really did love my job. It made me feel smart, and the large paychecks made me feel appreciated. But what I do now is *deeply* fulfilling in a way I wasn't really looking to find, but now I wouldn't want to ever write without.

I've received hundreds of e-mails from readers telling me how much of a difference I've made in their lives (mostly men and women who are now happier in their marriages, or women who were taught to be ashamed of sex but now feel more confident, and therefore better, about themselves). Readers are people, and *people want more from life.* I write stories that offer an immediate escape, and help them feel alive. I stimulate imagination; I stir senses; I promise naughty fun.

And I do it all with my words.

Storytelling is essential to a happy human psyche. I probably have it easier than you do. I create a stylized hyper-reality and a place for people to imagine what they can't have in real life, or are maybe too embarrassed to ask for. I give readers courage, and that feels amazing. But the end result is better. In the end, my readers are bonded to me.

This isn't intentional; I wasn't looking for this to happen at all. I'm a girl who knows her marketing, loves sex, and is a curious entrepreneur. I created my Lexi pen name because I wanted to write my naughty little stories and make a little sideline income. I didn't expect to fall in love with my audience, or feel so inspired to elevate my craft. I care about my readers, and that means I care about every word I write. Yes, it's easier for me than it probably is for you because my genre allows me to hit readers at an immediate, visceral level. But my readers are people, exactly like yours. Like my readers, yours are looking for more from their life, so give them stories that offer escape, and help them to *feel something.*

Stimulate imagination, stir their senses, promise *fun.* Do it with your words.

Love your readers.

Lexi Maxxwell is a pen name and is a supercharged version of who I am day to day. When I started writing as Lexi, I didn't care about the readers like I should have. I wasn't trying to do things the wrong way. I really just didn't know any better. My stories were good for what they were, and nothing more. They were quick and dirty, like I assumed readers probably wanted. For the most part, that worked. I would never hit the next level, but that was okay. I wasn't really trying to. Lexi Maxxwell was about earning me a little extra income in addition to my job, and nothing more. I didn't care. As long as I was writing stories that were *good enough* and I could keep up with my 9-5, I was happy.

Eventually, the personal e-mails started, first at a trickle, then at a flood. They made me *want* to be a better writer. "Good enough" started feeling like giving up, and before I knew it, the e-mails started to make me feel better than the sales. For the first time, I put more of *me* into my stories. And that *me* was all the marketing I needed.

I can't tell you that marketing won't be scary. It was easy for me because that's what I did for a living. Yet, it was only after I stepped out of my old heels and into new ones that I realized I'd been doing it all wrong.

Love your readers, and they will love you back. You have an intimate relationship with them already. If a person is on your list, you've probably already whispered stories in their ear. Your stories might not be quite as intimate as mine, and the need they served might not have been as immediate, but if you wrote a good story then you've touched that reader in some way. Just as you would with a lover, nurture what's already there to make it better.

There is no intimacy when you have sex with a stranger. Don't treat your readers like one-night stands. Make sure that your author/audience relationship has a fair amount of give and take. Know their anatomy so that you can tell by their reaction exactly when you're touching your readers in just the right spot.

The best part about marketing to your readers like lovers is that it leaves you free to be the most authentic version of *you*, and unleash your truest inner artist. Until I treated my readers like lovers (rather than one-night stands), I didn't even know what type of art I wanted to create. Since then, Lexi has gone from a hobby and maybe sideline income to what I do, and I couldn't be any prouder of the work I'm producing. My thousands of lovers have helped me to go wild, cross boundaries, and get creative.

I love my readers, and my readers love me, but that's only because I did what all great lovers do: *I listened.*

Listen to your readers, and they'll tell you exactly how they want to be marketed to most.

CHAPTER TWELVE:
Gathering Your Tribe

AFTER READING THAT, DOESN'T SOME of the pressure associated with marketing go away?

You don't have to be too literal about marketing like a lover for the idea to make sense, though. Our intention in this section is to show you that while there are certain *tactics* you may want to learn in order to implement your 21ˢᵗ century marketing, the *strategies* behind those tactics will probably still be relevant in the latter part of the century — perhaps in 2097, after the world has flooded and an omniscient and omnipresent AI network called The Beam rules the North American continent.

Cut past the surface details, and marketing isn't much more than psychology 101. You don't have to ever have read a psychology text to understand it; you have to be a human and remember one thing: *Marketing is about offering things a certain section of people want, then finding the best ways to let those people know those things are available, priced at a fair exchange for them.* It's not inherently complicated, brilliant, sleazy, deceptive, win-lose, tricky, difficult, or anything else. It is neither good nor bad. It is presenting offers to those people most likely to respond. The rest is details.

With that in mind (read it again and force yourself to breathe if the marketing makes you nervous), let's drill down, starting with the idea of those people we mentioned — the section of folks who might like what you have to offer. Before you can offer them anything, you must find them. And before you can do that, you must create a place where they can gather around you. It's not true that "If you build it, they will come," but it *is* true that if you never build it, they'll never even know you're there.

This chapter is about building that place, finding those people, and establishing exactly who you are — both as an author, and as a community with your readers.

Building Your Own Platform

A "platform" is what it sounds like: any place you can metaphorically stand atop and speak to your people. You're a writer, so you'll probably speak via the written word. The larger your platform, the more people you can reach.

All of the online booksellers are platforms: places where readers can find your books. If you tend to rank highly on bookseller lists and hence have a lot of exposure on those bookseller storefronts, your platform will be larger than a lesser-known author's.

But your books probably aren't your only speaking vehicle, right? If you're on social media, that's a platform, too. Writers with zillions of Facebook fans or friends or those with huge Twitter followings have big platforms as well. If you're engaged on the social media platforms you use, you have that much more ability to talk to your people. There are writers who can post about a new book on their Facebook page and get thousands of sales. You can also use your platform to announce live events, fuel anticipation for upcoming projects, advance causes, or simply to further engagement with your audience. It's about how many people you can reach, and anywhere you can reach folks is part of your platform.

All of that's great, but there's a problem with relying on booksellers, social media, or various other online communities for your platform. Anyone have a guess what it is?

Bueller? Bueller?

So many writers fail to understand this to their significant detriment: All of the above are examples of platforms owned by other parties, and it's a *big* mistake to rely on a platform you don't own, and hence control.

We first heard Sonia Simone from Copyblogger use the term "digital sharecropping," referring to the idea of building your assets on someone else's property, and the term encapsulates the danger perfectly. Right now, in 2013, Twitter is a big deal. But I hesitate to even write that last sentence, because I can feel it dating this book. Will Twitter be a big deal in 2018? Maybe, but we kind of doubt it. Ask Myspace if things ever change, and if the fickle public ever jumps ship and abandons a once-popular platform. Many musicians built empires on Myspace, and while Myspace was

230

thriving, they did well. Today, after Facebook more or less replaced Myspace for the majority, those same musicians are struggling. And so might soon be the case for businesses and artists who rely heavily on Facebook in a few years.

Don't simply try to stay ahead of change, because you'll never do it efficiently enough without a crystal ball. The people on Myspace couldn't have known how complete the transition to Facebook would be, and today you're only rolling dice by trying to predict which of the infinite possible successors will one day supplant today's popular networks.

Building your platform on a social network is a house of cards. The same is true of building it on booksellers exclusively. What if all of your content was suddenly pulled from one of the big sellers, or the ranking algorithms change such that you're suddenly invisible to browsers? It can happen; just ask people who relied heavily on ranking in free lists when Amazon's changes began to bury free's visibility. Ask authors whose erotic work was deemed obscene and yanked from retailers. Something could happen through no fault of your own. Do we think Amazon will shutter its domain anytime soon? No, absolutely not. But if it does, there's nothing *you* can do about it.

Build *your* own platform that *you* control. Stop relying solely on sharecropping and start planting crops on your land. You can and should use the other platforms out there — currently places like Facebook, Twitter, and obviously the big booksellers — but your axis of connection to readers should ultimately be your own website and mailing list. If you build your own platform, you'll have a buffer against change. Facebook suddenly vanishes? No problem; you'll still have your e-mail list, and can direct your readers to the next great social network you choose to join. The bookselling world implodes, and there's literally nowhere to buy your books? It's not likely, but just about the worst thing we could imagine happening. If you've built your own platform, it's not even a death blow. There are ways to sell your book files directly to readers if you must. Hell, you could implore them to support your next book via a Kickstarter campaign. But those things are only possible if you have your own platform.

Before we move on to "how," let me give you one more "what" about platform. Sean and Dave have a continuing debate over their CollectiveInkwell.com website. Dave wants the site to reside on Wordpress.com, which is the shared, hosted way to get a Wordpress blog. The alternative is to buy your own website hosting plan (currently $5-10 per month) and have your provider install Wordpress software there. Dave's argument is that independent sites can be hacked and infested with viruses and whatnot, but Sean's response is the digital sharecropping argument we've been making throughout this section. If Wordpress (the company itself) owns the "land" your Wordpress.com blog is hosted on, they make the rules. And they *do* make rules, even if they don't touch your content. There are restrictions on content; there are restrictions on the software ("plug-ins") you can add to your site to increase its functionality. For example, you can't do e-mail marketing from the site because you can't put an opt-in form on a Wordpress-owned page, and therefore can't collect addresses. Even beyond that, it's entirely within their rights to simply shut down your site. What they say goes, and you don't get an opinion. This happened to me once with an innocuous family Blogger.com blog. One day it vanished, and everything we'd posted was suddenly gone.

Of course, this makes Sean want to fly to Dave's undisclosed location and sock him in the jaw, but he loves the old curmudgeon enough to sigh and say whatever. But I'm sure you know where the RealmAndSands.com site — for Sean's and my company — is located. It's on a hosting plan that I own.

(For the record, we also don't agree with Dave that independently hosted websites are especially vulnerable to hacking. It can happen, but it's not a significant enough danger to warrant building your empire on loose sand in order to avoid it. Just keep good backups, have good security in place, and keep your website software up to date.)

Let's put a finer point on this: You should have your own website, and there should be a place on that website for people to sign up for your e-mail list. We'll cover how that works a bit later, but that's the arrangement we suggest. You can and should use platforms you don't control (social media, etc.) as well as having your own site, but be sure to use them as *secondary* platforms. So, yes, *do* have a Facebook page and a Twitter following. *Do* participate in outside communities and on other websites if doing so suits your time and personality. But never *rely* on those places. If you have a huge YouTube following, find ways to get those people to your website, then get them on your mailing list. Same for every other outlet. When working on a platform you don't control, always ask, "What would I do if this went away?" If you can't answer that question, fix that.

Our current recommendation is that your website be a blog, and for that blog to be a Wordpress blog hosted on your own website hosting plan. (If you're not paying a small hosting fee each month for your site, you don't have a self-hosted blog no matter what your domain name is.) If you're not familiar with blogs, or if blogs confuse you, don't worry. You don't need to write regular blog posts. Blogging software simply happens to be the easiest way right now to build a website.

You might be panicking because you're not technical and/or are getting confused. Let's solve that by giving you two options for getting your site built with a minimum of pain:

Option #1: If you want someone to set up your site for you, we recommend FixedPress.com. They do complete WordPress setup, optimize your website, and get it going right from the start. The business is owned by Sean's friend, Danny Cooper, whom he's known almost as long as Dave.

Option #2: If you'd rather save a bit of money and build your website yourself in around a half hour tops, I've created a pretty simple and painless seven-step tutorial for how to do so at SelfPublishingPodcast.com/hostgator. (NOTE: The link to get hosting on that page is an affiliate link. I'll get a commission if you use it to buy hosting, so if that bothers you, just go directly to Hostgator.com.)

Once you've set up your website, you're in business. The site becomes your platform, and you can start sending readers to it. We'll get specific later on about how to build an e-mail list on your site, thus capturing those readers so you'll always have (and be able to nurture) a direct connection.

Direct connection to your readers.

Doesn't that phrase just make you feel secure, as if your future is no longer subject to whims and happenstance?

Deciding on Your Brand and Your USP

Branding gets a bad rap in the minds of many who don't really understand what it is. Brands are not necessarily corporate, stale, dry, or impersonal. Your brand, simply put, is the coherent impression people get of you and your books whenever and wherever they encounter you or them, nothing more and nothing less. *Whether you want or cultivate a brand, you have one.* We think it's a lot smarter to get in front of yourself, consciously decide what you stand for, and work hard to make that impression consistent and firm across the breadth of your reach.

Brand has a feel. Done well, it conveys one or a few primary ideas. Volvo's brand is all about safety. From top to bottom, end to end, Volvo has done all it can to become synonymous with smart automotive engineering that keeps families safe if the worst should happen. Disney — especially their parks — is about a pleasant family experience. Disney parks are well known for being clean. Think that's just because they want clean parks? Nope. It's because it's part of the brand — visitors equate a spotless park and friendly employees with an overall stellar family experience that feels safe and leaves a lasting memory. Disney does nothing by accident. Look into the parks' history and you'll see how much specific thought went into (and continues to go into) enhancing that one particular impression.

But hey, Disney and Volvo — those are big corporations, right? Single writers don't have much to learn from the likes of them. Not true. Think about Dan Brown, author of *The Da Vinci Code*. His brand is largely plot-driven, religious-themed thrillers. Just as people expect safety when they buy a Volvo, they expect a highly plotted, fast-paced adventure when they pick up a Dan Brown book. If you still think Dan Brown is too big and unrelatable, our friend Joanna Penn also happens to have a similar brand. Joanna has actually put a slightly finer point on it: She says her books are "Dan Brown meets Lara Croft."

But there's more to a writer's brand than the kinds of things they write. There's also their public image, their perceived approachability and friendliness (or lack thereof), and other things. Hugh Howey, author of *Wool*, has a very positive brand; just do a search, and you'll find videos of Hugh doing dances to please his readers, surprising a random teen reader in a bookshop at the boy's parents' request, and various appearances on shows and podcasts, including ours. By all impressions, he always answers e-mails no matter how big he gets. Now: If you're a Hugh fan, doesn't that matter to you, and doesn't it bond you better with Hugh and his books?

Your USP, or unique selling proposition, is largely an outgrowth of your brand. Your brand is who the public considers you (and your publishing company, even if said company is just you) to be.

Your USP is the corresponding reason your readers should have for buying from you rather than anyone else. What are you that nobody else is (your brand)? And what can you offer a reader that no one else can (your USP)?

Our favorite example is the brand cultivated by Lexi Maxxwell. There are a lot of erotica authors out there, and when she was on our podcast Lexi talked a bit about how difficult it was to stand out in such a crowded marketplace. If she was just going to write sexy books, they'd have vanished into the erotic soup that was already out there — some of it quality writing and the rest absolutely horrible and unprofessional.

Lexi is a smart marketer in addition to being a very good writer, so she quickly moved from one-off sex scenes into what she called "smut for smart people." And it really is. We know Lexi and her catalogue pretty well at this point, and Sean has worked as a sort of mentor to her. Let's just say that in addition to being sexy, her work *is* smart. Bad erotica often plays down, figuring that the whole point for the reader is to get off and that nothing else matters. Lexi's work doesn't do that. It's sometimes hilarious (*The Autumn Diaries, I Fucked Tucker Max*), sometimes soul-wrenchingly sad (*Divorced*), sometimes sweet (*Anticipation*), sometimes edgy (*Bitten, MILF*), and sometimes satirical and adventurous (*Cheated*). When you consider *The Future of Sex,* which we map out and write the non-sex parts of, Lexi's catalogue extends to flat-out cerebral. *The Future of Sex* is as much social commentary and techno-thriller as it is erotica.

Within her main genre, Lexi hops subgenres as much as we do, but the one thing that stays consistent across all of Lexi's work is that it's *smart* and presumes an intelligent, well-read reader. Lexi loves sex, and that's clear in her writing, but she loves life even more. People looking for whacking material and nothing else will get little from Lexi. Her readers like to be stimulated above the neck as much as they want to be stimulated below the belt. *That* is Lexi's USP. *That* is what she offers that not many others do.

I'll just mention one more thing about Lexi's brand before moving on, because she discussed it on our show, and it's pretty relevant. Lexi wants to change the world, and her truest fans know that. She's incredibly unapologetic about her sexuality and says that it's her mission to make sex less shameful and more accepted. This is an empowerment issue, and she believes it with all her heart. As a result, Lexi's fans gain that much more identity, that much more bonding with her and her brand. They aren't just reading erotic literature. They're part of a movement.

The key thing to remember about brand is that above all else *it must be consistent, and you must not flinch from it.* Lexi's decision to advocate unapologetic sexuality rather than simply spin dirty yarns means she sometimes comes under fire. It also means that Lexi sometimes fails to appeal to readers who don't care about larger issues (or about "being smart with their smut"), but it doesn't matter. Her unflinching brand won our affection, which means that we talk about her a lot, co-write with her, and promote her. She was able to convince a huge erotic website with enormous influence to partner with her on a few forthcoming projects because they believe in her and her message. And as to readers, it's true that she's not casting the widest possible net ... but the solid anchor of her brand makes the people who love her *really* love her. They buy everything she sells. They sing her praises. They're on Team Lexi. They're in it with her to the end.

We'd all be lucky to have more fans like that.

Finding Your Peeps

So you want to find those raving fans, right? Awesome. Here are a few places you can:

Your Other Books

We're about to give you the most boring advice in this section. You're probably going to be disappointed that we're not going to offer you a magic way to get a ton more readers, but unfortunately that's not how it works. Ideal fans and readers are gained a few at a time, and it *takes* time to build that bond even if you experience a sudden and serendipitous burst of exposure. Our friend CJ Lyons hit Amazon's Top 5 and #2 on the *New York Times* bestseller list 1 1/2 years after starting indie publishing and, as a result, sold over a million books in two years — but that didn't mean that her base of true, pure fans grew overnight. She has a mailing list of 15,000 highly engaged and responsive readers, but she started building that list four years before her first book was even published.

Bonding always takes time. Because of that, *writing more* is almost always the best way to find readers, and *writing more* is almost always the best way to turn some of those readers into true fans.

The truth is seldom glamorous. Nobody wants to hear that, but it's a fact. I stopped doing online education when I realized a sad truth: Nobody is interested in hearing the boring reality about what it takes to succeed. People will buy bogus quick-fix solutions all day long, but few want to hear that the way to build a business or make money is to work hard for a long time and never surrender.

We run into authors all the time who say, "But I don't want to write more books. I want to find readers for the book I already have." This is often said desperately, and we can sympathize. Writing books, especially when you're new to the craft, can be difficult. The last thing many new authors want to hear after the hard slog to finish their first novel is that it's time to turn around and do it again. But here's the painful truth: If you have one book, your chances of making enough to live on from that one book are next to nothing. Your footprint is simply too small, and you'll get lost in the noise.

We've written these tips in order of importance, and "your other books" is first for a reason. If you can write another book and another book, your power is multiplied with every release. The effect is exponential. After enough books and time (no promises as to number or duration), you're likely to reach a critical mass, where you've cast a wide enough network that your ideal readers will find it hard to miss you. That can, in some cases, lead to the erroneously named "overnight success" some writers see after spending thousands of nights writing.

So yes, write more books. Each book is a little funnel, and it's out there scooping a few people toward you at a time. Some will stick, and read your other works. If you actually *have* other works for them to read, they'll bond with you further. If you have nothing? Well, then what reason is there for them to stick around?

For advanced writers, the "other books" lead generation method can be split in half. You may have books you sell for profit as well as those that are out there for free. The for-sale books will give you a more qualified reader (hey, they plunked down money!), but plenty of free readers will convert in time. So, be sure to write more, write well, and put solid calls to action in the backs of all your books prompting readers to join your e-mail list.

Friends of Your Readers

I said that we put these in order, but this one is enmeshed with and just as important as the final item. Unsurprisingly, you activate and maximize this method by writing more excellent books.

One day this summer, I was sitting at a Bob Evans with my family when my phone vibrated in my pocket (after editing, Sean asked me *Why in the hell I was eating at Bob Evans* and *What in the hell was wrong with me.*) I hate myself a little every time I feel compelled to check my texts when I'm out to dinner, but in this case I'm glad I did. It was from my friend Kyeli. I don't have the original text message, but I kind of wish I'd thought to save it. The gist was that Kyeli had been at a Target and overheard two people ahead of her in line talking about this ridiculous series wherein a gunslinger rides a unicorn. Kyeli, you may remember, was the fangirl who made the request that we include a prophetic owl in the *Unicorn Western* finale. She's also really outgoing, so for a few minutes in one city, two of our fans found each other in public and convinced a third person to read the books.

I've not had a random encounter like that yet. There's a story Chuck Palahniuk tells about a caving guide saying, "The first rule of the caves is that you don't talk about the caves," making an homage to *Fight Club* without realizing he was guiding the book's author. That's pretty cool, but for now I'll take a second-hand story about people at Target. I texted Sean. We both high-fived Kyeli in Texas from all the way up in Ohio (this was before Sean moved to Austin and was allowed to officially start dissing Bob Evans).

People may not be discussing your books in line at major retailers with low, low prices (and, according to Dave, checkers who lick their fingers) yet, but hopefully they *are* discussing them. If they are, you'll gain fans automatically. You want a money machine that works while you sleep? Friend, word of mouth *is* that money machine. It may churn pennies rather than fat stacks at the start, but it's out there working for you, and builds with every passing day and every fresh release.

Word of mouth is *huge*. If you're an avid reader (and if you're a writer, you'd *better* be an avid reader), ask yourself the last time you got a book recommendation from someone you know. Now, ask yourself the last time you were persuaded to read a book by an advertisement. Unless you're a very odd case, you get your recommendations from friends and family, not objective third-party sources. (Book recommendations on bookseller websites are somewhere in between. They're automated, but they only recommend your books if enough of someone else's readers also like your books, pointing to similar reading tastes.)

Here's how you get more word of mouth. Here's how you get more of your readers to tell their friends that they absolutely *must* read your books. Here's how you get an army of devoted readers out there doing your selling for you:

Write books that are worth sharing. Then more after that.

There are ways to make it easier for your best fans to talk about you, but they only work when those best fans are *already* predisposed to talk about you. You have to be good enough at your craft that your books move your readers to feel something that they want others to feel. Reading takes a lot of time, and accepting a book recommendation is therefore an act of trust. Most people will only suggest books that give readers an excellent experience, not just an interesting story. Do your books make readers want to stand up and cheer? Do they make them think and ponder? Do they make your readers excited, or thrilled, or sad, or aroused? It's all about conveying emotion. You will get better at conveying emotion by writing more and practicing your craft, and will deepen that emotional connection every time you publish something new. Taking *Unicorn Western* as an example (yes, *again*), I have my doubts that many people would talk about the first book in public like that. The first book is fun and quirky and interesting, but around the end of book 4, it grabs readers by the heart. If you've made it that far, you're flat-out invested through the rest of the series. We never would have forged that bond with those readers if we'd stopped at the pilot.

Now, because this section would be empty without a tiny bit of tactical talk, we'll just add that you need as many easy entry points into your work as possible. All of our starter books are free (*every* title has one), and that means that when Jane tells Jerry to check us out, it's more likely to happen because *checking us out costs Jerry nothing.* We've also made print versions of our work as inexpensive as possible. The *Unicorn Western 1* paperback costs around $4, and we can get them for $3 each. You can bet we'll hand those suckers out like candy when people seem interested in reading them.

You also need solid CTAs at the back of your books to drive new readers to your list. You're trying to capitalize on word of mouth (and hence being exposed to new readers), so make that call as compelling as possible. Ask yourself what new readers might want, then find ways to give it to them.

In our main call to action — which steers readers to RealmAndSands.com — we offer free books. They can pick up as many of our pilot books for free as they'd like (*The Beam: Episode 1, Unicorn Western 1, Namaste: Prelude,* and a bunch of others), and if they actually join our mailing list, we'll give them any book priced at $4.99 or less from our catalog as a thank-you. Put yourself in a new reader's shoes and ask yourself if our kind of fiction sounds interesting to you, if that call to action would compel you — and ultimately get you that much closer to being one of our 1000 true fans.

Goodreads

Goodreads.com — an online social network devoted to readers discussing and sharing books — is somewhere between an ordinary social network and normal word of mouth. We give Goodreads its own mention in this list because it's far, far more aligned than Twitter, Facebook, or any other flavor of the month. People on Twitter are looking to waste time and will *maybe* listen to book suggestions. On Goodreads they are actively looking.

We've been somewhat negligent on keeping up with Goodreads, but you may want to spend some time cultivating connections there. At the very least, sign up for an author account and claim your books, which may already have rankings and reviews piling high. (Goodreads readers are voracious and proactive and can list books on their own. We've been astonished to see the obscure stuff that has activity on Goodreads.) Once you've done that, you can add a bio and a photo, link your blog, respond to reader reviews, post in discussions, and so on.

Don't try to game Goodreads. The way to use it properly is to act like a human, talking to readers one-on-one or in small groups. Remember, a writer's brand builds slowly, person by person. If you show up regularly, are polite and respectful, have an intriguing personality, and keep producing new work, you can end up with a nice network of connections. But it's still just about groups of readers and authors, not about broadcasting or spamming your releases. Goodreads members won't like that, and you'll lose following that way.

One last thing to note: The rating scale at Goodreads is different than that at Amazon. It took me a while to 1) figure this out and then 2) to make peace with it. Your ego may take a hit when you see that your 4.5-star book on Amazon has a 3.5 star average on Goodreads, but those rankings are actually more or less equivalent. On Amazon, most reviewers will only give 3 stars or less if they were "meh" about a book or actively disliked it, but a 3-star review on Goodreads means that a person liked your book a lot but didn't consider it particularly earth-shattering. A 5-star review on Goodreads is really something to celebrate.

As we'll say when we talk about reviews, always be positive and respectful if you interact with Goodreads reviewers. Don't argue with bad reviews. Accept them and move on, only engaging — *maaaaybe* — if the reviewer says something factually inaccurate.

Other Social Networks

I feel like writing this as "You can go to [current social network favorite] and [some other trendy place] to find your ideal people," but I'll reluctantly fill in the blanks with a few of the current contenders: *Facebook, Twitter, LinkedIn ... Pinterest, maybe.* Whatever else.

The blasé way we're treating the issue of social networks may seem dismissive, because everyone knows that social networks are super-important and that there is magic power in the latest big thing, right? I mean, there's course after course out there about how to use [flavor of the month network] to make your fortune, so clearly that's where the Easy Button is.

But if you've read this far, you know that's total bullshit. You also just had to sit through several "find new readers" tips that amounted to us telling you to write better and write more.

Within that set of expectations, let me tell you what online social networks are: They're networks of people. Who are being social. Online. That's it. The minute you start to think that you should build your business' lead generation around Twitter, stop and ask yourself if that's remotely intelligent. You should *use* Twitter, sure, but don't you dare *depend* on it. It's a tactic, and you should employ tactics while they exist as long as you aren't putting them before strategies. The strategy here is to find people who might like your work and connect with them. Searching Twitter, using automated follow programs, and direct messaging movers and shakers are all tactics. The tactics may change, but the strategies won't. If Twitter vanishes or if its efficacy changes, the sky won't fall. You'll simply find another way to find people who might like your work and connect with them, just as storytellers have been doing since the dawn of selling stories.

That said — and with the caveat that we consider the use of any given social network to be a tactic (and admitting that Sean does an absolute shit job with social media since he quit doing it for a living) — definitely take advantage of modern tools.

We'll discuss social media a bit more later, but the short version for now is don't overthink it. It's not a magic bullet, and for most people, it's firmly in the 20 percent. Don't try to game Facebook for ten hours and write for five. Writing is always more important.

A Precautionary Note

Be careful whom you cultivate as fans and readers. It's tempting to embrace an "all who will have me" sort of mentality, trying to find ways to please the maximum number of readers.

This is usually a mistake. In order to gain truly widespread approval, you must be as neutral as possible. No type of fiction is universally loved, so in order to move closer and closer to universal approval, you have to offer less and less of a "type" of fiction. Everyone is OK with a blank piece of paper, but the minute you start putting words on it, you'll start losing the people who don't like those words.

Writers desperate for readership (and money) will often compromise what they stand for by attempting to tell the world that "anyone with $5 to spend" is the right audience for their book. Resist this temptation. It's fine if you end up discouraging the wrong readers by standing firm in what your books truly are, because doing so will gain you more of the right readers.

Don't change who you are, what your books are, and what your brand represents in order to make a quick grab for an audience who doesn't (and won't) suit you. You will automatically grow both your truest fan base and your e-mail list by staying authentic and standing firm to your USP and brand.

Proudly Alienating Those Who Aren't Your Peeps

Let's put a fine point on that last section.

If you've been paying attention, you've probably noticed that a strong brand will, as an unavoidable side effect, drive away at least as many people as it attracts. This is OK.

Go back to the "Knowing Your Market" section from earlier and read it again. Smart marketers understand that no matter *what* you do, you're going to attract some people and repel others — so you might as well declare who you're going to be and stand firm, so that you will attract the *right* people.

In other words, you don't want millions of potential readers to be *OK* with you. It's better to have even just a few hundred readers who truly *love* you. Those are true fans, and you don't attract true fans by playing it safe and never being gutsy enough to stand out.

Realm & Sands decided to hop all over the place, writing in many very different genres. Listeners told us that we'd alienate the people who only wanted to read one of those genres, and of course they're right. But we'd also *attract* people who loved to read different kinds of fiction — or even nonfiction, in the case of this book.

Sean started the Guy Incognito imprint because he wanted to write some things specifically for children. He started his fiction career writing for kids, and launched his WriterDad.com business the day after hearing back from a literary agent, who wrote, "Your work is great, but your vocabulary is too rich for children." Sean thought that was crap, so Guy's brand is about never playing down to kids. That will alienate some kids and parents, but it will resonate strongly with another segment of the audience.

You can't please everyone, so don't even try.

Entrepreneur Derek Sivers — who was talking about music, but whose words apply to any art — wrote the following:

> Every contact with the people around your music (fans and industry) is an extension of your art. If you make depressing, morose, acoustic music, maybe you should send your fans a dark brown-and-black little understated flyer that's depressing just to look at. Set the tone. **Pull in those people who love that kind of thing. Proudly alienate those that don't.**

The emphasis is mine, but read that bold sentence again. Get a tattoo of it on your arm. Get it? Be authentic, and work to attract the people who like what you do *as it exists in its purest state*. Others won't like it and will be alienated, but go ahead and wear that truth with pride. Don't be a jerk, but in the safety of your mind, feel free to think, "That's right; this stuff is too awesome for you. Don't let the door hit you on the way out."

CHAPTER THIRTEEN:
Building Relationships and Having Conversations

IF BEING AN INDEPENDENT AUTHOR was a board game, the end goal — the way you'd win the game — would be to get your 1,000 true fans. True fans will buy everything you sell (including special editions, signed copies, collectibles, merchandise, etc.), go to your live events, support and donate to your fundraisers, sing your praises in public, defend you when you're attacked, and tell all of their friends about you.

I got giddy just writing that list of true fan attributes. Now: Just imagine having a thousand of those people.

You can make a good living well before you have your 1,000 true fans, and you'll get plenty of sales other than those to true fans, but the faster you build "Team You," the better and easier your journey is going to be. True fans are like gold — meaning that they're valuable, rare, and that you usually have to put in a lot of time to find them. That's what this section is about.

The last section was about finding your people, but finding them isn't enough. Once you have readers' attention, your goal is to make them like your writing … and the last section was sort of about that, too. Readers will bond with your writing first, but true fans aren't usually satisfied with just knowing and liking your work. If they're to invest so heavily in you (read that list above again), they need to like *you*.

Getting your fans to like you more and more will be this section's topic, but first I'd like to frame the situation with a connection-building tip that's so simple, it's nearly impossible to believe: *Most people don't respond to the fans who take the time to contact them, so simply answering your fans will make you stand out.*

I wouldn't have drawn this one from the pile first, but it's true. I was a popular blogger before I was an author, so I'm used to a certain degree of F-List notoriety — that odd species of exposure we call "Internet famous." I also know a lot of "Internet famous" people, and we've traded stories about this. Over and over, I hear reports of people who contacted one of us and were shocked that they got a response. One time in particular, I remember an incident with my friend Pat Flynn, who runs SmartPassiveIncome.com and the very popular *Smart Passive Income* podcast. Someone sent a tweet to Pat and me on Twitter, and Pat and I both replied with some species of thanks. The guy who sent the original message was flabbergasted. It was honestly kind of embarrassing. He said he couldn't believe we'd responded. As if we were big Hollywood types, too important for such things as gratitude.

This is good news for those of us who understand the power of interpersonal connection. It wasn't some notion that Pat and I were "big deals" that made the encounter unbelievable to our mutual fan. The only reason he was so surprised we'd responded was because *nobody else does*.

This isn't a case where you have to do something amazing to be a superstar. This is a case where your competition is, frankly, being a bunch of jerks, and you can be a superstar simply by not being rude or dismissive. The guy above contacted us on *Twitter*. On Twitter, you're limited to 140-character messages, so it's not like responding took any effort. I probably said, "Thanks!" and was done. Three seconds, no more. But as crazy as it seems, most people won't bother.

You don't need ninja tactics. You can build true fan connections now, for free, simply by being a reasonable human being.

Here are a few ways to start.

Email

People may want to e-mail you, and we think you should let them. If you're protective of your e-mail address, you can create a special address specifically to put in the back of your books. We handle this by putting an "About the Author" page in everything we publish, and include our e-mail addresses in it. We also indicate how pleased we are to get e-mail from readers, and that we'd love it if they'd drop us a line.

When they do, treat those e-mails like gold. The idea that a reader would take the time to write to you is a supreme vote of confidence, and the day you start getting regular e-mails is the day you should realize you're doing something right. We get several very nice e-mails every week, some from readers and some from podcast listeners. We cherish those e-mails because they prove we're making a difference to our fans.

There are really only two rules for building relationships through e-mail. The first is to actually respond, as indicated in the previous section. If you have a dedicated account for reader e-mails, remember to check it, too.

The second is to remember that while fan relations are important, e-mail can be a productivity sinkhole. Dave writes e-mails long enough to be bound and set on a shelf, but Sean and I are more frugal. Readers like your writing, and every minute you spend on e-mail is a minute you stay away from creation. Your readers should understand that, and probably won't expect long, chatty e-mails. Sean usually limits e-mail replies to five sentences — that's plenty for most e-mails. Never be dismissive. You can use five sentences to intelligently (or compassionately) reply to even the most lengthy e-mails as long as you validate and respect the sender.

Social Networks

We won't spend a ton of time on social networks. One reason is that we're hardly experts, if there are such things, and you can find out plenty more in other, better places. (For free. Don't pay for the Facebook Super Secret 2000 product or something.) Besides, going into a ton of detail will imply that social media is more important than it is.

As stated earlier, there's nothing magic about proper use of social networks. Think about it: Social networks have existed since people started getting together to talk about things. The term simply refers to people being social. Putting those networks online, in the form of interactive software, hasn't changed the way they work best. Don't let bells and whistles confuse you. Twitter, Facebook, Google+, LinkedIn, and all of the others are simply places for people to meet and talk. *That's it.* You can try whatever super-secret ninja techniques you want, but none will do a better job of finding and fostering relationships with your true fans than simply acting like a human who's using some kind of intermediary technology to exchange thoughts, ideas, or pleasantries with other humans.

Because we like to make shocking statements, we'll start by saying that social networks are a waste of time.

Then, because we believe in qualifying our shocking statements, we'll add the qualifier *" ... in the way that most people use them."* And we'll add that if you use social networks properly, they can help you out with a minimal time investment.

The key, really, is knowing what works for you and being honest about what you're trying to do with the networks you've chosen. There are two primary ways marketers use social networks, and neither is helpful. The first is to try and game them, using whatever ninja trick they've heard about to spam people into paying attention. There are techniques that can work (highly targeted Facebook ads under certain conditions, for instance), but most are pointless and make you look bad. Marketers also use social networks for leisure disguised as work, fooling themselves into wasting time as distraction.

Authors, in our experience, do too much of the latter. We understand it because efficient, business-minded use of social networks looks a lot like wasting time on social networks. But let's face it: Screwing around chatting with friends or strangers online is easier than writing, and a lot more fun than crafting calls to action, so you have a vested interest in self-deception. The human mind can craft all sorts of justifications for avoiding work. "But I'm networking with readers," your brain will insist. When you hear that, stop and honestly ask yourself if that's true. And even if it technically is, ask yourself if the time you're putting in is in alignment with the importance of social networks to your business.

Most of the time, you're probably burning minutes in pleasant distraction. On the flip side, if you try to "use social networks for marketing," chances are you'll do it in a bogus, spammy way. And spammers eat alone. People hate spam. Become a spammer, and you'll be hated, too. You shouldn't have any difficulty avoiding this trap, as long as you treat Twitter, Facebook, and any other social media hub the same way you would any real-life gathering.

Think of social media as a cocktail party.

You enter the room, look around, and see different groups mingling among themselves. You wouldn't burst into the room, throw your arms in the air, and yell, "Hey everyone, I'M AN AWESOME WRITER!! Read my new book!! Check out my blog!!"

Now imagine that same cocktail party. You grab a drink, mosey over to a crowd of interesting-looking people, then stand there quietly and listen.

When you sense a break in conversation and have something intelligent and relevant to add, you speak, showing everyone around you how witty, helpful, and on-point you can be.

The sweet spot, in our opinion, is to use networks in a (wait for it) *social* way, but to be very, very careful about how much time you spend doing it. Don't think "marketer"; think "person chatting with friends." And if you have a tendency to go down rabbit holes, time yourself with a stopwatch, stopping when the alarm sounds.

Social media isn't a magic bullet.

Stories of social media rock stars who burst forth from nowhere and exploded overnight make for great reading, but it's a lot of hype and sawdust. It usually takes a couple of years to find "overnight success." Inflated expectations lead to broken hopes. Social media won't solve all your problems, set your marketing on autopilot, or eliminate the hard work of establishing and maintaining a strong online presence.

You won't get the results you're looking for overnight, and may not even be able to see tangible results for some time — as long as six months to a year. But once you have a steady base of community sending traffic to your blog, it will get easier. Your most avid fans will click your links, and reTweets will multiply, sometimes seemingly overnight.

The value of your community will grow exponentially once your members are actively participating. But be conservative when setting expectations and remain realistic so you can adapt to the needs, desires, and expectations of your audience. In short, grow with them.

We use four primary networks: Facebook, Twitter, Google+, and YouTube. We've ignored a lot of other networks that have popped up lately, despite cries that those networks are the next big thing. They may be, but for now our time is spent better elsewhere (like writing) than in learning to swim through a new ecosystem.

Here's how we use each ... with a keen note ahead of time that we are in no way saying that our ways are the best ways.

Twitter

Twitter is my prime social network, mainly because it's so easy. The fact that messages can only be 140 characters long makes it easy to maintain. Still, I only spend maybe five minutes a day on Twitter, if that. Honestly, that's plenty for me. I have a lot of Twitter friends I actively engage with and feel I know at least reasonably well. I get a lot of random messages because I encourage readers to contact me in the "About the Author" section in the back of my books, and I love those messages and always answer them, even if it's just with a "Thanks."

I don't follow everyone back who follows me. Maybe this makes me a diva, but the hassle simply isn't worth it. I tried for a while to keep up, and then Robin said she'd handle it. After she got several hundred behind for the fifth or sixth time, I told her to forget it. Currently, I follow anyone who "@ mentions" me. I have no idea if they follow me back, but following someone who talks to me and replying seems like the respectful thing to do.

I usually check Twitter once a day and reply to the latest people who've mentioned or replied to me. I follow the folks who are new. Every once in a while, when I'm out, I'll Tweet a picture or a thought, but that's rare.

I don't watch my main feed, filled with the updates of everyone I follow. It's too much information, I could never keep up with the backlog, and if I'm being honest, I don't care about most of the random, undirected things people tweet about. I'd rather spend that time writing. Instead, I just watch the "mentions" screen. You might ask, "If you don't care about what people Tweet about, why should they care what you Tweet about?" It's a good question, and I have two answers. The first is that some people are going to care anyway, so when I have something to say, I say it and am not offended if nobody cares, though some usually do. The second is that I don't broadcast much. Usually, when I Tweet, it's to reply to someone. That keeps our exchange closer, one-on-one, and more meaningful anyway.

I don't use any fun tools designed to game Twitter. I use the Twitter.com website instead of one of the fancy apps that I hear are great. I don't schedule Tweets. Again, I'm not saying this is right. I'm saying that it's what I do.

Just don't spam. Most of your conversations on Twitter should truly be conversations.

Sean uses Tweetbot for Mac. It's a simple app that lets him know when someone's mentioned him so he can reply. He has alerts turned off so he doesn't know when someone follows him. Like Johnny, he doesn't auto-follow, but does try and follow everyone who mentions or engages him in conversation.

Facebook

I suck at Facebook, but I'm there. My public account is not the same one I use with family and in-person friends, so I accept all friend requests without reservation. People tell me I should have a "page" instead of a normal account, but I'm far too precious with my time right now to figure out how to do that. I use that account like most people: upload photos, post random status updates, and occasionally comment on other people's stuff if it's at the top of my feed when I log in. A lot of people are very social on Facebook, but I'm more broadcast-only. This is a time-efficiency decision. I just make sure I post a lot of stuff that is friendly and social and only occasionally post with links to buy my stuff.

As with Twitter, we don't recommend trying to game Facebook. We also recommend that you let readers come to you on Facebook rather than trying to seek them out. Facebook is personal by nature, and the network uses the word "friend" to name connections for a reason. Readers friending authors makes sense, but authors friending potential readers feels wrong on so many levels.

Also, as with Twitter, using Facebook as an author should be about genuine connections, not mass-broadcasting spam.

Facebook is the most social of all social media sites. Use the site to have fun, observe, and contribute where and when you can. Hang out, make friends, and genuinely connect. Facebook is bigger than any other social media site, and will only continue to grow. What started as a small place for students to socialize is now a massive global network. Stay smart with your time, and Facebook is the best social media spot to let your readers see who you are.

Google Plus

If I barely use Facebook, I *baaaaarely* use Google+. I'm on the network, but am a total whore who is using it wrong. I pretty much never go to Google+ unless I have a special deal I want people to know about. Yes, I know I'm breaking my "be social" rule. It is what it is.

In contrast to Twitter follows, I do add people back to Google+ circles when they add me, mainly because the flow of new adds isn't overwhelming. Sean thinks Google+ would be his favorite social media site if he actually used it.

We use the Hangout feature to host our podcasts. That way, we can all see one another, and Sean and I can rib Dave to his face. Our Hangout is then uploaded directly to YouTube, and my assistant puts the audio up on iTunes later. Because of Google+, the three of us get live audience interaction with our podcast each week, and that's pretty terrific.

Hangout for podcasts?

YouTube

YouTube might seem like the last place for a writer, but used effectively, video can be *very* powerful — especially for nonfiction writers.

Google is always refining their algorithms and improving their search abilities by the hour. By using YouTube's metadata options (where you get to insert information about the video that search engines can see), you can make your videos rank for specific search terms. Searchable video makes it easier to find how-tos, tutorials, and general information, making it simple for nonfiction writers to market themselves through video.

For fiction authors, audience bonding means everything. When people know you, they enjoy buying from you, and the video format allows a writer to communicate with the audience in ways that aren't possible with text.

YouTube also allows you to embed videos on websites, meaning you can easily copy and paste code to put your latest awesome video right there in your blog for all the world to see without worrying about hosting large video files on your own site.

Even though we never set out to use YouTube as a social network, and use our Google Hangouts only as a broadcast vehicle to capture our podcast, the live comments have turned it social for us anyway.

A Note
The above are simply ways that we use social networks — *not* recommendations. We are in no way saying that the above are the correct ways to use those networks, or suggesting that those are the best networks to use. But there's a message in there nonetheless.

Neither of us spends much time on them each day, and neither of us has chased the shiny pennies of the new, hot networks. Still, somehow, we manage to sell a lot of books.

The next time you think you need to "solve" social networks — invest in an expensive ninja course, or spend a bunch of time on them — we'd suggest you keep in mind how half-assed we are as successful self-published authors.

Your Email Newsletter

We're going to talk about newsletters a bit later, but the short version for now is that you should start broadcasting regular e-mail bulletins to the people who join your list. Don't gather e-mail addresses and wait months to contact your readers. The worst thing you can do with an e-mail list is to let it go stale. You need those people to grow accustomed to hearing from you and opening your e-mail because there are always goodies inside.

If your newsletters are personal and engaging, which they should be, you'll get a few responses. This is more likely if you encourage responses — which, again, you should from time to time. Treat those e-mails as you would any other. Respond to all of them, and know you're also building relationships with the readers who never e-mail you back. They're hearing from you each week, and you're becoming part of their routine, like a friend.

Podcasting

We absolutely love podcasting. It's not for everyone, and it's far (far!) from necessary, but if you have a big mouth, some time, and a few hundred dollars to invest, it can be a fun way to connect with fans.

We have two podcasts. Our primary podcast is the one that spawned this book: *The Self Publishing Podcast*. After doing *SPP* for a while, we decided we wanted to try a guerrilla marketing experiment and launched a podcast for fans and potential fans of our fiction, called *Better Off Undead*.

We've gone around and around with *BOU*. Because the only genre I had in common with Sean and Dave was horror (though my horror was half satire), we decided it should be a horror podcast. The idea was that if we talked horror topics (our favorite horror movies, recaps of popular horror shows running at the time), we'd attract an audience who would be predisposed to buy our books. The topics would revolve around horror and that would be an attractor, but our personalities would also hopefully sift those who listened into ideal readers. We intended the show to be funny from the start, so the perfect listener would be interested in horror while having a dumb sense of humor that matched ours, and hence might like us as people.

It made perfect sense. Podcasting is an intimate medium, because listeners spend hours with your voice in their head and will come to feel like they know you in a way. It can make for fantastic bonding, and we were already seeing that with *SPP*. But despite our best intentions, *BOU* ripped at the seams almost immediately. We ran out of horror topics, and our best shows were ones where we went wildly off topic. We followed this collapse through a few iterations, eventually settling on what *BOU* is today. Our introductory script each week now reads, "Welcome to *Better Off Undead* — the horror podcast that's not about horror, the fan podcast without any fans, and the show that's not afraid to tackle any topic even if we can't stay on topic." The tagline is entirely accurate, and the show has literally no value. As a result, the people who have stuck with us and still listen are truly, truly *our people.* It's not a huge crowd, but it's a highly loyal crowd. And the show, while strange in concept, is usually the hardest I laugh during any given week.

We did an episode of *SPP* with Cliff "the podcast answer man" Ravenscraft that you can look to for more podcasting information, and we'd suggest that anyone interested check out Cliff's excellent and free video tutorial series at LearnHowToPodcast.com.

A word of warning: For most authors, podcasting isn't worth it. Only do it if it excites you outside of its marketing potential, and if you're not sacrificing time you should be using to write or do more important, impactful activities.

As with anything, it's essential to know what you're doing and why. Sean loves podcasting because it now gives him what blogging used to. He wants to connect with an audience but felt that blogging (for him) was largely unrewarding, and that it took valuable time from his writing. A blog's time requirement is undefined. He now reaches more people in a more intimate way, and spends exactly an hour a week.

Blogging

Sean and I both started our online lives by blogging. There are many benefits to blogging that don't apply to books, and there are times when we miss them now that we blog less. People can comment on blog posts and spark discussions, which isn't possible with your books. Blogs tend to be highly sharable; readers will tell their friends when something on your blog touches them or makes them think. Blog content can go viral in ways that books can't. As of this writing, my blog post "The Universe Doesn't Give a Flying Fuck About You" has over 6,300 Facebook shares. Those aren't "likes"; they're shares, where someone posted it on their wall for their friends to see. You'll get word of mouth with books, but not in such an immediate, sharable way. Blogs tend to form communities, and those communities are unique and different from book readers, so you'll reach people with blogging that you won't reach with books.

Blogs also benefit from searchability by search engines like Google. When you put text on a page on the Internet, search engines will find and index the copy. There's a lot that goes into search engine optimization (SEO), and we're certainly not going to go into it here, but in general the more content you have online about a topic, the more likely people are to find you by searching. That means more people who probably wouldn't have found you otherwise.

So, should you blog? Well, maybe and maybe not.

In short, it depends on you. Sean and I moved away from blogging when we started writing a lot of fiction because writing takes time no matter its form, and we decided it was essential to complete funnels and put more words up for sale. Blogging, not so much. But now that we're completing our initial burst and have more or less gotten our storefront in order, we'll return to a smarter, more streamlined blogging schedule.

As with just about anything, this ends up being an 80/20 issue, and highly dependent on what you're writing about. Nonfiction authors should definitely consider blogging, because the search engine benefits are much, much greater for nonfiction. If you write about cabinetry and blog about cabinetry, there's an excellent chance that you'll start getting search engine traffic for "how to build a cabinet" and other terms, which will likely lead to book sales. That doesn't happen as much with fiction. Searches are much less specific and targeted in fiction, and tastes are much more subjective, meaning that a blog that centers around a fiction author (whether your blog's contents are stories or not) will behave more like our *Better Off Undead* podcast, building community within a small and slowly growing but loyal contingent of readers.

We're in the enviable position of being able to use the best from both fiction and nonfiction, so if you're the same, definitely consider blogging.

Here's how this works for us:

Our primary business is fiction, and selling fiction is where we make most of our money. But we also love discussing our craft with other writers enough that we started a weekly podcast. After a year and a half of podcasting, we began to realize that while the show is a great resource, it's not easily searchable or as "bottom line" as a writer might want. We decided to write the book you're reading now. That foray into nonfiction opened the spectrum of nonfiction promotion opportunities to us, including blogging. Because while we're unlikely to start a blog and earn search traffic for terms like "science fiction" and "western novels," we're very likely to get traffic for "how to self-publish" and similar terms. We'll start writing blog posts about those topics, and everything will grow that much more. (Side note: For the same SEO-related reasons, we'll probably start posting transcripts of our podcasts on the same website. Search engines can't search audio files, but can search the same content in text form.)

Here's the synergy: We're betting that some of the people who read this book (or read our nonfiction blog, or listen to our nonfiction podcast) will check out some of our fiction titles, thus raising our overall exposure. If you're in a position like ours, we'd strongly suggest writing a book that advances your profile in the way this book does for us, even if it doesn't do so directly.

Real Life

There's life outside the Internet. It's true. I heard it online.

This book is mainly about digital self-publishing and online promotion, but sarcasm aside, some of the best promotion avenues often have more to do with real, interpersonal connections that you'd have even if the Internet died tomorrow.

If you're part of organizations in your normal life, make sure they know you're a writer. Maybe you want to speak at a local library or bookstore event. Maybe you want to have a book signing. Maybe you just want your networks to know what you do, because you never know who knows whom, and who's interested in what.

Our favorite offline networking event is the South by Southwest (SXSW) conference held each March in Austin, Texas. When we went in 2013, we told everyone what we were doing with indie publishing, showed off our professionally illustrated book covers, and piqued a lot of interest. In 2014, we'll print up maybe a thousand copies of our "first episode" books (*Unicorn Western 1*, *The Beam: Episode One*, and many others), and deepen that interest by handing those books out like business cards. Again: You never know who knows whom, and who's interested in what.

We've also spent over five years in our respective fields, making a lot of friends. We've had dinner with these people; we've partnered with them; we exchange gifts at the holidays; we text them with amusing anecdotes. Some of those friends have rather large audiences of their own who might be interested in what we're doing. We didn't forge any of those connections in a quid-pro-quo way, anticipating "using" them some day, but regardless, those kinds of connections come in handy when you ask them for help spreading the word at the right time.

Boundaries and Maintenance

Regardless of what methods you decide are best to start deepening connections with your community of ideal readers and fans, be sure to use common sense.

For one, keep up a few boundaries. You don't need to be like Dave, electrifying fences and stocking decoy wallets in case of incursions by rape gangs, but it's probably not a good idea to post your personal phone number or your kids' Social Security numbers online. The decision of where to draw that line is personal. We know people who hide their families entirely, people who talk about their families using aliases (Sonia Simone from Copyblogger refers to her son as "Little Dude"), and people who share much more. Sean and I share a lot, for instance. By contrast, neither of us is sure if "Dave" is Dave's real name. (I'm kidding. We know his name is actually Raoul.)

But regardless of how much you share, respect a few boundaries. We'd never share anything that our families weren't comfortable sharing; we're extremely careful about giving out mailing addresses; we use simple common sense when answering communications. It's easier than ever to truly *know* people via the Internet, but there are limits.

The other precaution we'd urge is to know your own capacity as far as maintenance is concerned. In other words, only start what you know you can finish. Most of us can answer e-mail (in five sentences) and social network messages (if we keep it sensible), but blogging and podcasting are much more time-consuming. Remember, *Write. Publish. Repeat.* Adding to your available catalogue of excellent books should always come first, and developing passive marketing around those books (like CTAs and funnels) should be running immediately behind, waving her arms and yelling, "Wait for me!"

Yes, we have two podcasts and have a blog, but we also do this full time. If you only have a few hours a week to work on your indie publishing business, you shouldn't be spending those hours on 20-percent activities like blogging and podcasting — or, for that matter, delving into more social networks than you can manage (that might mean two).

One final note: If you found the social networking advice in this chapter lacking, there's a reason. We're hardly "good" at social networking, and hence don't have a ton to say. It's not that we consider social media unimportant, but it's certainly not a major part of *our* individual strategies. Other writers use those tools very effectively. If you'd like to hear from someone who uses social media much better than either of us, check out Joanna Penn's guide *How to Market a Book.*

CHAPTER FOURTEEN:
Understanding Funnels

WE'VE TALKED A BIT ABOUT funnels, but this chapter will more specifically detail what funnels are, how we use them, and how you can do the same.

In our opinion, putting your work into product funnels is the very best and most important thing you can do to increase your sales, assuming you've created an excellent and professional-looking family of products. This chapter is easily one of the most important in the book, so be sure to pay close attention.

Let's start with a definition.

What a Funnel Is

Simply put, a product funnel is way of organizing your works so that one product leads logically into another. You'll do this by setting up a series of pointers — in the backs of books, in product descriptions — in order to steer readers to the places you want them, and to give them compelling reasons to do so.

Understand: A good funnel isn't a straight chain, where Product A simply leads to Product B. It's a *funnel* — which, like a kitchen funnel, is wider at the top and narrower at the bottom. You want to scoop as many people into the top of your funnel as possible, then understand that they will sift apart — some sticking with you and others deciding your stuff isn't their cup of tea — as they move downward.

To put some labels on this, think about three products you have for sale: Products A, B, and C. These products can be books, novellas, short stories, short story collections, or other written works. If you write nonfiction and sell consulting or are available for speaking gigs, those products can also be speaking and consulting.

Now, think about something for a second: If you ultimately want to sell a big book bundle for $9.99 or consulting for $499, does it make sense for the very first thing people see from you is that big-ticket item? Absolutely not. Ten bucks is a lot to pay for an e-book by an unknown author, and $500 is a lot to pay for anything. If you want to sell those later items, you'll need to sell them last — which, to bring this metaphor full circle, is what happens at the very bottom of your funnel, where a few die-hard devotees (or true fans) remain out of that huge group who entered the funnel.

Let's call that big-ticket item Product C, at the bottom of the funnel. You can't usually sell that right off the bat. You must prove yourself to the customer with Products A and B, which they've already passed by on their way down the funnel, before you can hope to earn that sale.

Products at the top of the funnel must be easy to consume. Product A, which casts your widest net and scoops in as many prospective readers as possible, should ideally be free so that there's no barrier to entry for anyone even remotely interested in what you eventually want to sell. Product B can be a bit more expensive, and you work your way down further and further until, for a certain focused segment of customers, they're invested and confident enough to pick up your Product C ... or D, or F, or however deep your funnel goes.

Here are two age-old sales principles behind why this works:

It's Easier to Keep a Customer Than to Gain a New One

What do you think loyalty cards are for? What do you think "returning customer discounts" are for? The merchants you shop with, if they're smart, know that on average, it will cost them five times as much to get a new customer as it will to keep an old one. That's why intelligent merchants constantly bend over backward for their customers.

For you, with your funnel, this means it's easier to sell a customer on Product C if they've already bought and enjoyed Product B — and they'll be much more likely to buy Product B if they've already found Product A worthy of their time or attention.

The best way to sell any product in your catalog is to sell it to someone who's already a customer, and you can do that by hooking them in with the ones at the top of your funnel, which are easier for them to consume because they're cheap or free.

Each Time Someone Says "Yes," the Next "Yes" Becomes More Likely

Old-school vacuum cleaner salesmen asked prospects a lot of questions. If they were classically trained and good at their craft, they would only ask questions that they knew in advance would be answered with an easy, straightforward yes. The questions didn't have to have anything to do with what they were selling: "Isn't this a beautiful day?" "Don't you love it when your house is clean?" Etc. Those questions were easy for people to answer yes to, so they tended to do so. When the salesman finally got to a much harder question to answer in the affirmative ("Would you like to buy this vacuum cleaner?"), the prospect's mind would already be used to saying yes, and their likelihood of buying would be higher.

If you think this sounds like crap or voodoo, look it up. It's legit. Your product funnel asks those questions for you. Product A, which should be free, is very easy to say yes to. Product B might be a $3-$5 book. That's a harder yes, but they already gave an affirmative to A and liked it, so they're an easier sell. After *that* yes — again, for a smaller but more ideal segment of the buying population — you'll have an easier time getting buyers for the big bundle.

Things You Need to Know About Funnels

I can already feel a torrent of "But what if ... ?" questions flying at us. I can also sense a lot of hair-pulling frustration, because this all seems so complex. *How can it all work? How the hell can I possibly figure all of this out?*

Take a deep breath. Here's some stuff you should always keep in mind as you read this, no matter how mired down in nitty-gritty details you feel.

You Already Understand Funnels

Sean and I both have wives who really like the sitcom *Friends*, so we both own the full DVD set, containing all 10 seasons' worth of episodes.

(OK, we really like *Friends,* too. Sean, Lexi, and I have laughed repeatedly about the episode where Ross can't fit his couch up the stairs and keeps yelling "PI-VOT!")

But the process that led us to buy all those DVDs — not a cheap purchase — was a funnel. So, if you were getting confused in the previous section, just allow yourself to forget about it, and instead think of us with our DVDs. At first, the networks gave that show to us for free. Sure, the show was getting paid, but we didn't pay that price. We just sat back, on our over-the-air-with-no-digital-converter TVs at the time if that's all we had, and absorbed all of that entertainment for free. We said yes to that show over and over, because there was no barrier to entry. And then in the end, we bought in

276

because we'd been given a taste and knew we liked it.

Want another? I heard about the Angry Birds app, decided to see what all the fuss was about, and then saw that the app was free for iPad and iPhone. I downloaded it and thought it was amusing. More importantly, my son thought it was amusing, and he played until he'd 3-starred every level. After that, we decided to download Angry Birds Seasons, which cost 99 cents. He played that one to death, too. He got so obsessed that we ended up buying all sorts of Angry Birds plushies — including for my daughter, because she had to have some if he was getting some. We got an Angry Birds birthday cake that year. We bought Angry Birds Space, Angry Birds *Star Wars*, you name it.

That's a funnel. We paid nothing, then paid 99 cents, then paid more and more for merchandise. Oh, and here's an important thing to note about the Angry Birds funnel: If the first game hadn't been free, I never would have gotten it, and the whole thing would have fallen apart. Even a 99-cent price tag would have been too much. It's not that I'm too cheap to spend a dollar; it's that I was only curious, but not curious enough to spend any money.

Keep that in mind. You may reason that a few dollars (or 99 cents) is such a small price that no one will think twice about paying it, but that's only partially true. It's equally true that the most casual of visitors will turn away from 99 cents because they're curious … but not curious enough.

Funnels Require Multiple Products

We've just implied that you might consider making your book free, like the original Angry Birds game. And you might think that's a hideous idea, because although a 35 percent commission on a 99-cent sale isn't much, it's better than nothing.

Well, right. If you only have one book, that's true. But if you have several, it matters a lot less. Let's say you have two related books, and each sells one copy per day. Wouldn't you make the first one free if, by doing so, you thought you could sell three copies a day of the other?

The more books, stories, novellas, etc. that you have, the more options you'll have at your disposal for ways to promote and funnel. You must be able to send readers from one book to another to another — and, if you want a really *good* funnel, to a bundle of many books — and that only happens after you've ushered plenty of product to market.

Different Kinds of Funnels Require Different Structures

The more expensive the "deepest" product in your funnel, the more items you'll need upstream. If you're a consultant who also writes nonfiction books and your prime consulting package costs $1000, you'll need a lot of stuff in the funnel ahead of that package. The part of the funnel that this book covers will be at the very top, because self-publishers (at least with Amazon's current commission structure) generally don't price above $9.99 because that's where the 70 percent cutoff is.

But if all you have is a book and a short story, you can generally make a two-step funnel: an entry product (the short story) that's free and a book for $5 or so. You could also make the short story 99 cents, but that will mean a lot fewer people in your funnel.

As long as it goes from a low-barrier entry point designed to catch as many prospects as possible to a higher-barrier product that will appeal to fewer people, it's a funnel. The rest will depend on your specific situation.

Funnel Sequences Must Be Logical

I have one book with no funnel: my first novel, *The Bialy Pimps*. Not coincidentally, it almost never sells.

The reason there is no funnel with that book is because nothing is related to it. If I find the time some day, maybe I'll write a short story featuring one of the characters from *The Bialy Pimps* and use that as my entry point. It's quite a dilemma, because with only one book in the product line I'm unwilling to make it free, and as of now I have nothing to stick into the funnel with it.

If you have a free product and a paid product but they're not at all alike, that's not a funnel. It's a free product and a paid product that stand alone.

An Average Writer With a Tight Funnel Will Always Beat a Brilliant Writer With a Poor Funnel

... or no funnel whatsoever, which is the case for most indie writers.

Artist types hate to hear this, but it's true. You can be an excellent writer who creates brilliant art, but unless you know some serious heavy-hitters who can tell the world that your book is awesome, your brilliance will never be seen without a solid marketing strategy.

To be appreciated, brilliance must be seen. Have you ever heard that koan about how if a tree falls and nobody's around to hear it, does it make a sound?

Yeah. That.

Calls to Action

A call to action, typically abbreviated as CTA, is simply a request for your reader to do something. You can have a CTA that leads a reader to your book's sequel or a bundle, a CTA to join your mailing list, a CTA to review the book they just read, or anything else you want them to do.

CTAs are the engines that drive your funnels. If you have a logical, coherent constellation of products for readers to buy their way through, that funnel will never function if it simply *exists* and you tell no one.

We could get really tricky and technical here, but it's far kinder to you and far more helpful to say that crafting CTAs is simple human psychology. You don't need a marketing degree to craft a quality CTA. Put yourself in a customer's shoes and imagine encountering each of your products in turn, making your way through them, then asking yourself, "OK, what next?"

In the core *Unicorn Western* series, there are nine books, not including the prequel, *Unicorn*

Genesis, or the sequel trilogy, *Unicorn Apocalypse.* <u>The first book in the core series — a novella of about 25,000 words — is free on all of the major platforms.</u> Books 2-9 are $2.99, and the upsell we really want people to buy is the *Unicorn Western Full Saga,* priced at $9.99.

Here's how *Unicorn Western's* CTAs are set up:

No CTAs on the Unicorn Western 1 Product Page

We want entry into the series to be totally and completely frictionless. If someone knows nothing about *Unicorn Western,* we don't want to distract them with extraneous information, and don't want them thinking in advance about future purchases. So they see that there's a book with a cool cover about a grizzled gunslinger riding a badass-looking unicorn. They read the summary and customer reviews. They see it's free — and then, hopefully, they download it.

A CTA at the End of Unicorn Western 1 That Gives Two Options

Here's what it says:

> GET COOL STUFF!
> If you liked Unicorn Western #1, you'll LOVE *Unicorn Western #2* (this saga gets better by the book!). <u>CLICK HERE</u> to start reading *Unicorn Western #2* right now, or (and this is DEFINITELY SMARTER) <u>CLICK HERE</u> to spend 60% less for all 9 books in the *Full Saga.*

Psychologically, people are more likely to make a decision if you give them options, so that's one reason we've given them the choice between just getting #2 or getting the *Full Saga*. But even more importantly, we want them to have some contrast so they see how great a deal the bundle is. If they investigate both options, they'll see that book 2 is $2.99 and that the Saga can be had for triple that. If you enjoyed the book you just read and are planning to buy more, isn't it sensible to save money now?

We've built similar notices into all the stand-alone volumes.

CTAs in the Product Descriptions of Books 2-5

At the top of the product description (on the actual sales page) for *Unicorn Western 2*, in big, bold type, is this:

> SAVE 60% WITH THE *FULL SAGA*!
> This book is also available in the UNICORN WESTERN *FULL SAGA*, which contains all 9 books in the series. Saddle up and get it here: http://unicornwestern.com/saga

Basically, this is our way of grabbing someone who's about to buy *Unicorn Western 2* and yelling, "WAIT! Wouldn't you like to Super-Size that?" We have them on books 3-5 as well, but don't generally bother to add them to the later volumes. If you've made it all the way to *Unicorn Western 8* or *9* and still haven't gotten the bundle, learning about it for the first time before you buy will only piss you off.

A Generalized CTA at the End of the Full Saga and Book 9

You should always be thinking about where else you can send people, so when we reached the final book's end, we thought, "Well, that's all of them. Now what might they like?" The answer was *Unicorn Genesis*, which is its own book: a prequel in the same universe. So, that's where we send them.

If you don't have anywhere else to send people, send them to your mailing list. Or if you have other product lines that people who've finished your entire epic might enjoy, you can steer them toward those products. I did both — sending people to our mailing list and pitching our other lines — at the end of the final *Fat Vampire* book. Here's what it looks like:

SO WHAT'S NEXT?

It sucks finishing a series, doesn't it? Reginald's journey (as I wrote it, anyway) is now complete, but there's plenty more great stuff to read. **And you can get that great stuff FREE.** Just go here to get your next read for free: realmandsands.com/free/

I recommend *The Beam* if you're into science fiction and/or thrillers, or *Unicorn Western* if you like stuff that's really, really epic ... and has the same basic serious/funny vibe as *Fat Vampire*. But hey, it's ALL good stuff!

Thanks so much for reading!

It's also worth noting that we have specific versions of our manuscripts for each bookseller platform, all with different CTAs. We want the version we upload to Kobo to link to the Kobo version of that title, and we want the Amazon version's CTA to link to the books on Amazon. It's a bit of extra work, but it's worth it. The Internet makes people lazy, and if you can give them one-click access to what you want them to do, you absolutely should.

Across all of these CTAs, it's really not that complicated when you get down to it. All we're saying is, "When a reader or prospective reader reaches place X, what do they need to know about and what would appeal to them most?"

Using Free

If you have the inventory to spare and don't mind sacrificing income on a single title to gain income on others, free is the best way to get your books into as many hands as possible. If your free book, story, brochure, or whatever else stands as a quality product, a significant number of people who read to the end will buy your follow-up product. The good folks at Kobo told me that their stats show that over half of the people who finish *Fat Vampire 1* will buy either *Fat Vampire 2* or one of my bundles. Those are fantastic odds.

Making a book free is a bit tricky. You can upload a book to Kobo and set the price as free, but can't currently do the same to Amazon, Nook, or Apple. To cover those other marketplaces, the best option as of this writing is to upload your book to Smashwords.com, set the price as free, and set Smashwords to distribute that book to Nook and everywhere else (except Kobo and Amazon) for you. Upload to Amazon directly, set the price to whatever makes sense (they won't let you make it free), and wait. If you do everything right and don't get rejected by Smashwords's meat grinder, your book will eventually appear in Apple and the Nook store with a price tag of $0.00. When *that* happens, you can report the free price to Amazon and hope they lower their version of your book to match the free price tag. It's hit or miss, and the details in this paragraph could change at any time.

But even with all of this said, free can be dangerous. You do want to give people a way to taste your product, but definitely *don't* want to train people not to pay for your stuff.

As mentioned earlier, Amazon has a program called KDP Select, and you used to be able to make your book free for a few days, then end the free run and rack up follow-up sales. Because of this — and because we wanted to reward the people on our list — we used to launch all of our books at free, then raise the price with the intention of making our money down the road.

This was a good idea at the time, but quickly soured. For one, you may fill your list with free-seekers. Die-hard free-seekers want everything for free and refuse to pay for books. In order to give our books regular boosts, we'd run free promotions on all of them from time to time, and the free seekers would wait whether they were on our list or on the bookseller sites in general. We started getting e-mails like, "When will title X be free? I want to get it." But they wouldn't cough up $2.99.

We're pretty hard-line on this kind of thing. Dave is a pleaser despite his surly exterior, and wanted to pacify those people — some of whom grew angry when we tried to charge for things — but Sean and I didn't share his sentiments. We wanted those people to get off our lists. If they're never going to buy, the relationship isn't equal. They want to take and take, so if they're not telling their friends and leaving you reviews — basically, giving back — then how is that fair?

Making a title permanently free as the start of a funnel is an awesome way to drive sales further down your sales funnel, but we want to kick "promotion via temporary free" in the teeth over and over again. We suggest you think the same way. Reading your work should not be a matter of charity; you do not need to bend over backwards and not be paid if someone will deign to read your book. If you don't have a good reason to make your book free, don't.

OK, time for a caveat we've not mentioned in a while: This is all a very *tactical* discussion. Remember at all times to base what you do around *strategy*, not tactics. For now, the above is how free works. And for the foreseeable future we think that some version of "first book free" (whether or not it's done exactly as above) will be a winning tactic. But you'll need to be prepared to adjust as needed, because your bigger strategy is "make it easy for people to get into your funnel, then upsell them when it makes the most sense."

Making your books free on the major booksellers isn't the only way to get people into your funnel using free as a lure. Here are a few more ways to seed your funnel-starter as far and wide as possible:

Short Stories in Your Story's World

You might be able to write multiple short stories to exist within your story worlds, and if you do, you'll be able to steer people to your upsells through several avenues.

For instance, the very first seed that spawned *The Beam* came from one of Collective Inkwell's *Dark Crossings* (*Twilight Zone*-inspired) short stories written by Sean called *Respero Dinner*. We put this short up for free as an additional entry point — a *pre*-funnel piece that actually serves to send people *to our other free product*. We also had a standalone *Unicorn Western* story called *The Outlaw Hassle Stone* that was just laying around (we wrote it to encourage social shares when we launched the original saga), so we put that up as an additional entry point to that funnel.

Offering Free Books on Your Website

Our default is to offer books and stories for free on the major sellers, but you can also offer the files (.mobi for Kindle, .epub for other readers, and PDFs for just about anything) for download on your website. We also use them as an enticement to join our mailing list. If people join the Realm & Sands mailing list, they can choose any of our $4.99-or-less books as a thank-you. We simply e-mail the file after they do.

Podiobooks and Podcasting Your Book

A lot of people like to listen to audiobooks, so if you record an audio version of the book at the top of your funnel, you can distribute it that way. Your CTA needs to be verbal, but we've all done it. People finish the audiobook, want to know what happens next, and buy up.

There's a site called Podiobooks (short for podcast audiobooks) that will distribute it to their network and put it on iTunes for you, and that works well and has a good-sized audience. Alternatively, you can put the podcast on iTunes yourself. Sean and Dave did this with their horror serial *Yesterday's Gone* (before selling the rights for a pro version), and the advantage is the ability to post new audio episodes as you go rather than finishing them all first, which Podiobooks requires.

These options can be very time-consuming and require quality audio equipment and some know-how, so keep that in mind if you decide to try them.

Online Reading Sites

Wattpad.com, for instance, is a popular website where people can read free books uploaded chapter by chapter by the authors using apps available on their computers or various mobile devices. Wattpad readers typically like their content in nuggets, and they may follow a book's posting live, reading a chapter or two per week as it's slowly uploaded.

You can upload your free funnel-starter to sites like this to expand your reach, then include a link at the end of the chapters (or at the end of the larger work) to get the rest of the series.

Creating Pilots

When we launched Realm & Sands, we wanted to write a few projects in addition to the large ones we already had planned, but weren't sure which of our many ideas we wanted to write to completion. We had six ideas — three for serious serial projects (*Namaste, Robot Proletariat,* and *Cursed*) and three for comedy series we thought of as sitcoms (*Space Shuttle, Greens,* and *Everyone Gets Divorced*) — but probably only had time to write two of them.

The original intention was to follow television's model one step further (Sean and Dave had introduced the idea of episodes and full seasons to the e-book world a year earlier), so we created "pilots" for all six of our ideas. The theory was that some of those pilots would be green-lit by our readers and be written out fully while the others would die and live their lives as smaller stand-alone shorts. We asked our readers to vote with their reviews.

Of course, because we love all of our projects and are masochists, we decided to flesh out all six. *Namaste* became a novel, *Robot Proletariat* became a serial, *Cursed* became a series of novellas, and the sitcoms all got six-episode first-season treatments.

Here's where free comes in: Because we'd already structured all six projects to have pilots, we kept the pilots online and made them free, with the upsell being the completed first season or bundle. *Namaste*'s pilot became a part of the larger novel, but the original pilot worked as a self-contained story within a story, so we released it as a free prelude.

You can always try stories out this way, seeing how well the pilot lands with readers before deciding whether to flesh it out. If the pilot does well, you can then write the larger work and leave the free pilot as the entry point to your funnel.

Establishing Authority

You may or may not have known about us before you bought this book, but in many cases, writers will buy *Write. Publish. Repeat.* only after listening to our podcast for a while. That makes this book plus our podcast an odd kind of free-to-paid funnel. You can create something similar if you already have exposure or authority out there in the world. Our podcast is our free, and it shows listeners that we know what we're talking about and that they'd get significant value from our book.

The funnel goes the other way, too. As mentioned earlier, we're hoping that some of you reading this book will be intrigued enough by who we are and what we do to pick up some of our fiction — probably beginning with the free products. It's like a funnel on top of a funnel, this one attempting at the funnel's bottom to convert a few of our nonfiction readers to our fiction.

Upsells, Next Steps, and Bundles

An upsell is simply the purchase you're trying to entice a reader to make at the end of completing any given work. It's called an upsell because they're already sold on you to some degree, and you're trying to get them buying up to the next thing.

Upsells are everywhere in everyday life. If you've ever gotten a car wash and been asked if you'd like the hot wax, that's an upsell. If a waiter has ever asked you if you'd like desert after finishing dinner, that's an upsell. An upsell can be anything that's a natural next step. It's your job, as an author/marketer, to make that next step as obvious and attractive to your reader as possible. Once you have an easy-entry (ideally free) product plus a CTA leading to an upsell, you also have yourself a funnel.

You can make your funnel a simple series of novels or novellas introduced by a free first book if you want to. We actually like this structure for our *Future of Sex* serial with Lexi because if readers get hooked on the series (which they do; the cliffhangers between books are killer), they'll gobble new installments as they're released. One significant advantage to this model — especially for people like the three of us, with many projects on our plates — is that it allows you to take your time. Once you have two books, you have a rudimentary funnel, and although that funnel will improve with a third book, there's no rush to get there.

If you want to supercharge your funnel, you can make the deeper products inside easier to say yes to by bundling them for a lower, can't-pass-it-up price. Staying in Lexi's sexy realm, this is how our other product with her works. *Adult Video,* our "*Clerks* in a porn shop" collaboration, sells in three-episode packs for $2.99, but the entire 12-episode season is just $5.99. If you read and enjoy the first three-episode group of *Adult Video* episodes (the entry point to our funnel) you flat-out are *going* to buy the bundle if you buy anything, because the deal is too good to ignore.

We try to make our upsell a bundle whenever we can, but as implied, the disadvantage of doing things that way is that we really want to have the bundle complete — or at least on the calendar to complete soon — before we publish the pilot. The nature of conversion (whether or not people buy an upsell through a CTA) is such that you'll lose people if they can't act instantly. We didn't want to have *Adult Video 1* out there for free, gaining fans eager for more of Heather's hilariously slutty antics, without having our upsell available for immediate purchase. If we'd done that, most of those people eager to pull the trigger would have lost their urgency, moved on, and forgotten the series (as hilarious as it might be).

Because of this, we always feel some sense of urgency between the time a funnel is opened and the time it's completed. As I write this, we're operating at full capacity thanks to a bit of self-imposed funnel-related pressure. The new year is approaching, and January is typically a very big month for e-book sales. We want our funnels complete by the time those holiday shoppers arrive, and we have a lot to finish. But once we close a funnel — ideally by creating a value bundle at its bottom — the pressure is relieved, and we move into a situation where things become as automated as they currently can be in digital publishing. Despite the extra work now, the thought of having nine complete funnels between us and another two with Lexi (plus another for me on my own and several more between Sean and Dave in Collective Inkwell) makes it worth doing.

Just remember that whenever you can bundle products and offer them as an upsell, you make it that much easier for a pleased reader to buy them. That means stuffing your upsell with value and discounting it heavily over the alternative ways of purchasing the same content. The stronger the bundle and the better you convey that inherent value in your CTA, the better your funnel will convert free readers to paid.

CHAPTER FIFTEEN:
Email Marketing the Non-Sleazy Way

DAVE HAS A DEEP SUSPICION of scams, and in his mind the Internet marketing community might be the biggest group of liars and scammers to have ever existed. We get it; there are only so many claims of expensive products that promise instant riches and boner medication ads you can see before you start to feel the same way.

For this reason, we're pretty sure that Dave dies a little each time he thinks about the fact that he's sending product-related announcements to an e-mail list for Collective Inkwell. It means that he's *marketing* on the *Internet*, and that makes him an *Internet marketer.*

OH, THE HORROR!

If you're a Dave on the idea of Internet marketing, we kindly suggest you get over it. As is true with anything, there will always be bad apples who spoil the bunch. Marketing isn't evil, and doing it on the Internet doesn't increase its evil (although it does make evil easier). If you don't make fake offers of easy wealth and operate inside the latest, grayest areas, the fact that you have product funnels and operate an e-mail list doesn't make you a bad person, and the readers on your list aren't going to think you are. They joined your list because they *wanted* to know when you had new books for sale, so give them what they were hoping to get.

Minute for minute and dollar for dollar, adding e-mail to your marketing plan is the best way to bond with your readers and make them *want* to buy from you. It's only sleazy if you make it so.

This chapter is all about how to do e-mail marketing the right way, ultimately making it not that different from e-mailing your friends.

Think of it that way — as e-mailing friends to let them know about something cool rather than as something scammy done by the people Dave hates — and you can kill it in this aspect of your business. All it takes is good writing. And you're a writer, right?

Let's begin.

Why Email is Non-Negotiable

You need to build yourself an e-mail list, and do some form of e-mail marketing. Period.

You can ignore this chapter if you want to. You can be so turned off by the idea of sending a mass e-mail that you'll skip past it, eagerly moving on to reading about customer reviews and leaving this nastiness behind. You can decide that it sounds like too much work, that you'd rather be writing. You can reason that you're "not a marketing type" and that you can connect with people on social networks instead. That's your choice, but that's a massive mistake. Building a list isn't a step you *can* take, it's a step you *must* take. Without it, everything else you do to promote and sell your books will only have a fraction of the effectiveness it should have. Without it, you might as well not have bought this book, because you won't be using what it teaches in any meaningful way.

E-mail is that important.

The reason doesn't even have to do directly with selling. It's not like we're saying you need an e-mail list so you can do some crazy, top secret Internet marketing techniques. By now, you should realize that we don't believe in top secret techniques. As with everything else, our insistence on e-mail comes down to a simple, real-life-relatable, strategic concept: You don't want someone else to be able to suddenly take away your ability to talk to your readers.

Remember the concept of digital sharecropping from earlier in this section? We discussed it in terms of building your own platform, and think we made a convincing argument. If you don't build an e-mail list, you won't be creating a direct means of contact with your readers. And if you don't do that, you'll always be sharecropping. You might reach your readers on Facebook, but what if Facebook falls out of favor or if your account gets inexplicably suspended? You might count on your books to speak for you, but what if your books get pulled? It happens. I once had my Amazon KDP account locked, meaning I couldn't make any changes to anything until I e-mailed Amazon support and asked them what was up, which took a few days. The problem got resolved, but the experience felt like Amazon rattling its scythe, reminding me exactly who owned the land I was planting on.

Yes, you want to take advantage of all of the platforms available that will help you reach your ideal readers, but you should rely on none as your sole means of contact. This is one area where Sean and I are as paranoid as Dave. When it comes to the pipeline between you and your customer, *be* paranoid, and trust no one. As long as you have that connection, you can steer readers around any obstacles that land in your path, telling them what you're doing and where to find you. Without that connection, your entire business is a house of cards.

If you do have an e-mail list, though, all of your marketing efforts will work much better. You can tell the people who like your work most when new titles are available. You can ask your best fans for reviews. You can let them know when you're doing a book signing or when you're having a sale and need as many purchases as possible to drive yourself up the bestseller charts. If you have a series, rest assured that some people are eagerly waiting for the next book. You want the ability to tell those people that it's available, because they're as eager to buy as you are to make sales.

How To Do It Wrong

E-mail marketing usually gets a bad rap because it's handled in one of two crappy ways. Either it's full of bullshit promises and high-pressure salesmanship (traditional Internet marketers) or it's boring and impersonal (major retailers). It's not e-mail (the medium itself) that's the problem. Only how it's done.

If you write a nonfiction book and promise that it holds all of the secrets your readers have ever wanted and that it will make them rich/famous/fabulous/you name it, you're doing it wrong. If you tell them that they have to buy your novel NOW NOW NOW or else they'll miss out, you're doing it wrong. If you lie in general, you're doing it wrong.

But similarly, think about how the big, "respectable" folks do e-mail marketing and you'll see that they're doing it wrong in an entirely different way. Are you on Victoria's Secret's mailing list? Target's mailing list? Even the mailing list of most big-name mainstream authors? If you are, do those e-mails engage you? Do you even pay attention to them? Or are you the way most people are with regard to that kind of digital mailbox clutter — totally uninterested, but not irritated enough to bother unsubscribing?

Even when bigger names create unoffensive e-mail campaigns that are in many ways the exact opposite of most Internet marketing e-mails, they fail just as hard because they go too far in the other direction. The L.L. Bean e-mail newsletter isn't pushy; it's forgettable. The newsletters of certain unnamed major authors aren't full of lies; they're full of announcements so dry and generic that even those who aren't insulted by how little they seem to mean to the sender are bored stiff.

Don't do this stuff, and your e-mail marketing will already be halfway there.

Again — and we keep saying this, so we hope you've caught on — none of this is rocket science. You're a reader in addition to being a writer, and you're a person who is marketed to as well as doing marketing yourself. That means you know perfectly well what it's like to be on the other side of the fence. Do you *like* traditional Internet marketing e-mails? Do you *enjoy* the Walmart newsletter? If not, it's not like you need to hire a team of experts to figure out why. You probably dislike the former because they're pushy and disingenuous and you probably dislike (or are neutral about) the latter because they're mind-numbingly bland and mean nothing to you as an individual. So, when you're on the other side of the e-mail control panel, don't create those kinds of e-mails. Do unto others as you'd have done unto you.

How To Do It Right

There are two parts to doing e-mail right, and one may sound like it contradicts something we said in the last section. One of the parts of a successful e-mail campaign should almost feel like common sense; the other may require you to fight a bit of internal programming.

Let's tackle the hard one first. In the previous section, we said you should use your own feelings, as a receiver of e-mails, as a guide when you write e-mails of your own. If you don't like receiving e-mails of a certain type, don't send them. So far, so good.

Problem is, a lot of people who read this will trip over the idea of "what they wouldn't like as a receiver" and end up being overly timid when it comes to selling. Dave would, and he'll *tell* you he would. Because we've been so conditioned to hate sales from the likes of used car salesman and high-pressure Internet marketers, the tendency for most people is to swing too far in the other direction. If the way most high-pressure folks sell feels bad, you might reason that *any* selling feels bad. But that simply isn't the case, and you'll need to learn the difference if you're to effectively use e-mail to reach your customers.

Here's what I mean:

As I write this, I'm listening to the four pre-released singles from Eminem's *The Marshall Mathers LP2* on repeat. Most of this book has been written to those four songs, because I'm so eagerly anticipating the album's release on (and watch me date this manuscript) Nov. 5, 2013. I happen to have pre-ordered the full album on iTunes, but if that wasn't possible — if Eminem were an independent artist like all of us and could only sell the album when it came live — I'd have signed up for an early notification list. I would be salivating to receive that e-mail. In fact, before I pre-ordered the album, I told Sean to be sure to let me know when the album was out because I didn't want to miss it by even a day.

If Eminem were in our position (and if he could refrain from calling me a motherfucker), do you think I'd remotely mind when he sent me a link to buy? Sean would want the link *and* think being called a motherfucker was funny.

The people on your e-mail list are your readers, and they joined the list because they were interested in your work. You must not feel timid about letting them know when you have new work for sale, and giving them links they can use to *buy what they already want to buy.* You must not feel that you can't remind them about work they may have missed. You must not fear singing your own praises, seeing as they're on your list because they agree your praises deserve a few musical notes. If you're timid about selling, you're doing those readers a disservice. They won't be mad at you if you tell them about your books, but they might be mad if you *don't*, since that's exactly why they signed up in the first place.

That's the first part: *You must not be afraid to sell.*

The second part is common sense. This is the antidote to the high-pressure Internet marketer half truths and the milquetoast mumblings of your big-name competitors. If you want a newsletter that truly connects with readers, *be a human being.*

That's it. Once you understand that you need to add selling to the mix, the rest is writing e-mails like you would to a friend. "Hey Joe, you asked what I was up to, so let me tell you about some cool things." *Like that.* No magic. If anything, you may need to un-learn some of the crap you've heard about e-mail marketing. The best e-mails are personal, funny, engaging, even vulnerable. The best thing you can do in your e-mails is to be honest, especially when you wonder if you shouldn't be. Level with your readers. Shoot straight. People can smell crap, and appreciate it when someone finally delivers straight truth. Don't blab on and on, but don't be afraid to tell them about something amusing that happened in your life that has nothing to do with your writing. Remember, the idea is for them to bond with *you*, not just your books. Give them some of yourself.

I like Louis CK. Sean has a boner for him — not just as a writer and comic, but as a thinker and businessman. If you're not subscribed to his list, you should be. If you like him on stage, or in his absurdly stupid (and super-smart) show, you will like him in his e-mails. Sean also goes to boner town with Louis because he's one of us. An entrepreneur, *and* a self-publisher. He went direct, giving HBO a Dirty Sanchez when he went straight to the fans (his list) and dropped a comedy special direct to the tune of a million dollars. Here's what he said to his list after it happened:

> People of Earth (minus the ones who don't give a shit about this): it's been amazing to conduct this experiment with you. The experiment was: if I put out a brand new standup special at a drastically low price ($5) and make it as easy as possible to buy, download and enjoy, free of any restrictions, will everyone just go and steal it? Will they pay for it? And how much money can be made by an individual in this manner?
>
> It's been 4 days. A lot of people are asking me how it's going. I've been hesitant to share the actual figures, because there's power in exclusive ownership of information. What I didn't expect when I started this was that people would not only take part in this experiment, they would be invested in it and it would be important to them. It's been amazing to see people in large numbers advocating this idea. So I think it's only fair that you get to know the results. Also, it's just really cool and fun and I'm dying to tell everybody. I told my Mom, I told three friends, and that wasn't nearly enough. So here it is.
>
> First of all, this was a premium video production, shot with six cameras over two performances at the Beacon Theater, which is a high-priced elite Manhattan venue. I directed this video myself and the production of the video cost around $170,000. (This was largely paid for by the tickets bought by

the audiences at both shows). The material in the video was developed over months on the road and has never been seen on my show (LOUIE) or on any other special. The risks were thus: every new generation of material I create is my income, it's like a farmer's annual crop. The time and effort on my part was far more than if I'd done it with a big company. If I'd done it with a big company, I would have a guarantee of a sizable fee, as opposed to this way, where I'm actually investing my own money.

The development of the website, which needed to be a very robust, reliable and carefully constructed website, was around $32,000. We worked for a number of weeks poring over the site to make sure every detail would give buyers a simple, optimal and humane experience for buying the video. I edited the video around the clock for the weeks between the show and the launch.

The show went on sale at noon on Saturday, December 10th. 12 hours later, we had over 50,000 purchases and had earned $250,000, breaking even on the cost of production and website. As of Today, we've sold over 110,000 copies for a total of over $500,000. Minus some money for PayPal charges etc, I have a profit around $200,000 (after taxes $75.58). This is less than I would have been paid by a large company to simply perform the show and let them sell it to you, but they would have charged you about $20 for the video. They would have given you an encrypted and regionally restricted video of limited value, and they would have owned your private information for their own use. They would have withheld international availability indefinitely. This way, you only paid $5, you can use the video any way you want, and you can watch it in Dublin, whatever the city is in Belgium, or Dubai. I got paid nice, and I still own the video (as do you). You never have to join anything, and you never have to hear from us again.

I really hope people keep buying it a lot, so I can have shitloads of money, but at this point I think we can safely say that the experiment really worked. If anybody stole it, it wasn't many of you. Pretty much everybody bought it. And so now we all get to know that about people and stuff. I'm really glad I put this out here this way and I'll certainly do it again. If the trend continues with sales on this video, my goal is that i can reach the point where when I sell anything, be it videos, CDs or tickets to my tours, I'll do it here and I'll continue to follow the model of keeping my price as far down as possible, not overmarketing to you, keeping as few people between you and me as possible in the transaction.

(Of course i reserve the right to go back on all of this and sign a massive deal with a company that pays me fat coin and charges you straight up the ass.). (This is you: yes Louie. And we'll all enjoy torrenting that content. You fat sweaty dolt).

I probably sound kind of crazy right now. It's been a really fun and intense few days. This video was paid for by people who bought tickets, and then bought by people who wanted to see that same show. I got to do exactly the show I wanted, and exactly the show you wanted.

I also got an education. And everything i learned are things i was happy to learn.

I learned that people are interested in what happens and shit (i didn't go to college)

I learned that money can be a lot of things. It can be something that is hoarded, fought over, protected, stolen and withheld. Or it can be like an energy, fueled by the desire, will, creative interest, need to laugh, of large groups of people. And it can be shuffled and pushed around and pooled together to fuel a common interest, jokes about garbage, penises and parenthood.

I want to thank Blair Breard who produced this video and produces my series LOUIE, and I want to thank Caspar and Giles at Version Industries, who created the website.

I hope with all of my heart that I stay funny. Otherwise this all goes to hell. Please have a safe and happy holiday, and thank you again for all this crazy shit.

That, son, is how it's done. It's easy to see why Sean would want to jump rope with Louis. As much as we want to emulate and improvise upon what authors like Stephen King have done with their ethic, artists like Louis CK are worth paying close attention to because they represent a new way of communicating with your fans, and making the middleman wait in the corner where he belongs.

How To Set Up Your List

This is the part that scares a lot of people. Setup can be a bit technical, but the setup itself is really the only part that's kind of sort of (not even really) difficult. Find a way to get through the setup (there are probably tutorial videos for whatever service you're using, either on the site or on YouTube), because maintenance really isn't much harder than sending a normal e-mail.

We'll give you the broad strokes of *what* you need to do to set up your e-mail list and get it working, but we're not going to tell you *how*, specifically. There are too many variables for us to give you a comprehensive tutorial here, and doing so would be pointless anyway. You can find much better how-to in other places — probably from your e-mail service provider itself. In this section, we're going to tell you what to do, and leave it to you to find the details of "how."

So... here's the "what."

Step 1: Set Up a Website

The first step is to get yourself a website so you have a place to put your e-mail signup form. Technically, you can often send people to a hosted version of the signup form provided by your e-mail service, but you should put it on your own website. That way, you can control its function and appearance, and you need a website to act as your "platform" anyway.

Launching a website can be very easy. Take a look back at the section on building your platform for our advice on how to do it, but be sure to get it done. Again, we strongly suggest getting your own site on your own hosting plan rather than opting for a hosted solution like Blogger or Wordpress.com. (Wordpress software installed on your own website is good, but the free version on Wordpress.com is still digital sharecropping, and by now you know that's a bad idea. One out of every 2,314 intelligent people will disagree with this. Don't be a Dave.)

Step 2: Choose a Service Provider

You can use just about any e-mail service provider. Our favorite by far is aWeber, which has a stellar record in the industry and goes to great lengths to have good "deliverability," which means that the maximum amount of messages will make it past spam filters and into inboxes.

I have an already-somewhat-dated aWeber tour video at SelfPublishingPodcast.com/aweber if you'd like to check it out. It'll show you the basics of how to use the service, create a form, send e-mails, and so on. (That video is "Johnny 1.0" from before I was an author. I'm sure it's amusing in its own way.)

You can absolutely use other e-mail providers, too. Two that come to mind are iContact and MailChimp. Both have their limitations, real and rumored, from low volume hurting deliverability (low deliverability = little point in sending) to missing e-mails and unhelpful customer support. aWeber has fantastic people on the phone. Our experience with them is aces. If you think you may end up with aWeber in the end, start there for sure. You'll thank us later, when you don't have to try and migrate (losing most of your list in the process).

People new to e-mail marketing usually complain about the expense, but this is smart money to spend and keeping it in your pocket will only mean you won't be filling it with more. We suggest sucking it up as an inevitable cost of business. If you're extremely price-conscious, you can use MailChimp despite the limitations because they'll let you get started (with a list up to 2,000 people) for free. That sounds like a really good deal, and it is — if that's all you'll ever need.

If you have more than 2,000 readers already, you know the right place to go. If you don't, picture where you want to be a year from now. Do you want at least, if not more than, 2,000 readers? If so, this is a tiny investment in your future. If the service won't fit your needs once the free window is closed, don't open it.

Ultimately, what matters most in a provider is that you can add people to your list and send e-mails, so if the provider you choose can do those two things (hint: they all can), you're doing great.

Step 3: Create an Email Signup Form

Once you've signed up with an e-mail service provider, you'll need to set up a list and create a signup form that will allow people to join that list. You'll need to consult your provider's documentation for information on how to do this (or watch the video I linked to in the last section if you go with aWeber), but in the end you'll be given a snippet of code to copy and paste onto your website.

Create a new page on your site and paste the code onto it, then add some descriptive text above the form that tells people why they should sign up. Make it compelling; "Join my list for updates and newsletters" isn't good enough. Put yourself in the shoes of a random web surfer — someone who probably already gets too much e-mail and doesn't want more. What would *you* need to read before you signed up? Use that as a guide when crafting your own copy.

We suggest adding an enticement, then spelling it out. People who join the Realm & Sands e-mail list can pick out any of our books priced at $4.99 or less for free as a thank-you, and they'll get that as soon as they sign up and e-mail us back with their choice. They also get first crack at our new books, often at a discount, and will receive an ongoing e-mail-only serial (*Caveman Timecop*) that isn't available anywhere else. You can check out our signup page for ideas at RealmAndSands.com/free.

Our offers will change over time, so if you visit that page when this book is brand-new you'll see the *Caveman Timecop* and $5 offer. If it's a few years later, you'll probably see a signup for an app, and maybe a $10 book because we can afford it, and we'll always love our readers.

Always be listening.

We asked our readers what type of serial they wanted. And because our true fans love that we can and will write anything, we let them pick the name (and therefore the topic) of our e-mail-only serial. We said, "Throw us two words or a one-sentence pitch." Our example was, "Dinosaur Romance." Readers sent in their entries, and the one with the most votes — *Caveman Timecop* — won.

We're 10 episodes in as I write this, and the story is a lot of fun. We treat the time travel aspect seriously, so it's made for some cool paradoxes and loops, and has us seriously wanting to write a longer, deeper time travel tale. We will continue to write *Caveman Timecop* and deliver the story in 500-word snippets each week, as long as readers want it. When they tell us they're ready for something else, we'll pivot to that.

Use your list to make your readers happy, because for people like you and me, happy readers are the best thing in the world.

Step 4: Create an Immediate Reply Message

After your signup page, you will need to create an automatic reply message (sometimes called an autoresponder) so that readers who join your list will get an e-mail from you immediately. This is important for PR reasons (everyone likes being thanked and welcomed), but you'll also need it to deliver any bonuses you've promised for joining, such as a link to a free book, instructions on how to contact you, and so on. Write this e-mail in a casual tone — one person e-mailing another. Don't try to be "professional," because for most people, professional equates to dry and boring. You want them to like you as a person, so be who you are. Yes, it's an automatic reply, and nobody is going to be fooled into thinking that you personally, instantly responded to their signup. But that doesn't mean you can't be cool.

Here's the text of our e-mail signup message, keenly noting that we call our people "Outlaws" as a nod to *Unicorn Western*:

Hey there, Outlaw!

We're so glad you're here with us.

We appreciate you reading, and want you to love our words.

There are two ways we want to thank you right now (plenty more later).

First is with our e-mail-only serial, *Caveman Timecop*. You can catch up with *Caveman Timecop* here:
http://realmandsands.com/caveman-timecop

Second is with a book from our catalogue. Please pick anything from this page priced $4.99 or less:

http://realmandsands.com/books

Just hit reply to this e-mail with your choice, and we'll get it to you as soon as possible.

Thanks!

Johnny and Sean

For details on how to set up this first message, we'll again refer you to your provider's documentation. (Or, if you're using aWeber, how to do it is covered in the tour video we linked to in step 2. aWeber refers to these automatic replies as "follow-up messages.")

Step 5: Put a Link to the Signup Page in Your CTAs

Once you've set up your list and your automatic reply and have put your signup form on a page on your website, the last step is to start giving that link out to readers. The main place you'll want to do this is in your book's back CTA.

You can download any of our free books to see how we do this, but it's pretty straightforward. You already wrote some copy to put on the opt-in page itself, so you'll recap that same copy in the CTA. Think of your reader, who's just finished your book. What do you need to tell them to make them want to go to your site right now and sign up for your list?

Be sure to make the link in your CTA clickable. Few people will walk to a computer and type your URL into a web browser. Many more will click a link in an e-book to open their e-reader's browser and sign up on the spot. If you use Scrivener, adding clickable links is easy. You just highlight the text you want to link, go to Edit > Add Link, and type it in. Test the link to be sure it works, and you're in business.

Feels good to be a pro, right? Now you can sit back and watch your e-mail list grow. It will happen slowly (maybe very slowly) at first, but keep in mind that every person on that list is an asset you didn't have before — a hot lead who likes you and would have otherwise gotten away.

Optional: Using Placeholder Pages

This one is a sorta-ninja trick I'm proud of. We use it on Realm & Sands, but Lexi took our idea and used it more hilariously, so I'll tell you about how things work with the series we co-write with her, *The Future of Sex*.

At the end of each episode of *The Future of Sex*, there's a significant cliffhanger. They're the kinds of cliffhangers that have fans of the series clawing at their readers because they're so eager to see what happens next. At the end of each episode, we capitalize on that enthusiasm by including a CTA pointing to the next book. The CTA includes something specific about the cliffhanger, then tells the reader that the thing they want to know about will be resolved in the next episode, and then we give them the link.

That works great for finished books with a published sequel, but we'd normally run into problems when we get to the final book in the series for the time being. If *FOS 5* isn't out yet, how can we link to it at the end of *FOS 4*? In the absence of a link, we'd normally have to let them know that the next book would be out soon and suggest that they join Lexi's list if they want to know when that happens. But if we do that, we have to output all of those *FOS 4* versions again — this time with the link and the more immediate "get it now" language — when *FOS 5* comes out. It's an administrative pain, and it leaves us with a weak CTA in between books, as "join our list for later updates" is nowhere near as compelling as "get it now."

To solve the problem, we had Lexi install a plug-in called Pretty Link on her website. Pretty Link lets you create links (leximaxxwell.com/fos5a for the Amazon ("a") version of *FOS 5*) and then determine where those links send readers. When *FOS 5* is released, we make sure that link points to the *FOS 5* sales page on Amazon. But before that time, the same link is directed to a generic e-mail opt-in page on Lexi's site that indicates that the book they're looking for isn't out yet, then gives them the e-mail form they can use to join her list.

On Realm & Sands, this page is fairly straightforward, but Lexi, being the minx she is, changed the text to make it more suggestive. Specifically, it says, "Oops! You came too early!" Which, we can assure you, is something her ideal readers think is clever and funny.

The beauty of this method is that it doesn't require changing the book files at all. The link itself stays the same; Lexi just goes into the Pretty Link control panel on her site to change where it sends people. It also makes the CTA itself more compelling, because they've clicked the link before they see if the book is available yet or not.

How to Use Your List

Once you have your e-mail list, you have to send stuff. Some people collect e-mail addresses and wait until they have something to announce for sale. That's a mistake. At best it's a waste of many excellent opportunities to build bonds with your readers, because weekly e-mails will become part of your readers' lives. If your e-mails are engaging, they'll become a *pleasant* part of your readers' lives. We send our e-mails on Thursdays, so we hope our people look forward to them. Judging by response, they certainly seem to.

At worst, failure to communicate with your list on a regular basis will cause it to wither. People are busy, and it's easy to forget about some random list that they signed up for months earlier if they've heard nothing since. Let your list go stale, and readers will likely ignore you when you finally do send them something. A smaller but not insignificant number may actually be angry with you. They'll forget that they signed up on purpose, the memory of finishing your book or hearing about you long gone, and they'll mark your e-mail as spam or actively turn away from a book they might have otherwise bought.

The least, least, *least* often you should e-mail something to your list is once a month, but we think weekly is better. Unless you produce extremely fast, that means that most of the time you contact them, there will be nothing new for sale.

With that in mind, here are a few of the types of things you can send to those on your list:

Weekly Newsletters

Don't put too much emphasis on the word "newsletter." What you send out doesn't need to be formal — and in fact, we absolutely think it shouldn't be. At some point, the readers on your list fell in love with your voice, so give them something that sounds like it. Don't be dry and boring and informational. Be yourself.

You're a writer and a creative person, so chances are you'll always have something new to talk about. Respect your readers' time and think twice before you blab on and on about some pretty fountain you saw and its sculptural significance, but you might have visited a place in the past week or two that inspired something that will later show up in your current historical romance project, so maybe you spend a hundred words mentioning it, building anticipation for the project.

A newsletter's job is to build attention and habit. You want people to get used to seeing your e-mails on a regular basis, and want people habituated to opening them. Over half of our people open every Realm & Sands e-mail, and that's a great number in the world of e-mail marketing, where often 15 percent is considered very good. This happens because we tend to keep our e-mails brief and quippy, written in a friendly tone like an e-mail from a friend, and we try to always include something worth opening the e-mail for. Lexi once shared that her open rate was 84 percent. That number is ridiculous. As we've said, Lexi has it easier than most of us.

The best way to get people opening your e-mails is by using intriguing subject lines. Don't be deceptive, but try to write something curious that a fan couldn't help but check out. When I released *Fat Vampire 5: Fatpocalypse*, the subject line was *Are you ready for the fatpocalypse?* When we were building anticipation for *Unicorn Genesis*, we sent the cover we'd had made with the subject line, *Now THAT'S a pretty cover!* At Realm & Sands' launch, when we debuted the *Unicorn Western Full Saga*, our subject line was the unicorn pun, *Are you horny?*

Make your e-mails worth opening. "Worth it" might just mean that it breaks up their day with amusing distraction. This again goes back to writing casually, being yourself, and sharing stories when you can. We usually talk about what we're working on, what's inspired us, or amusing and sometimes irreverent discussions we've had lately, like the time I told Sean I'd punch him in the dick if he priced *Writer Dad* incorrectly (he wanted to charge 2.99, I've read it and think it should be 4.99). Our fans dig this stuff. It shows them who we are, and they respond to our e-mails often. This is very good. Person by person, we're taking care of our readers and creating true fans.

You can include pretty much anything in your e-mails that you want, as long as it fits your brand (who you are). We like to use visuals when we have something for sale (a nice, big shot of the cover, usually), but otherwise we stick to plain text. We know people who go the way of a full, fancy HTML newsletter (I used to do that for my old business), but plain text works fine. The readers on your list are there for updates and bonding. Words are perfect for that.

Book Release Announcements

This one you'd probably already figured out. We talked about the dangers of digital sharecropping in terms of losing contact with customers, and *customers* are people who buy stuff.

This is the default way that many indie authors use their lists, and while we think that *only* sending out new product announcements isn't at all ideal, it's miles better than not having a list at all. So, if you really can't stomach writing a weekly or biweekly e-mail newsletter, you can at least do this.

Before your book announcement, though, see if you can build some anticipation for the title in advance, by e-mailing updates, telling people when the book will be released, maybe sharing the product description or cover ahead of time if you can. Teasing can work well if you aren't a jerk about it. When I finished the first draft of my highly anticipated series enders *Fat Vampire 5* and *6*, I sent out an e-mail with the subject line, *"Fat Vampire 5 and 6 are done!"* But of course they weren't *for sale*; they were just *done*. I got a few good-natured replies chastising me for being a ball-buster, saying that they'd gotten all excited. But see, that's the point: *They'd gotten all excited.* That meant that when I actually did release the books, people snapped them up like cheesecake balls at a buffet.

When you send the actual book announcement, you can probably keep things brief. Visuals are powerful, and we've already argued how vital a professional cover is to a book's success, so go ahead and show off the cover if you're sending an HTML e-mail — something that's easy via any professional e-mail service provider. Then include direct, clickable links to the major places where readers buy your books. For us, that's Amazon U.S., Amazon U.K. (yes, separate links), Kobo, and Nook. We always also say something awesome about the book to sell them on it and get them salivating. Sometimes, that just means cutting and pasting the product description into the e-mail.

If you just do this and nothing else, each of your book releases will be bigger than the last, all other things being equal. How's that for an asset worth tending?

Other Announcements

In the same vein, you can use your list to announce anything else you have going on. Remember, the idea is to keep your list from going stale and members from forgetting you, so having something — *anything* — to announce is a good thing. If you're doing a book signing, tell your list. If you have a sale on an existing book, tell your list. If a story has gone free, tell your list. Sean and I hit the South by Southwest conference every March. When we do, guess who hears about it?

How To Grow Your Email List

How do you get more people to join your list? You might as well ask how to get more people to buy your books. It's one of The Big Questions, and accordingly, it has no simple answer. Or rather, it has an answer that's *so* simple it's almost disappointing. How do you get more people to buy your books? You write more, build smart funnels, stay true to your brand, your USP, and what you stand for. You stay patient. You get more people on your list the same way.

Don't expect miracles. Your 1,000 true fans won't be gathered in a day, and neither will a big, responsive, highly engaged e-mail list. You can't game this. It's not hard to get a ton of mildly disinterested people on an e-mail list, but adding the *right* people *will* take time. You don't want wrong people on your list. That increases your e-mail provider fees and gets you nothing in return.

Don't worry about what the gurus say. There are no super-secret tricks to building a quality e-mail list, and it's not technically difficult. This is about building relationships like a human, one reader at a time.

There are some things you can do to accelerate quality additions to your list, though, and we'll go through them now.

CTAs in the Backs of Your Books

We've covered this one enough by now, right? People read your book, they get to the CTA (generalized, to get the next book, or the upsell, if one exists), and they join. Let's move on.

Using Free Books as Lead-Gen

This strategy piggybacks on the one before it. You need good CTAs in the back of your main product lines, but you can also put them in the back of works that are out there solely as lead-gen.

Lead-gen, if you're not down with our insider language of marketing-ese, refers to lead generation, which in turn is simply the process of generating new prospective readers, or leads.

If you have a book or story out there that really doesn't fit into a funnel, you can make it free, stick a CTA in the back, and see if you can use it to feed new readers in your direction. I did this with several e-books I put online when I was a motivational blogger. The e-books are essentially repurposed blog posts, and they no longer fit me as an author.

They fit me so poorly, in fact, that I actually asked Amazon to remove them from my author page so they wouldn't distract my fiction readers. I kind of wanted to pull them down, but they're all very popular (as of right now, "The Universe Doesn't Give a Flying Fuck About You" is downloaded more than 100 times every day), so I wanted to see if I could use them. They aren't fiction, but they *are* written in my unique voice, so I figured there was a chance that people who enjoyed those e-books might also like my fiction. I expected conversion from those nonfiction, hard-line e-books to our fiction list to be poor, and it is. But after changing the CTA in their backs, we started getting a few extra e-mail subscribers per day. Hey, I'll take it.

You can always trade the opportunity to make money on a book for the ability to make it free as lead-gen. If you have a book that's not performing for you otherwise, maybe you should try it.

This strategy is easy if you have a workmanlike approach to the craft. Some writers feel very precious about their work and don't want to devalue it and price it for free. But words *are* free, and you can make more. It probably wouldn't be that hard to make thousands a day for a week. BAM! You have something new to publish, that can lead people to your bigger works.

There is no limit to your imagination. Your bricks of thought can lead readers to find you. Build better roads to make this easy.

Creating quality freebies is simple. Like life, your book has endless unexplored roads. People are mentioned, and questions are asked. Go out and meet some of those people and answer some of those questions. For *Unicorn Western,* we wrote a story called, *The Outlaw Hassle Stone.* This is a freebie we wrote for our fans, but it's also a freebie we're making free to lead more people onto our list and drive them toward *Unicorn Western.*

Using Other Free Stuff as Lead-Gen

We talked earlier about podcasting your book, using free audiobook distribution sites like Podiobooks.com, social reading sites like Wattpad, and other ways of using free to find new readers in the last chapter. Those are also potential lead-gen sources. If it's pure lead-gen rather than a focused product funnel, you can broaden things like I did with my barely-related blog posts in the previous section.

You have a creative mind. Open it up and consider the potential. There is no limit. There are plenty of ways to use social media for lead gen. For example:

You could give a character a Twitter account. Be careful, because this could be stupid. Or it could also be awesome if you have 1) a character that is popular enough to warrant the account, who has a strong enough personality to fuel it, and 2) the ability to maintain the account.

Sean took his and Dave's most popular character, Boricio, and gave him a Twitter account. They'd had many requests for Boricio solo adventures, and for a Boricio quote book. Sean unleashed him on social media instead.

WARNING: *Borcio Quotes Ahead.*

For a while, it was awesome. Boricio Tweeted his own quotes from the *Yesterday's Gone* series like, "Do we want to make shit straight, or pack our bags, tuck our dicks in between our legs, and cluck the fuck out of here?" "The meek shall inherit the Earth is just another way of tricking the sheep into not fighting back when the wolf comes" and "Sarcasm is a fair substitute for when Johnny Law keeps you from beating someone's face with a shovel."

Sean tweeted these along with things Boricio came up with in the midst of his workday like, "Change your car horn to sound like gun shots. That'll get people the fuck out of your way," and "Fucker asked me if he could use my phone to call his sister. I said sure, then told him to hit redial."

But Sean got busy and let Boricio's account grow cold. Boricio made just 44 tweets, the last one posted over a year ago. Time spent in the early months building Boricio's account was totally wasted.

Boricio is very quotable, and if his online presence grew he would likely earn reTweets often. His bio could lead to an e-mail opt-in with a free book of Boricio quotes. That book would be perfect for readers of *Yesterday's Gone*, and *Yesterday's*

Gone is perfect for readers of *everything else that Sean and Dave have written* (the best argument for staying in a single genre). Lexi wanted to record herself reading (using her voice without revealing her identity), and post the audio to YouTube, with links to get additional readings by joining her list. She's not done this, but she absolutely should. As with all of us, it's a matter of making sure it fits into her 80 percent.

There are a ton of ways to distribute free content online. Find the one that neatly fits your best ideas. Language is powerful; you're already great at that. Giving Boricio his own Twitter account is an excellent idea, and so is reading stories on YouTube. But that's the danger: They're *all* great ideas. Know what's right for you, but only start what you can finish.

Blogging

Sean and I built our original lists (not the Realm & Sands email list) almost entirely through blogging: another reason we decided that we will make a 2014 return to blogging on the Self-Publishing Podcast site. Blogging takes time and mental brainpower that we'd really rather save for writing books, so the fact that we've decided to use that brainpower for blogging anyway says a bit about how much we ultimately believe in the power of that specific form of broadcast.

Blogs reach people who don't necessarily read ebooks, and are sharable and social. If people like your blog, they might be interested in joining your list.

If you write nonfiction, building your list through blogging is easier than it will be for fiction writers. Nonfiction blogs are about a specific topic, and it's usually a subject readers can see themselves using in their real lives in a tangible and obvious way. Often, nonfiction topics have a return on investment. Learn to build your own deck and you'll save the expense of construction. Learn to cook and you'll save money and probably end up being healthier. Nonfiction's "results" are usually things readers can point to and say, "That benefitted me in this way." Fiction's slippery. Whether your blog's content is stories, writer's-life pieces about what you're crafting, or story world stuff (a pop culture vampire blog by a vampire novelist), people "get" enjoyment. That matters, but it's harder to justify the spend in time or money.

Regardless, the ways to use your blog to grow your list are the same. My blog at JohnnyBTruant.com has become a ridiculous hybrid and is no longer a proper example of how to use blogging to grow your list as it is today (mainly because nothing on the blog — from re-postings of my podcasts or the older, real blog posts — appeals to the same audience as my fiction) but it'll give you an idea of how to use CTAs on a blog.

I've tried to "convert" that blog to suit my current career as a novelist (because those old posts still get a lot of traffic and I'd like to capture some of it), but back when I was in the "human potential" business, the CTAs made more sense. All of the CTAs used to point to my *How To Be Legendary* manifesto, which you can find at HowToBeLegendary.com. That manifesto, unlike *The Beam* and *Fat Vampire*, was *very* aligned with my old blog and my old business. So were the repurposed ebook blog posts I mentioned earlier, like "The Universe Doesn't Give a Flying Fuck About You." The blog, the *How To Be Legendary* manifesto, and those free ebooks on the ebook sellers were all funnel pieces to get people onto my list. It worked well, and I could often count on 500 or so new list subscribers each month. I then used the list to bond with the people who'd already said "yes" to the top parts of my funnel, and sold down the line.

As you look at JohnnyBTruant.com, you'll see notices about my books or fiction list. But for the purposes of this lesson, pretend they're still notices about *How To Be Legendary*.

There's a CTA at the end of every blog post. It used to say something like, "If you liked this post, you'll love this free manifesto."

There are small ads in the sidebars. They used to be for the manifesto.

There used to be a very prominent email signup form at top of the right-hand sidebar, offering an alternative bonus that was similar to the manifesto.

And if this is your first time to JohnnyBTruant.com, you probably also swatted away my annoying pop-up like a housefly. I acknowledge that those pop-ups are obnoxious, but holy crap do they work well. The software I used is called PopUp Domination, and it's highly customizable so as to suit your obnoxiousness tolerance. I know that the idea of a pop-up will strike a lot of you as hideously Internet marketingy and you won't want to consider it, and that's totally fine. But personally, I can't say a bad thing about it. Mine only shows up once every 30 days. If a visitor is so sensitive that they hate me due to 3 seconds of advertisement every 30 days, they're not the kind of person who'd ever buy anything from me anyway. I'd suggest something like that more for nonfiction bloggers than fiction-related blogs. Offer a special report or an audio interview that covers something you know your readers will want, then watch your list grow in proportion with your blog traffic.

If you write fiction and are trying to use a blog to grow your fiction list, you can still use JohnnyBTruant.com as a guide — with or without the annoying pop-up. Instead of imagining the book CTAs being manifesto CTAs, go the other direction and pretend that I actually use that site to blog about something related to my fiction. As long as the blog's content (and hence readership) lines up well with the list you're trying to urge them to join, this approach can work very well.

Guest Posting on Other Blogs

This is, by far, my favorite way to get new people onto your e-mail list. For the same reasons I described in the section above, it tends to work much better for nonfiction authors/bloggers, but it can work (usually to a much lesser degree) for fiction bloggers, too.

My friend Jon Morrow, who runs BoostBlogTraffic.com and who is a certifiable genius, compares guest posting to being the opening act for a popular band. The other band has the audience you want to reach, so if you go out there in front of that audience and give a truly bravura performance, some of them are going to buy your albums and generally move into your fan base as well.

The metaphor is about perfect, and holds the formula for effective guest posting.

For one, you need to make sure you're performing in front of the right audience. If your band is heavy metal and you open for the New York Philharmonic, you probably won't grab many fans. If you write about management techniques or zombies (I'm going to dodge the obvious joke of comparing the two), you want to be sure to ask if you can guest post on blogs that cover those respective fields, or at least have readerships that are likely to be highly interested in those topics.

Second, you must wow the crowd. Some bloggers who try guest posting opt to save their best posts for their blog and use their lesser posts as guest posts. Don't do this. Put everything you have into giving a stellar performance when you step in front of those new readers, and write the very best, most helpful, or most interesting post you possibly can.

And lastly, you need to give the people a compelling and obvious call to action. You're in someone else's house when you write a guest post, and you need to be respectful. Most bloggers won't let you put a big flashing arrow in the middle of your post that says, "GO TO MY BLOG NOW!" so you have to be more subtle. Typically, your author byline at the end of a guest post is your place to sell, so write a byline that gives a good reason for interested readers to follow you and learn more. When I was actively promoting my funnel-starting *How To Be Legendary* manifesto, I used a byline for guest posts that went something like this: "Johnny B. Truant is the author of *How To Be Legendary: A*

Realistic Guide to Being the Superhuman You're Supposed to Be, which you can download for free." And then there'd be a link to get it.

CHAPTER SIXTEEN:
All About Reviews

AH, REVIEWS. THE DOUBLE-EDGED sword of writing and publishing.

On one hand, authors love getting reviews. Good reviews make you feel great, make your book seem appealing, and generally fill you with the warmest of fuzzies a writer can feel. On the other hand, sometimes all it takes to ruin your day is one bad review from someone who clearly has issues that have nothing to do with you or your book. And perhaps the worst are those mediocre reviews, because they're not bad enough for you to dismiss as the vitriolic work of a pissed-off soul. Sometimes, those middle-of-the road reviews can be the real bone-crushers, because you'll wonder if they're true — if your prose *is* wooden, if your characters *are* flat, and if your story really *was* totally predictable. Reviews can lift you up and cut you to pieces. They can make your book's success, or crush it.

We get a lot of questions about reviews on the *Self Publishing Podcast*, and ethical ways to get more good reviews is something we end up discussing often. Make no mistake: Getting adequate positive reviews of your work is critical. You can't force people to like what you've written, you can't (shouldn't!) game the system with bogus positive reviews, and you can't make bad reviews disappear, but there *are* ways to maximize what you have and can get. That's the subject of this chapter.

We'll start with the big picture.

Why Reviews Are Important

Let's get the most obvious and least relevant purpose of reviews out of the way: to stoke the writer's ego. That does matter, of course. The more people like your work, the more you'll want to write it, and the better mood you'll be in when you do, which will probably lead to a better end product. But letting it matter, while human and almost impossible to avoid, is dangerous. Because while everything is hunky-dory when the reviews are good, it's a problem when a book falls flat. It's kind of hard to soldier on when your reviews suck. We'll talk about that in a bit.

Regardless of whether your reviews make you feel good or bad, that's not what matters in the big picture. Reviews mainly matter because they serve as social proof. The more reviews a book has, the more legitimate it will appear to people who find it, and hence the more likely they will be to investigate further. The overall review average matters, of course, but it doesn't matter as much as you might think once the sheer number of reviews gets high enough. When a book has 5000 reviews, most people will look with a serious eye toward purchase if something about the book grabs them even if a lot of those reviews are negative. In 2012, the biggest story in publishing was the breakout erotica title *50 Shades of Grey*. It didn't matter that around a quarter of the reviews on Amazon were only one-star reviews. Too many people were interested, and the individual (or curious) person declared they'd buy and decide for themselves, while E.L. James bathed in golden coins.

You're probably not going to get overwhelming numbers of reviews right away, and that means your average matters more. You need reviews, and you need those reviews to be pretty good. The more reviews you have and the better those reviews are, the better chances your book will have. With each new (good) review, resistance dims between a reader and your book. The safer they feel among a larger crowd of happy buyers, the more quickly they'll pull the trigger, and the more likely you'll be to be able to sell at a higher price point.

Review thresholds seem to break down in the following highly unscientific and unsubstantiated way:

0 Reviews: If your book is new, this isn't a problem. If your book has been out for a year, good luck selling it. You shouldn't cherry-pick reviews, but seriously ... your mom won't even review it?

1-9 Reviews: A lot of new indie authors — and newer books by established indies — fall into this range. Here, you really need a nice, high rating average. Single-digit review numbers will feel like amateur hour to more seasoned book buyers, so they may hesitate. Your audience will likely be confined to the people who are used to buying lesser-proven, largely independent books.

10-99 Reviews: This is where most of us will find ourselves, but it doesn't seem to matter much whether you have 10 reviews or 99; two digits is two digits. A lot of traditional books by non-blockbuster authors will end up here, so you're in more company. You need a high average to overcome a buyer's hesitations.

100-999 Reviews: This is where you want to end up as often as possible. It's not easy, but most buyers believe a book has proven itself once it hits three-digit reviews. <u>Buyers understand that only a small percentage of people will ever review a book they've read, so 100 or more reviews equals a reasonable crowd.</u> We always strive for 100 reviews on our books. For most of our series, we tell our readers that we'll start the next season or book once we earn 100 reviews on the previous one. On Amazon.com, indies currently want to maintain at least a 4-star average for best results. Even a 3.5-star average will look bad. 4.5 looks quite good, and the sheer volume you'll get at this point makes a solid 5-star average (meaning all 5 stars appear fully shaded, not necessarily that your average is literally 5.0) extremely difficult to achieve or maintain, so few people will expect it. If you can manage 200 or so reviews with 5 stars shaded? Holy crap; you're bulletproof.

1000+ Reviews: Four digits is where the truly big names head straightaway, with many getting more. Few indies other than the real breakouts reach four digits as of this writing, but that will change as the e-book market matures, simply because older books will have more time on market. Once you have this many reviews, buyers tend to understand that haters are weeds in every garden and will tolerate a slightly lower average. The higher your sales, review numbers, and bestseller rankings, the lower your generally accepted average can be. Don't content yourself with complacency if you ever make it this high. Always try for maximum good reviews.

Some prospective buyers will read through some of your reviews, but they'll probably only hit a few of those near the top. Amazon lets people vote on which reviews are most helpful and will also pull common quotes from reviews to display prominently. People will read these, but this is all FYI. You can't control this stuff.

One thing to consider is that Amazon also displays the most helpful positive and the most helpful critical review prominently at the top of your reviews. Critical reviews are 3 stars and below, which is an interesting thing because in many reviewers' minds, 3 stars is still a rather good ranking. As a result, you may have a "most helpful critical review" that sings your praises nicely. That's a good thing.

How to Get More Good Reviews

The very first thing you should do before embarking on any campaign for positive reviews is to write an awesome book that deserves them. It's amazing how many people forget this. "How can I get a lot of good reviews on a mediocre book?" isn't a legitimate question. Sorry, we can't answer that one — not in a way that's strategic rather than tactical, and not in any remotely intelligent way when considering the long term. Everything you're about to read is within the booksellers' guidelines and in no way amounts to gaming the system. You can only attract good reviews using our tips to the extent that your book itself earns those reviews. We can help you get more of what you deserve, but not more of what you don't.

Once you're certain that you've written the best book possible, you want to encourage reviews from those readers most likely to say something positive. These are the people who like you already — who would go into the review mindset already predisposed to enjoy what they've read. This is in no way cherry-picking reviews. There's nothing you can do about it if some of those reviews aren't stellar, but you can approach the selection process from the other end. You're not trying to pick the reviews; you're trying to pick who you encourage to leave them.

If you're trying to win a baking contest with your amazing cheesecake and you thought of a good way to encourage people to vote in the contest, doesn't it make sense to encourage voting from the cheesecake lovers rather than encouraging everyone?

When we released *Plugged*, which we think of as *The Beam*'s *Season 1.5*, we contacted our e-mail list and told them that we'd be happy to give them a review copy of the book for free. But we didn't just want to give that book to anyone who asked; we wanted to give it to people who'd actually be likely to review it, and do so favorably. Some people will take anything for free simply because it's free, even if it's not the kind of book they'd be interested in otherwise. We'd seen this when we made our books free in the past, and people who didn't like horror would pick up Sean and Dave's *Yesterday's Gone* and give it crap reviews that basically bashed it for being horror-ish.

To narrow our field of reviewers, we asked readers to send us a link to their review of *The*

Beam: Season One. Not only did this show us that we were sending the book to people who actually left reviews (we didn't want to waste them on non-reviewers), but those people were also likely to leave good reviews for *Plugged,* because anyone who'd read the full first season of *The Beam* would likely enjoy *Plugged.* As a bonus, this encouraged a new wave of reviews on *The Beam* from people who'd read it but hadn't yet left a review. They wanted to get *Plugged,* so they left a review for *The Beam.* Unsurprisingly, most of those new reviews were very good.

Note that this is *not* quid pro quo. We did not say, "If you left (or leave) us a good review on *The Beam,* you can have *Plugged* as a reward." But we needed to know that you actually left a review, to establish that we aren't simply wasting a potential sale on someone who grubs for free stuff without giving anything back. "A review," not "a *good* review." If someone leaves you a 1-star review and sends you the link in response to a call like I've described, you must still send out the review copy. *The book is not a reward. It is a review copy.* Keep that in mind, and act accordingly. Your job is to try spread the message to the people who are most likely to leave good reviews.

Think again of your funnel. You want the best reviews on the products further down in that funnel because those are the hardest to sell, but the fact that they are harder to sell will actually tend to work in your favor in terms of reviews. Assuming your deeper products are well-written books worth the price you're charging, you will earn disproportionately positive reviews because only "qualified" buyers tend to buy them. *Unicorn*

Western 1 is free, so people who don't know if they'll like the story or not pick that one up. They may or may not leave a review, but they definitely won't plunk down $9.99 for the *Full Saga*. Readers who buy the *Unicorn Western Full Saga* (or any of our upsell products that live "deeper in the funnel" beneath a free initial book) have been pre-screened, in a way. The free product sifts out those predisposed to not like the story, and as a result, our bundles always average a half-star higher — because the people who bought it already knew they liked the story, characters, and world *before they opened their wallets.*

Treat reviews as another kind of funnel, sending qualified reviewers to your bigger products. The word is *qualified*, not *duped* or *bribed*. If your books suck, even your best people will review it poorly. If you need clarification, flip back and read the first paragraph of this section again.

There are two parts to this concept: Come up with a way to encourage people to leave reviews on your stuff (just *reviews*; you can't structure this to reward only *good* reviews), *then* preferentially present those encouragements to the people most likely to leave positive reviews.

Here are a few ways to encourage reviews. Some we've had luck with, some we haven't.

Indiscriminately Give Out Review Copies

The simplest but least-qualified way to encourage reviews is to give away review copies. This is a common publishing practice even in traditional publishing. You give a book to someone, then hope they read it, like it, and leave a shining review. As we've already implied, this practice can be risky because the person you give the book to might not leave a review, thus costing you a potential paid sale — but that's nothing compared to them leaving you a bad review. If you want to try this scattergun approach, make sure your book is excellent.

You'll be using this strategy inadvertently if you follow our advice, because all of your free funnel-starter products are up for grabs to anyone who wants them. When a book is permanently free, you can't remotely control who downloads it. Some of the people who download it will be an orbit away from your ideal reader. If they hate it, there's nothing you'll be able to do. For this reason, we don't like this approach for our more important products. When the KDP Select program was viable, we might (*might*) have made one of our $9.99 products free from time to time in order to boost sales, but we wouldn't today. Some writers don't care who buys their work, reasoning that all sales are good. Long term, we disagree. We only want people who will love our most expensive products to buy them. Thanks to the structure of our funnels, readers who buy up to our full bundles have already digested the introductory product and liked it. This strategy is *only* for our permafree titles.

One thing we'll add: Lexi very successfully built momentum using free promotion — better than we ever did, for sure. She's mostly moved away from indiscriminate use of free but says she's considering dallying again here and there because Lexi, in the erotica marketplace, gets different results. When Lexi's products went free, she could count on 20+ reviews and an overall 4.9-star average, within the first few days. In her case, the huge boon of social proof from those reviews might be enough to consider the occasional mass-broadcast giveaway.

Give Review Copies in a Controlled Way

We do this fairly often. I've already described what we did with *Plugged*, but we've done it for other titles as well. Before we published the *Unicorn Western Full Saga* (all nine books), we made a point to finish writing *Unicorn Genesis: Origins* (the first part of the larger *Unicorn Genesis* novel). *Origins* wasn't due to be released for months, so we used an early look as an incentive to leave reviews for the *Full Saga*. If people left us an honest review on the *Saga*, we'd send them *Origins*. Then we put a CTA describing the offer in the back of the *Full Saga* book.

This was a highly controlled way to give out our review copies, because only people who finished the entire *Full Saga* would ever see the offer. The *Full Saga* is a quarter million words long. Anyone who read through it all was probably going to have enjoyed the book, meaning we were preferentially putting the offer in front of those readers most likely to leave us positive reviews. In addition, the bonus itself (*Origins*) would only effectively incentivize people who already liked the series. Why would someone who hated *Unicorn Western* feel incentivized by the offer of its prequel?

We were putting the offer in front of people who were *most likely* to leave us good reviews, not people who we'd somehow made sure *would* leave us good reviews. Those readers were perfectly free to leave bad reviews, and our offer said nothing whatsoever about the quality of those reviews.

338

Whenever we do this, we specifically state that we want *honest* reviews. You cannot ever refuse to give out a review copy if the rules are obeyed. If someone leaves a terrible review and requests a review copy as promised, give it to them, period. This should serve as another reminder to make sure your book is fantastic before trying anything like we've described.

This strategy can work very well if you write good books and foster bonds with your fans. It's never a bad idea to give away digital products — which cost you nothing to produce and distribute — if doing so might yield more of those oh-so-important reviews.

Offer to do Something Ridiculous or Fun

In January 2012, Hugh Howey's *Wool* was climbing in the reviews. Once it hit the high 80s, Hugh got hungry for 100. He made a promise to his editor that he'd do a silly dance in a very silly hat once he hit 100. He hit 99, donned his ridiculous cap, and danced to Soldja Boy on YouTube. His fans LOVED it.

This isn't just about the reviews; it's about bonding with your readers and showing your human side. Make your readers laugh, and they will love you. Sean danced like an absolute idiot to *Gangnam Style* when *Z 2134* cracked the Top 100 overall on Amazon

He has since apologized to humanity.

Offer to do Something Aligned

A much better way to present a mass incentive (something you'll do that will be publicly available rather than one-on-one) is to offer something aligned with the product you're trying to promote. Because while the world was obviously *dying* to see Sean dance *Gangnam Style*, there were probably some readers of *Whitespace* who wouldn't feel particularly incentivized to leave a review to see it. Dave dancing would probably be even funnier, but it's not necessarily something fans were willing to take action to see. He did offer, saying if *WhiteSpace* hit 100 reviews he would dance on YouTube. At the time of writing *WhiteSpace* sits with 95 reviews, a few more than when the offer was made a few months before.

Keeping in mind that you want to always incentivize those who are most likely to leave you good reviews, what would be a good incentive for people who really love *Whitespace*? The solution is simple, so long as you're willing to do a little extra work — to write an extra story to give out to people who will leave a review. Sean and Dave have been too busy to write a *WhiteSpace* standalone short, but it's on their queue because they know that readers of *WhiteSpace* love that world, and are most likely to leave a positive review of an existing work to spend more time inside it.

Fans of a series want more of that series. For *The Beam*, we told our readers that we'd write *Season Two* when there were 100 reviews on *Season One*, thus allowing us to reach the all-important three-digit review threshold where our book would seem "officially proven" in the eyes of more and more potential buyers. Our fans know we produce like machines, and that we have a lot on our plates. We can make this agreement with them because they know that once we start writing, it won't take us months and months to deliver. They also know that due to our many product lines, we have many other things to work on. They understand that 100 reviews is a satisfactory way to show us that more *Beam* is something with sufficient enough demand to divert our other projects

If you don't want to wager on a project as large as a book or season (*The Beam: Season Two* may top 200,000 words), you can do the same thing with a short story. In the world of *Yesterday's Gone*, the alliterative, profane serial killer and psychopath Boricio Wolfe is a hands-down fan favorite, whom readers always want to know more about. Offering a standalone Boricio story (there are three so far: *What Would Boricio Do?*, *A Very Boricio Christmas*, and *Boricio Goes Camping*) to incentivize *Yesterday's Gone* reviews is in perfect alignment.

Generalized Giveaways and Contests
We're including this one even though we hate it, because it may work for some authors.

When Sean and Dave were promoting *Season One* of *Yesterday's Gone*, they did a contest on Goodreads wherein they raffled off a Kindle Fire e-reader. The experience, in addition to being expensive at a time when Collective Inkwell couldn't afford expensive, was nothing but a headache. People complained that the giveaway was limited to the U.S. and gave them a ton of grief. They got the distinct impression that the people who entered the contest weren't potential or current readers of CI's books, but were instead people who wanted a free Kindle Fire. Confirming this, they learned that the guy who won had never read anything of CI's. He was nice, and told them that he did *then* buy their books, but did this work as a promotion? No, not so much.

Sean and Dave spent money they didn't have on a promotion that didn't work. You must be very careful with giveaways. The problem was twofold. First, the audience for their promotion wasn't specific enough, and they therefore got mostly people who only wanted the prize, not people who cared about their books. And second, it was a monetary gamble. Giving away digital products like e-books is free, but giving away a tangible prize can be expensive.

Aligned Giveaways

You can give away physical prizes, if you do so in a way that's more aligned. We're not down on giving away non-digital content by any means; we're just down on doing it in such a non-targeted way as Sean and Dave did early-on with their Kindle Fire giveaway.

Although we haven't employed this tactic for Realm & Sands yet, Lexi told us about a giveaway she did to encourage reviews on her book *Cheated*, which she describes as "Quentin Tarantino's *Kill Bill* with sex." She e-mailed her list and told them that she'd send a print copy of the book to a random reviewer.

Lexi's *Cheated* giveaway was much, much more aligned than CI's Fire giveaway. For one, she announced it to her mailing list rather than broadcasting it on a popular website, meaning she was reaching people who already liked her. Secondly, she was offering a print copy of a book to people who actually cared about it, because they'd read the e-book. And finally, the people most likely to be incentivized to leave a review by the promotion would be those who wanted the print book ... and hence would have *enjoyed* the e-book ... and would therefore be most likely to leave a good review.

The book plus shipping cost Lexi $20 at most, but it was worth it. Thanks to the magic of fan bonding, the woman who received that copy of *Cheated* became one of Lexi's most reliable reviewers, leaving glowing reviews on book after book ... including one she searched for and found on her own, then bought, read, and reviewed before Lexi even had time to e-mail her list about it.

A $20 gift earned Lexi a true fan. That sounds worthwhile to us.

Ask

Ask and ye shall receive. We've all heard that, right?

We've saved this technique for last, but it may be the most powerful of all. Writers need reviews. People read their books and hopefully enjoy them, but few typically leave reviews if left to their own devices. So, why not ask? They're your fans. They may just be willing to do it if they know how much it matters.

At the end of all of our books, we include a small paragraph that briefly explains how much reviews matter to independent writers, then we ask the reader to leave one for us. We include a clickable link that will send them to the review page on the platform the book was compiled for.

This will net you some reviews, but you can also ask more directly. Whenever someone sends me an e-mail or a Tweet or a Facebook message about how much they enjoyed one of my books, I check the book's reviews, and if they haven't already left one I politely ask if they could and often give them a link. This may seem a bit forward, but it works. And remember, this is a person who liked your book enough to take the effort required to e-mail or message you, so the chances that they'd mind the effort to leave a review are slim. If they've gone to the effort of contacting you, they're probably also interested in helping you out. Show them how much reviews mean to indies, and chances are good they'll agree. Be polite, don't be pushy, and thank them for their awesome words. I can't imagine anyone being mad at such a request.

We did something fun and in-world to get reviews for *Plugged*. Part of *Plugged*'s identity is that we created a fictional author to write it: a man named Sterling Gibson, who lives in our future world of *The Beam* and writes from in the year 2097. Gibson is a member of a group in our world called "Enterprise," and *Beam* readers know that Enterprise citizens are on their own to make their livings and receive no government support. So when we created the "leave a review" CTA for the back of *Plugged*, we wrote it the way Gibson's publisher would write it in the year 2097:

> As a member of the Enterprise Party, Sterling Gibson makes his living from the books that he writes. He needs help from readers like you.

Please review this book so he can write more books liked *Plugged*.

We've also asked our list for reviews directly, but again, Lexi's far better at this than we are. Once on *SPP*, Sean read one of her e-mails. It was kind of a ball-buster of an e-mail, but at the time Lexi was using free promotion a lot, thereby making a strategic decision to forego profits in exchange for improved social activity and (you guessed it) reviews. She wasn't making much money, she'd quit a damned good job to write full time, and was counting on a few of the thousands who downloaded her books for free to step up with an occasional review. That wasn't happening, so Lexi e-mailed her people in a respectful-but-firmly-worded way. She said we could we could include that language here:

> Last week's freebie generated only two reviews, so I have to pull back this week.
>
> Delivering free smut each week is super expensive for me. One of the biggest reasons I do it is to generate reviews. Two simply isn't enough.
>
> Hopefully I'll get more reviews this week and can put a few additional titles out there for free next week.

Lexi had been giving away free books in exchange for reviews, but wasn't getting the reviews, so she cut her readers off. That may seem hard-line, but we agree with her decision. If you're giving your books away for free in exchange for reviews and aren't getting them, your readers aren't keeping up their half of the bargain. You're within your rights to respectfully call them out. A few people will be put off, but your ideal readers and true fans won't be. And yes, Lexi's rate of reviews went up dramatically after that e-mail. (Note: You can't ask this directly if your books aren't free. You can *ask*, but you need to be much more reserved when you do it because paid customers *are* keeping their half of the bargain. They paid; you gave them the book. Whether or not they leave reviews is up to them.)

Dealing With Negative Reviews

It can be incredibly frustrating to not get any reviews, and for the most part you can only deal with it by reminding yourself that building a self-publishing career is a long-term game, being patient, trying some of the techniques from the last section, and continuing to write.

But as annoying as a lack of reviews can be, getting negative reviews can feel much worse. And here's the bad news: You're absolutely *going* to get some if you keep writing.

Dave takes all of his bad reviews personally, and has to find ways to soldier on in the face of them. But even Sean and I, who can sometimes look like optimistic balls of sunshine and rainbows, feel the sting of poor reviews, and sometimes they'll even ruin a part of our days. But it happens, and you have to let the feeling go.

Here are some tips for dealing with bad reviews in the meantime.

Ignore Them

The best thing you can do with bad reviews is to read them and then forget them. Or, if you're particularly sensitive, don't read them once you see the 1- or 2-star rating. We do suggest reading all of your reviews — including the bad ones — to see if there's criticism that you should consider addressing, but it's not required. The review already exists, and all that's left is for you to decide if you're going to let it bother you. It *is* a choice, and changes nothing. If you know a review will only upset you, don't bother. You being upset does nothing to change the review; it will only impair your ability to work and feel good.

Don't keep returning to bad reviews or dwell on them. You have our permission — and, in some cases, our outright encouragement — to stick your head in the sand. Writers usually default the other way, feeling a masochistic need to do some strange form of penance, flogging themselves with bad reviews. You don't deserve that. Have more respect for yourself.

Don't engage negative reviewers, or argue back. If they are saying something that is factually inaccurate or if you feel you can clear up a simple misunderstanding, you may choose to reply, but if you do, keep a level head. Don't get angry or defensive. And again, our first recommendation is to simply ignore 100 percent of them. Just let them go. You may disagree, but that's OK. It's not your business to convince someone to love you, and you probably can't do it anyway. Lastly, some negative reviewers are instigators anyway, and nothing would make them happier than to rile you up. As the expression says, "Don't feed the troll."

Understand That You Are Not Your Art

We had Tucker Max, author of *I Hope They Serve Beer in Hell*, on *SPP* once to talk about bad reviews and haters. Tucker gave excellent advice: You have to divorce yourself from your art, because your art is its own thing, and you are something — *someone* — separate from it. Your art is going to get bad reviews, but that's not the same as *you* getting bad reviews.

In short, don't take it personally. Books — especially fiction — are subjective. It's unrealistic to expect everyone to like any of them, and irrational to equate someone's not liking your story to something that you should give the ability to wind you up personally.

Understand That Bad Reviews Are a Sign That You're Relevant

The only way you could never get any negative reviews would be if you were so incredibly irrelevant that no one thought you were worth talking or thinking about. Wouldn't you rather have those negative reviews than no reviews at all, no sales, and no base of readers?

If you have trouble saying yes, you're not alone. Most of us, in the logical parts of our minds, understand that having a career pocked with some negativity is better than not having a career, but it's hard to feel that way in the face of bad reviews. But you must, because they're a sign that what you're saying matters.

Seth Godin said, "You will be judged, or you will be ignored."

You get to pick one or the other. Which will it be?

Understand That Many Bad Reviews Aren't Actually About You

Tucker Max, whose unique breed of humor is divisive in the extreme, also talked a lot during his *SPP* interview about how, in many cases, negative reviews are about the reviewer, not you.

Tucker's books and stories are all based on his being an asshole. That's not me saying that; Tucker's website text begins with, *My name is Tucker Max, and I'm an asshole.* When your stories center on what Tucker calls "fratire" — mainly tales about sex, getting drunk and in trouble, and treating women like crap — you're going to get a lot of hate. But here's the interesting thing: Most of the hate Tucker gets isn't about his writing, but about his actions and him as a person. Tucker's haters don't hate his books so much as they hate *Tucker.* In other words, his negative reviewers *do* feel that he is his art in contrast to the section above, and *do* want him to take it personally.

Tucker *was* that asshole in his stories, but he was also a law student, a writer, a reader, and a guy who was interested in world events, health and fitness, business, and many other things. He selectively sifted his most obnoxious stories for publication. He hand-picked his very worst parts and didn't show the parts that weren't about him being an immature asshole because they didn't fit his admittedly controversial brand.

With all of that considered, why do so many reviewers hate Tucker when they don't know him personally? Hate implies connection, and this man, to the people who read his books, is a writer who put words on a page … and isn't connected to them at all.

The answer — and this is not a judgment in either direction — is that we can't help but take most things personally when we read, view, or otherwise experience them. When a movie makes you happy, you're happy because you're imagining the things in the movie happening to you. When you read a creepy story, you get scared because you can't help but picture those same things in real time. When you read stories about some misogynist asshole screwing some girl and running off, it might upset you because you can imagine being in the girl's shoes, or being in the shoes of that girl's friend, father, or whatever.

I'm not arguing that there's anything "right" about Tucker's stories, but I'm also not arguing that there's anything "wrong" with them. They are stories: words on a page. Readers who don't like them can turn away. Most readers don't know Tucker personally and have never literally been the people in his stories. What makes the difference between a person who reads those stories and either laughs or is unaffected and a person who gets furiously angry and leaves a scathing review?

The answer is that it's something *inside the reader*. If you once knew someone like Tucker as portrayed in his books and hated that person, his stories will make you angry. If you didn't, they probably won't. There's a middleground wherein someone could argue that what he writes about is morally wrong and that they object on that basis — but again, which personal experiences shaped that moral opinion in those readers?

We're using Tucker Max to exemplify this point because his case is so extreme, but it's also possible that something you write will spark something inside a reader in such a way as to really piss them off. It's not you or your writing that did that; it was the wound that was already inside the reader, aggravated by something they read.

What you say doesn't have to be something widely considered to be "bad" to cause problems, either. I once said in a blog post that I believed in "something like God," and I got two or three comments on that post that were actively angry. It wasn't even a main point in the post, and I certainly didn't argue for my position. The post was about something entirely different, and the God thing was literally a passing thought that most people probably flew right by. Why did those few people get so mad? Was it really about me or my post? Wasn't it far more likely that they'd had some experience in their lives that caused them to loathe spirituality or a church?

Yeah, that certainly seems more likely.

If that's true, given that I'd made such a glancing mention of the subject in making a very different point, wouldn't it have been absurd for me to obsess about that negativity? Wouldn't it be more sensible for me to understand that those negative comments had to do with the readers' disposition, and that they would have reacted to a million random stimuli in exactly the same way as they did to me, regardless of who'd said or written it?

Understand That You Are Distorting Reality

It's natural to be bothered by a bad review in the moment, but in order for you to *stay* upset, you must actively distort reality. You have to ignore all of the positive reviews you've ever gotten, and believe on some level that the negative review you just got is more real, relevant, or representative of your overall average.

If you have 10 reviews and nine are 5 stars while one is 1 star, it's human nature to focus on that 1-star review. But what about the other nine? Don't let the weight of the people you didn't satisfy nullify opinions from those who loved what you wrote. Doing so is insulting to your fans and their opinions, which are every bit as valid as those of your haters.

Things You Should Never Do

Okay, so those are some of the "do's" about reviews. Let's cover some of the "dont's" that we've learned through trial and error, and through the public errors of others.

Don't Argue With Reviewers

Arguing and being defensive about your work always makes you look bad. Don't do it. If someone doesn't like your book, that's their opinion. If they hate your book or even if they hate you, that's their opinion, too. It may hurt, but there's not much you can do. If they're saying something factually incorrect or defamatory about your work, that's unfortunate, but all you can do is try to set the record straight, and if they persist, (having said your piece) let it go.

Arguing, being defensive, and engaging in public flame wars is exhausting and infuriating, futile at best, and actively damaging to your reputation at worst. If I feel something is worth a reply (not an argument), I'll respond once and only once, no matter how they answer back. Turning the other cheek is always best, especially given that many negative people are only trolls — folks who act up specifically to get a reaction. Don't give it to them.

I'll add that once you have enough fans, they may end up going to bat for you. This is the best of all worlds, as long as your fans and readers aren't intimidating or abusive. It shows the public that people like you and disagree with the troll, and doesn't cost you brand capital by arguing yourself. Your fans may also intercept criticism that is outright absurd. Once, a critic said that they thought we were hacks because we didn't use enough passive voice sentences. *What?* Excessive use of passive voice is widely considered to be the mark of a crappy writer. Still, Sean and I didn't want to engage. One of our readers did, though, and the resulting zing was brilliantly effective in handling the objection.

Don't Buy Reviews

There was a huge to-do in the self-publishing world in 2012 when author John Locke admitted that he'd paid a service to leave glowing, high-star reviews on his books. The entire industry then embarked on a witch hunt against bogus reviews and so-called "sock puppet reviewers," some of it justified and plenty of it overblown. But the incident underscored two things for those who were paying attention: That it was possible to buy reviews and that intelligent self-publishers shouldn't do it.

This is a case where in addition to being morally wonky, the tactic doesn't justify the risk to the underlying strategy. You might get away with buying reviews, yes. But the strategy is supposed to be about pleasing readers and building social proof behind your brand. That strategy crumbles if you're caught. Shoot straight. The risk to your reputation — which can be a death blow to your entire catalog and career — isn't worth it.

To a lesser degree, this includes truly quid-pro-quo reviews. You can incentivize reviews as described earlier, but you absolutely should not reward positive reviews disproportionately. Doing so is essentially the same as buying reviews. If you say, "Leave me a 5-star review, and I'll give you X," that's bad mojo. Knock it off. There's a fine line; be honest, and you'll know where it is.

Don't Fake Reviews

Same as the above. Don't create extra accounts (the sock puppets from the preceding section) and leave yourself reviews. Amazon figures this out in most cases and will pull them. This (stupid) tactic suffers the same risks as buying reviews.

Don't Send out Print Copies for Review

This is the e-book age. That means you can send out e-books for review. There are still places that require physical copies, but unless you know for certain that a review by one of those places will make a significant difference in your sales, we suggest you don't bother. Creating print books is a 20-percent activity for most writers, and buying and shipping can get expensive.

Yes, you might gain a few good reviews doing this, and those reviews might send you some sales. But will the sales offset the expenses of creating and sending out the books? In most cases, the answer is no, so we suggest sticking to digital.

CHAPTER SEVENTEEN:
Ways to Supercharge Your Marketing

EVERYTHING YOU'VE READ SO FAR in this section will help you establish a strong marketing base. Done well, you'll be ahead of the vast majority of self-publishers … and, honestly, much of traditional publishing as a whole. You won't outsell James Patterson or other big names, but there are plenty of authors signed with traditional publishers that no one ever hears of. Those authors could be you if you'd published traditionally (always assuming the publishers would have you), but you wouldn't have had the control over your product and marketing that you do as an indie. Setting up your business as we've thus far described will greatly improve your chances of killing it.

This chapter is filled with big-picture things you'll want to keep in your marketing mind. You may or may not make changes to your positioning or strategy after reading this chapter, but do let it sink in. Every time you write a new book or add to a funnel (or have the beautiful experience of completing one), knowing what follows will make a big difference in getting the most juice from every squeeze.

These are our best tips for taking your existing marketing machine — no matter how established or complete — and cranking it higher.

Understand What Marketing Actually Is (and Isn't)

This is probably a boring way to start a chapter on "supercharging," but by now you've probably figured out that our advice is more nuts and bolts than fireworks. You've probably realized that we're not going to tell you THE ONE AMAZING THING that makes a writer successful. There is no such thing, and if anyone offers to tell you about that one amazing thing — typically just before dropping a large price tag — you should run in the other direction.

Most writers live at the more artistic end of the spectrum and don't consider themselves marketers, or even businesspeople. As a result, many writers end up with all sorts of skewed perceptions about marketing, and expect it to be something it isn't. So, they do what they can, notice that nothing is happening, and decide that they've failed. In our opinions, any competent writer who's willing to do the work, produce lots of content, make continuous tweaks to their marketing, and take the time to build their audience should have a respectable income stream from book sales within a handful of years. There are plenty of writers who fail simply because they don't forge ahead. That happens because they don't understand what marketing really is, and hence don't know what to expect.

Marketing isn't sleazy and pushy, as we've already discussed in detail.

Marketing also isn't magic. It is not something that will instantly make lemonade from lemons.

Marketing is not a switch that is either on or off. We've seen writers who build their first small product funnel, then complain that it's not making them money. That's not how it works. You don't turn your marketing "on" one day and watch money roll in. You take a step, and then another.

Marketing means informing people who might like to buy your product that it exists. Optionally, you can also inform those people that your product is a great deal, that it'll make them happy or change their lives, that its price is discounted, or that other people liked it. *That's it.* Standing on a street corner with a bullhorn is marketing. Facebook ads are marketing. Handing a print copy of your book to someone at a party is marketing. Having casual discussions about what you do at a party is marketing.

Once you understand what marketing is, a lot of the misperceptions surrounding it become obviously false. For instance, marketing doesn't require an advanced degree or a genius mind. If you're human and know how humans tend to think, you can do it. You don't have to burden yourself with conversion percentages and tracking pixels; you have to ask questions like, "Where are people who read books like mine?" and "If someone has just finished reading my first book, what would make my second book easy to find and buy?"

Once you truly get that marketing is about people being people, you should lose any unrealistic expectations you may have. Does it make sense that your magic marketing campaigns would hypnotize people into buying *en masse* if it's about simple human tendencies? No? Then you shouldn't get frustrated when the going is slow. If you start to wonder if what you're doing is sensible, put yourself in the shoes of your prospective customer.

Think: Have you ever seen a book, thought it looked interesting, but not bought it? I know I have. I might be in the middle of something at the moment; I might be reading another book; I might not be in the mood for that kind of book. The marketing for the book isn't "wrong"; I'm just not receptive enough yet. Ask yourself the next logical question: If you *were* that prospect, what would eventually make you buy the book you thought was interesting? For me, I'd probably just need to be reminded when I'm ready for a new book and am in the mood for a book of that type. If you keep putting that book in front of me, in other words, I'm eventually going to pick it up.

There's a principle in advertising that says that a customer needs to be exposed to your message seven times on average before they actually notice it. You don't need that metric — you know it's true because you've been a customer before.

The recommendation engines on the bookseller sites will do a lot of that reminding for you, continually putting your book in front of people who bought other books like it. Practically speaking, this means that most of what you have to do is to wait. And write the next book, of course.

You should periodically examine your marketing and funnels, but we want you to have realistic expectations. Even good marketing strategies take time to mature. Don't sweat every passing day. Keep producing, and be patient. If you're building your indie publishing business right, you're in it for the long haul. If you don't expect to get rich quick and commit to putting in the time and effort no matter what, sooner or later your smart marketing will bear fruit.

Marketing is also cumulative and can hit a kind of critical mass. When we had Hugh Howey on *SPP*, he talked about the power of having multiple books in the charts at the same time. One book by an author is easy to ignore, but if you see that author's books everywhere, something is going to click. When that happens, readers will suddenly see you everywhere, and so will their friends. Sean and Dave once ran a promotion on *Yesterday's Gone*. They wanted to earn a lot of new readers, sure, but one of the key parts of their strategies was moving several titles at once. They put all four seasons of *Yesterday's Gone* on sale because they wanted all four to place in the Top 100 for horror. For a while their names were on four out of the five top horror pages. That's a lot of exposure.

Get to Know Your Audience Better

We're always interacting with our Outlaws on the Realm & Sands e-mail list, asking them for feedback and replies. We also talk to readers on Twitter, Facebook, and via e-mail.

We do this because it's nice to talk to people, and because we like and appreciate having fans and readers. But we also do it because we want to know them. This is a true win-win. The better we know our Outlaws, the better we can serve them. The better we can serve them, the happier — the more "served" — they will feel. They will like us more, and like our books more. They will buy more titles, and we will be happier and want to write more books for them.

We never base our decisions about what to write on market demand (more on that later), but there's an odd give and take that happens when you're bonded with your ideal readers and they're bonded with you. It's almost like writing to demand. It's not, though, because Outlaws *are* our ideal readers, and ideal goes both ways. They are a perfect fit for our style, but that also means that we're a perfect fit for them. This relationship is developing all the time as we get to know our readers better. The result is an oddly coordinated synergy, where what we write tends to be what they want to read, and what they want to read syncs with what we want to write. Now, not everyone in our audience wants everything we produce, but it happens more often than not.

Readers don't influence our writing on high-level issues like topics and genre. They are micro-level influences, such as the inclusion of inside references. We've gotten a good feel for what makes our readers chuckle, for one, and because so much of our early readership also listened to one of our podcasts, we couldn't help but include a few podcast jokes, like references to Dave's decoy wallet and roving gangs looking for only one thing at the end of the world. We don't do this to pander; we do it because we feel a kinship with our readers, and including things that they're a part of feels right, like sharing a joke or fond memories with friends.

The better you know your audience, the better you can craft offers that you know they'll respond to. The more you know about what your readers like, the more excited you'll probably be for one project over another. Everyone loves positive feedback, and if you can work on Project A or Project B next, you'll probably work on the one you know your ideal readers want most — again, not because you're twisting your writing to market demand, but because your ideal readers' excitement can't help but infect you. The better you know your people, the better you'll get at pleasing them. At that point, not only will your existing marketing become more powerful, but your fans will also start marketing for you — singing your praises and telling everyone how awesome you are.

Sell Benefits, Not Features

Here's a feature available in certain vehicles: anti-lock brakes. You can also drill down on that feature, getting the details and sub-features, such as the type of computer control and how many times the system pumps the brakes per second.

Now here's the benefit of those brakes: You won't be as likely to slip and lose control when the roads are slick, and hence might avoid a collision and not die (you're safer, and so is your family).

When you do any form of marketing, be sure to emphasize the benefits of what you're selling rather than its features. People don't care about features; they only care what those features can do for them. There's a marketing expression that sums this up beautifully: "Don't sell drill bits. Instead, sell holes."

In other words, nobody buys a quarter-inch drill bit because they want a quarter-inch drill bit. Nobody wants to hold a piece of metal in their hand, put that piece of metal on their mantle to admire, or thinks that their drill is lonely without a bit to pinch in its grip. The people who buy quarter-inch drill bits actually want quarter-inch holes.

This may sound like semantics, but it's not. Selling features locks you inside of a box. If instead you think about what that feature actually does for people — what they *really* want, essentially — then you'll not only see new ways to appeal to them as customers, but you may even find new ways to meet those needs. In the drill bit example, what if a tool company came up with a safe laser drill that would create perfect quarter-inch holes with much less effort at a similar overall cost? Do you really think people would be so loyal to drill bits that they wouldn't make the switch? Of course not. Nobody cares about the bit. They care about the hole, and whatever meets that need best is what they're going to buy.

This thinking applies to books as well. If you're a nonfiction author, thinking about the "holes" your readers need to fill will help you position your book. You'll realize that you shouldn't tell them about the three chapters on conflict resolution in your management book, and should instead pitch it as a way to have a harmonious, happier, more efficient workplace.

For fiction, you might realize that your readers love romantic story lines. Romance, in this case, is the benefit — the "hole" in our metaphor. Do you really have to make it a romance between a man and a woman in Nantucket? Or can you kill two birds with one stone, indulging both your desire to write a romance and your desire to write paranormal fiction by penning a romantic story involving a ghost?

This thinking should extend past the actual work. You might be assuming your $9.99 product isn't selling well because it's too expensive, but price is a feature, not a benefit. Would $9.99 be too much for a new computer? Of course not. So, it's not the price of your book that's a problem; it's the fact that readers don't perceive enough value for that price. *Value* is the benefit. So, don't focus on the price. Instead, focus on the value, demonstrating how much a prospective reader will be getting for that price. We did this with *The Beam.* The individual 30,000-word episodes are priced at $2.99, so the product description and other marketing for the six-episode "full season" collection focus on the fact that taken separately, the episodes would cost almost $18. Compared to $18, our $9.99 bundle pricing on the full season looks like a value-packed deal.

Value, not price. Benefit to the reader, not features of the product.

Advertising

We don't suggest buying advertising for your books until you have at least one funnel completed and ideally another started. You're likely to make more sensible and objective decisions regarding paid advertising if you aren't married to the campaign's results. When Sean and I push any of our product lines, we're optimistic about the results but are in no way banking on them. If you are banking on one product line paying off, you're likely to overpay for advertising, thinking like a gambler trying to get lucky.

Most beginning writers shouldn't touch paid advertising, because advertising tends to have a halo effect: Promotion of one title will likely spill over into generating new readers for your other titles. For this reason, it's most effective if you have many titles on the market.

If you do advertise — and if your product catalog, funnels, and well-placed CTAs are all lined up optimally to take advantage of the extra attention advertising can bring — we've found that paid advertisements can be a fantastic boon for your sales.

We won't go into exhaustive detail on advertising options here because the landscape changes constantly (we can easily see the details of advertising programs or which players work best changing within a few months of this book's publication), but we will say that carefully chosen advertising programs — again, for writers who have everything in place — are almost sure bets. You may or may not earn back the cost of promotion during the sale, but chances are good that you'll earn it back after the sale on that book or similar titles — ideally those later in the same series.

Currently, the most effective paid advertising options require you to discount your book to 99 cents for at least a few days. The most effective promotions typically come from high-value deals ($6.99 discounted to 99 cents versus $1.99 discounted to 99 cents) on proven titles that have earned a decent number of good reviews. Advertisers have either mailing lists of deal-seeking readers or websites frequented by eager deal-seekers, and after you book a deal and lower your price, they will tell their subscribers and readers. If your book is intriguing to those readers (good cover, description, premise, and title) and if the deal's value grabs them, many people will buy.

Those sales benefits you in two ways. The first is that you will get paid for the books, but at 99 cents, using Amazon's current commission structure, your payment will amount to only about 30 cents per sale. The bigger benefit is that as more people buy your book, you will rise in the sales charts and appear in your buyers' "also bought" lists, hence becoming more visible to new buyers. Then, once you end the sale, you'll sell more copies at your normal price.

You'll also get a third benefit if you have other titles in the same series. If the series is any good, people will buy the sequels (or prequels). You can accelerate this benefit by discounting the other books in the series and noting those discounts in the product description of your promoted book. In this way, a successful promotion on a book or a box set in a popular, proven series can lead to a rising tide across all of the titles.

As of this writing — and here we'll remind you that this will quickly become obsolete and that you may want to listen to *SPP* for our more current thoughts — we've had the most luck with BookBub.com, EReaderNewsToday.com, and FKBooksAndTips.com's 99-cent promotion programs. We've also had lesser but substantial success with BookBlast.co (.co, not .com) and BookGorilla.com. We've either not tried or haven't had much luck with other players.

As of 2013, it's almost impossible to promote books on any seller other than Amazon through any advertiser other than BookBub. BookBub will send readers to any platform selling your book, but the others primarily or exclusively push sales to Amazon.

(Is it clear that the information in the two above paragraphs could change tomorrow?)

PART FIVE:
Thinking Like a New Wave Publisher

Go To Where the Puck Is Headed

READY FOR SOME BAD NEWS?

The moment you think you have everything figured out, the indie landscape will change. As of this writing, the e-book market is only a few years old, and it's already evolved tremendously. These changes create a neverending culture of reactivity, with indie authors scrambling to get a hold just as the game changes again. Fresh outrage and cries of falling skies greet each new shift: the death of KDP Select free promotions' effectiveness, the Amazon affiliate agreement change that further drove a stake through free promotion, and an endless tail of too many other things. People get mad when their world is shaken, and the self-publishing world gets shaken plenty.

But here's why this "bad news" is actually good if you're the right kind of author/businessperson: While your competitors are scrambling to keep pace with the changes, you, as a forward-thinking publisher, can stay one step ahead and reap an advantage.

There are definitely parts of this book that will be quickly obsolete, such as the preceding section listing our favorite book advertising options. But most of this book will be as useful in 2018 as it was in 2013, and we're betting the vast majority will still be true in 2023 and 2028 after that. This isn't because we're prophets. It's because most of the advice in this book — based on strategies rather than tactics — was as true 50 years ago as it is today. Strategies don't change much over time. You may find one day that our advice on the dollars and cents of pricing seems dated (prices may rise or fall; the dollar may inflate or drastically change against global currencies; the world may flood, and the North American Union may replace dollars and cents with universal credits), but the principles won't. People will always be less resistant to lower prices from unknown authors than they would be to high prices. People will always be more willing to try something for free than they would be to pay for it. People will always be psychologically predisposed to buy a bundle over single books in order to save money, and people further down your sales funnel will always be willing to pay more for your work.

Aside from always thinking strategically — employing today's tactics but staying ready to pivot if new ones serve your strategies better — the ability to think ahead will keep you in front of your scrambling competition.

We all *can* think ahead, but so few of us will. It's human nature to stick with what works as if it will always work — then to cling to it long after it stops. It's this thinking that led authors to repurpose public domain content in e-books' early days, trying to capitalize on the Kindle gold rush rather than building a brand and creating quality original works that readers would love. It's this thinking that led authors who felt that KDP Select had lost its luster to stay in the program instead of diversifying to other booksellers. And in the future, it's this thinking that will keep indies from seeing new advertising options while they keep using defunct ones, that will keep indies from exploring new markets and reading formats, and that will keep indie publishers' heads stuck firmly in dead paradigms like old men bolted to porches, jawing about how things were in the wayback.

Wayne Gretsky said, "A good hockey player plays where the puck is. A great hockey player plays where the puck is going to be."

That's very true, and it's what we all need to learn. Do you want to be a *good* indie businessperson who tries to chase ever-changing trends? Or would rather be *great*, always in front?

There's a concept in life, of zigging versus zagging. The idea is that while your competitors are zigging by going in one direction, you should consider zagging in the other. At face value, this means to buck trends, but we'll step back a bit and say you should always keep your eyes and mind open. Zagging for the sake of zagging can, in certain cases, be idiotic. You become like a punk rock poseur, distrusting everything simply because it's popular. Don't do that. Right here and now, Amazon is the big bookseller, and zagging away from it would be the height of idiocy. On the other hand, don't assume it will always be that way. We used to have all of our eggs in Amazon's exclusive basket, and it was our friend, Joanna Penn, who first said we should really consider putting our books on Kobo. Now Kobo sales are a significant portion of our income, far outweighing the benefits of Amazon exclusivity in Select. In our circle at the time, Joanna saw it first, because she's always looking for where the puck is headed. Now she's talking a lot about international book markets, and while we're not translating our work yet, it's absolutely on our radar, and we're ready to jump when the time's right.

Constantly reevaluate your tactics relative to the underlying strategies. Don't ask, "Is Amazon the place to be?" Instead, ask if selling on Amazon fits well with and best serves your *strategy* of selling as many books as possible to your ideal readers. As long as it does, stay. (For the record, it's hard for us to imagine a day when Amazon won't fit. This is only an example.) Don't look for hot tactics. Look for grounded, solid, time-tested strategies, then watch for marketplace shifts that suggest an old tactic may be on its way out while another's on its way in.

Here's an example: Our friend Jim Kukral, who runs author education site AuthorMarketingClub.com, is very forward-thinking, always doing exactly what I just described. Jim is a marketer first, and understands that human behavior ultimately dictates how people buy. Accordingly, Jim looks at the addiction we all seem to have to our cell phones and sees opportunity. He predicts that the future of reading will include a heavy emphasis on small-screen reading. Other things Jim is watching, and which he's discussed with us on *SPP*: a surge in audiobook popularity and a trend toward authors selling their work directly to readers rather than relying solely on booksellers, possibly through mobile apps.

You don't have to jump on every shiny penny, and we certainly don't recommend ditching the big booksellers to focus exclusively on direct selling and cell phone apps. But you should watch the horizon. Check in with your strategies, and never be unwilling to reevaluate even the most precious tactics if it looks like the tide might be moving elsewhere.

Always look to see where that puck is going to be, and you'll always have an advantage in the shifting indie landscape. Fail to do that, and watch your career flounder while clinging to outdated ways of doing business.

CHAPTER EIGHTEEN:
Mistakes That Writers Make (and That Publishers Usually Don't)

WE OFTEN THINK WE'RE SUPERIOR. "Ha ha," we say, "we are smarter than those outdated, slow-moving behemoths in traditional publishing! They are the past. We are the future. Hail the new wave of publishing!" I mean, talk about an industry that can't go to where the puck is headed. They might see the big changes coming, but they're giant organizations and can't be nimble like we can. Sean once said on the show, "They're the *Titanic*. It's not that they can't see the iceberg; it's that they're too big to steer away from it. All they can do is brace for impact." Yeah. That.

Well, don't be so quick to dismiss the big boys. It's true that they can sometimes appear slow and cumbersome while self-publishers are small and agile, but they still have some things going for them that most indies lack. Let's take a chapter to pay tribute to the traditional world and see what they're doing right that many indies are doing wrong. If you think self-publishing is definitely the way to go, awesome. We like it a lot, too. That doesn't mean there isn't a hell of a lot we can learn from those

375

who've been in the game for a lot longer than we have.

Not Treating Writing Like a Business

You wake up. You sit down to write. You peck at the keys for a while, waiting to see if you feel inspired. Sometimes, you do, and good words spill from your brain to the screen. Sometimes, you don't and decide you can't rush art, so you do something else instead.

If you have a day job, maybe this is where you go after calling it quits on writing for the day. You'll write when you get home, if you have the energy. But it's a rough day at work, and you don't. You watch TV instead, or maybe do some reading. Either can be justified as "research," so it's cool. You go on this way for a few weeks or months, figuring that the first draft will be done when it's done. Eventually it is, but it still needs an edit. Then maybe another. You have to pay for an edit, then another to be sure. You get a cover done by the best cover artist supposedly out there, and it costs you a grand, but hey, this novel is really awesome and you read somewhere (possibly a self-publishing manual with a catchy title) that covers really matter.

After everything is finished, you put your book online. Nothing happens, so you buy some advertising. There's no return, so you buy some more. Eventually, you start a second novel and repeat the process, but this novel's harder because you see how badly you're bleeding financially on the first one, and it's not exactly encouraging you that this self-publishing thing pays off. A few people buy that first novel, but not enough. They say nice things and ask if you're going to release another book. You try to keep up with these people but eventually lose their contact information.

We'll stop there. We've made our point; there was a ton done incorrectly in the above scenario. But it's not merely overpaying for a cover or the lackadaisical approach to production that's the problem. Those are symptoms. The bigger problem is that they represent someone treating writing like a hobby.

There are only a few big-picture themes in this book, with the rest being details and clarifications on those themes. One is that there is no get-rich-quick in publishing and that you must work hard to build a career. Another is that time-tested strategies (which seldom change) are always more important than tactics (which change often). A third is that this is a business, not a hobby, and that you need to treat it that way.

The best book we know about the workmanlike approach to art — the approach we advocate — is *The War of Art*, which we've recommended twice already. Get that book. Read it. It's a fast read; you can plow through it in a few hours. Pressfield's approach (which he put a finer point on in *The War of Art*'s sequel, *Do The Work*) sounds almost merciless. Making art *is* like a war. It's you versus The Resistance. You wage battle by surrendering hours, grinding through your art like you'd grind through the chore of moving a pile of dirt one shovelful at a time. You don't treat making art with kid gloves. You don't pamper it or wait for inspiration to strike. You work. And you work. And you work. Like you would if you were doing a job for someone else.

Do you treat your writing like that? Do you show up on time, put in a given number of hours, and stitch words together like you'll be fired if you don't? Most writers write when inspired, which is ephemeral and comes and goes. Some days they write a lot, and others they don't, but it's random. They have no idea how many hours they'll put in per week, and no idea how many words they can expect to produce during that time. They don't set deadlines for themselves, and if they do, those deadlines are solid as tissue.

Don't do this. We've argued that you can't just think of yourself as an artist; you must also be a businessperson and a marketer. If you buy that idea, drill down until you prove it with practice.

If you're doing a real job in a real business, you set regular hours, and unless you're deathly sick or unless it's a special, planned-in-advance occasion, you show up when you're supposed to and stay until it's time to leave. You're given deadlines, and if you expect to keep your job, you meet them — or if you don't, you give your boss a damned good reason for it and promise to bust ass until you get the job done.

Businesses set budgets. A business knows what it can expect to get out of an investment at the outset, and spends accordingly. A business will invest in projects that aren't expected to deliver a return, but only if that loss is in the service of a greater win down the road. This means that while a product line may be expected to run in the red, the sum of the business's products, over time, is always expected to end up in the black. Businesses never go into a venture, spend blindly, and hope. Businesses plan deftly. If a project is a pilot and carries risk, it's kept on a shoestring. Only blockbusters are given blockbuster budgets.

This is one area where indies can learn big lessons from traditional publishing. Their criteria for deciding whether to take on a project are a lot tighter than ours need to be, but at least *they have them.* Most writers write what they feel, publish when they get to it, and spend whatever seems right. A publisher won't budget for publication and promotion if it doesn't expect a return, and you shouldn't either. Your less-certain novels should be kept on tight leashes. Get a good cover, but nothing outrageous or extravagant. Don't dump a bunch of money on advertising for a single novel with no sequel or funnel because you're emotionally attached to its success. Publishers don't get attached to any one book's success. Books, to publishers, are line items on expense and income sheets. You're going to be somewhat emotionally invested in your books, and that's fine (it's sweet, really; we enjoy our own for sure), but you can't approach business with emotion in your equation. Will an expense pay off? If it won't, do you have a concrete plan to make it pay off down the road? If not, why are you doing it?

Set a budget on each book that is commensurate with its real, objective, non-emotionally-clouded expectation of return. Set regular hours for yourself as you would for an employee, and stick to those hours, keeping your butt in the chair, getting words on the page. Measure your stats if you can, noting how many words you can write in a day and extrapolating to see how long a book will take to complete. Set deadlines for projects (which also requires guessing at a word count for those projects and trying your best to hit those word counts) and stick to them.

The more you treat your writing like a business, the more likely you'll be to have a businesslike result rather than a starving artist's.

Making Your Books About You Instead of Your Reader

Joanna Penn shared a graphic on Google Plus that read: *Writing is about you. Publishing is about the book. Marketing is about the reader.*

We agree, on all fronts. Publishers agree with it, too — or at least the last two-thirds.

Writing *should* be about you. When you're coming up with your story ideas, creating beats for those ideas, writing the first draft, or revising, you should be acting according to your internal compass. That's the reason we write in multiple genres instead of making the "wise according to common thinking" decision of sticking to one. It's why, when producing his Guy Incognito children's book line, Sean doesn't edit out all the big words, because he got into writing in the first place after being told that his vocabulary was too rich for kids and thought that was utter crap. These are decisions we make without thinking of the market and what's most likely to sell. We think that's dangerous. Writing is both art and business, but they shouldn't mix. It's art *then* business — in order, non-overlapping.

Your written product stops being about you, your needs, desires, and emotions as soon as the writing is finished. Then it becomes a product, and you must treat it as such. Products must sell, and in order to sell, they must be positioned in the best possible way — even if that way doesn't totally jibe with your own personal artistic feelings. That's not always easy when those words feel like your babies — things you slaved over, loved, and gave birth to. But you need to take a step back, and if it won't work for readers, you must be able to see that and act accordingly.

Sean had the idea for *The Beam* over a year before we started work on the series you see on the shelves today. He produced an entire season of *The Beam*, working with another writer, well before I'd moved back into fiction. But when that season was done, Sean shelved it rather than publishing it. The end product meant a lot to him, but it wasn't good enough for his readers. Publishing it as-is, knowing it would miss the mark, would have been the actions of an emotional indie writer. Sean's not emotional about his books, and puts the reader first. He let it go until we could reinvent it, tossing an entire season's worth of copy into the trash.

Sean and Dave made a similar choice when they finished their first book, *Available Darkness*. Here they had a finished book after months of hard work ... but putting their full weight behind it in order to promote would have been a mistake, and they knew it. They only had the one book, and readers who loved it would have nothing else to buy. So, they published without promotion, letting it rust until they had a funnel in place. The next project ended up being their post-apocalyptic serial *Yesterday's Gone*, which truly paved the self-publishing road for all three of us.

Remember: Write for you, then act in the best interests of the market and your reader.

Thinking Short-Term

If you sign with a traditional publisher, your book will get a promotional budget, will spend a few weeks on bookstore shelves, and then in all likelihood will disappear. Your book can earn its way out of obscurity by selling well, but only a minority ever will.

While this may be heartbreaking, frustrating, and downright infuriating to the minor author whose book ends up dead in the water, it makes sense to the publisher. They have a crap-ton of assets (that's how they think of books), and any business knows that if it's thinking long-term, it must cut non-performing assets so it can focus time and energy on those that generate a return.

As an indie, you can choose to make the same choices. Now because keeping a book available in e-book form (or even in print-on-demand form) costs nothing, you don't have to pull non-performing titles from the shelves like a publisher in order to consider the big picture. And because when an indie does promotion he sort of ends up shining light on his entire catalog, there's also no real reason to ever give up on any one title. But the principle is still there: Don't just think of what might happen today; think of what will be best in the future. What assets are most likely to pay off later? What properties are worth working on and getting behind because they have potential down the road, even though they may stagnate now?

When Sean and I decided to write *Plugged*, we knew it wouldn't sell well in the beginning. We were writing it for three reasons, and none had to do with fattening our pockets in the short term. First, we wanted to reinforce our bonding with and satisfy true fans of *The Beam*, who had been salivating and demanding more since finishing the first season. We couldn't get to *The Beam: Season Two* for another four to five months, but *Plugged*, which explains *The Beam*'s entire backstory as well as much of its theme, would act as a holdover — and accordingly, we referred to it as "*Beam* Season 1.5." The second reason we wrote it was because we had our own questions about the world, which is very complex, and kept wasting research time when working with Lexi on *The Future of Sex*. Writing *Plugged* taught *us* the NAU's backstory at the same time we were teaching readers.

But the third reason we wrote *Plugged* when we did was because we knew that 2014 was going to be a huge year for *The Beam*. We were going to write the second and third seasons; Lexi's series was due to explode; we'd gotten some interest in developing the world for film or TV; several of our big-selling indie friends were due to write their own stories in our shared world, leading to a lot of promotion. We wanted to flesh out as much of *The Beam* as we could whenever we could find time, and writing books like *Plugged* — "fourth wall" books that, written as nonfiction, made our world feel more substantial and realized — was part of our larger strategy. We knew we could write *Plugged* in the time we had, but also knew it wouldn't sell well until the other pieces were in place.

We got a few e-mails about *Plugged*, all of which essentially said that we were ridiculous to write that kind of book about a world that was so new, while there still wasn't much demand for it. But see, we knew that before the beats were written. We also knew that by the time there *was* demand for books like *Plugged*, we would need them to already exist. If we waited, we would have been chasing the puck where it stood, and wouldn't be well-positioned to capitalize on critical mass. We wanted to go where the puck was *going* to be, like Wayne said.

If you only try to make money today, you might do well … and you also might sever excellent opportunities to make much more money later. Our decision to price full seasons of *The Beam* at the higher-than-normal price of $9.99 was a long-term branding decision establishing it as our premium series. We wanted to show the world from the start that we were only willing to keep writing in that world if people liked it enough to pay the higher price. Did that mean we lost some sales in the first months? Yep. Did we care? Not in the least. We knew it would pay off later.

You're an independent publisher. You don't have to have huge book launches, and don't need to manage your inventory to account for limited shelf space. You can afford to let books sit, arranging pieces of your publishing business like you'd arrange pieces on a chessboard before moving to take your opponent's king. Your book published today has the potential to earn money forever. You can write a book knowing it won't make you a cent, because its larger, longer-term purpose is to promote you, serve as a feather in your cap, or advance sales of another book (or series).

We'd take a month today to write a book that would flounder and fail ... but then, five years from now, would push big sales onto my entire catalog.

Would you?

CHAPTER NINETEEN:
Things You Can Probably Stop Worrying About

THERE'S NO SHORTAGE OF THINGS to fret about as a self-publisher. You're the captain of the ship, but that's both good news and bad. Because while everything about your success or failure is ultimately up to you, *everything about your success or failure is ultimately up to you.* Nobody will help you out unless you're partners or are paying them. Nobody will automatically be in your corner. Nobody will shake the pom-poms for you. If you were traditionally published, you might not get a ton of promotion, but at least you'd get placement, in a few places, for a while. Even though the publisher might barely know you exist within their huge catalog, you'd at least be there, and your success would be their success. At least someone else would have a reason for you to succeed. But as an indie? You're on your own, baby.

    Sean and I are deeply infected with entrepreneurism — so much that it's almost terminal. Just ask our wives. We've both driven our families through ruin to surface on the other side, but it doesn't occur to us that we were ever in danger despite the way our supportive but frightened wives kept screaming from the passenger seat. But if you're not like us — if you're sane enough to see potential hazards in the road rather than blissfully farting rainbows — the responsibility that comes with indie publishing can feel overwhelming. It's not just that you could trip and fall. You could also fail to keep an eye on everything you should. You could forget about something, position yourself incorrectly, or generally be blindsided by something you hadn't thought to watch out for. You might feel like a plate-spinner, trying to keep too much in the air lest something fall and shatter.

It's true that there's a lot to keep an eye on when you're an indie, and there are certainly many tasks you'll need to manage. But there are also plenty of things that indies worry about that we think aren't worth your mental bandwidth. Without further ado, let's go through our list of things we think you can stop worrying about, and instead spend that recovered time writing.

Picking the Right Genre (Or Even *A* Genre)

Convention says that writers should pick a genre — thrillers, horror, romance, maybe generalized literature — and stick with it. The thinking makes sense; it's based on satisfying readers of your current work by giving them more of what they already like.

The problem for us, though, was that Sean and I like to read multiple genres, and hence wanted to write in multiple genres. Obeying the stick-to-one-genre dictum would have violated so much of what we've said in this book. It would have been basing our art on a marketing decision (writing something profitable over something we wanted to write more); it would have robbed writing of its fun because we both love variety and value freedom more than anything; it would have been a stupid long-term decision seeing as neither of us wanted to be writing in one and only one genre five or ten years from now. Plenty of writers would love to stay in a single genre and find success there (Dave appears to love horror, sci-fi, and dark fantasy, all of which overlap, enough to stay in its gnarled shadows forever), but that wasn't us.

There are three main concerns with genre-hopping. The first is the idea of satisfying readers by giving them more of what they already like. There are people who only really like one type of book, and if you have some of those people in your audience, they may not feel satisfied enough by your output in one genre and may therefore go elsewhere. While that can be true, that concern mostly fades for people who produce at our volume. If you only write one or two books a year, hopping genres will indeed leave some readers wanting because they'll have to wait a few years between their ideal reads. But if you produce over a million words a year — a large book each month or three to four novellas a month — you don't have this problem. High-producing writers don't have to pick one genre *or* another. They can do one genre *and* another.

Critics also say it's confusing to readers. If your brand doesn't stand for a tightly focused style of work — like Collective Inkwell does in churning out a steady diet of dark horror — how will readers know what to expect from you?

First of all, readers are smarter than that. Realm & Sands doesn't have stupid ideal readers. Maybe there are readers who would see a book called *Unicorn Western*, with a gunslinger riding a unicorn on the cover, with a product description that describes it as, "*Harry Potter* without wizards but with gunslingers, talking unicorns, epic fights, and more turkey pie," and think it was a romance novel set in Bangkok in the 17ᵗʰ century. But if there are, they're not in our group of ideal readers — and frankly, we don't care if we confuse them right out of our lives.

But there's another thing: You know that expression "The only constant is change," which is all ninja-like in positioning the antithesis of "constant" as a constant? Well, does no one consider that there might be readers out there whose genre is a lack of genre? It's certainly true of both of us; the shelf across from me right now includes *Fight Club, House of Leaves, Catch-22*, the *Harry Potter* novels, and a fantastic young adult sci-fi romance Dave introduced us to called *Everyday*. We contend that a lot of readers' genre is "books they think are awesome," and those are the people who are Realm & Sands' core readers. They won't love every book we write, but they also won't automatically dismiss one (or be confused by it, furrowing their Neanderthal brows in a vain attempt to understand) simply because it has nanobots instead of talking unicorns. Our readers aren't fickle enough to run if we write something they don't want to read. Believe it or not, they seem willing to wait a few weeks or months for the next one.

The final argument against genre-hopping is about discoverability, and we contend this one is pointless to spend a minute fretting about. In a physical bookstore, it's true that proper genre shelving mattered, because you wanted people looking for romance books in the romance section to see your book. It's similarly true that if you wrote a sci-fi novel after writing dozens of romances, even your most loyal readers would never see it because it wouldn't be shelved with your other books. But in online bookstores — especially for writers who have their own mailing lists — this problem disappears. Thanks to various recommendation lists ("You might enjoy these books," "Customers who bought this book also bought these books"), cross-genre books will be "shelved" next to one another if enough people have bought them both — and, if you cultivate a list of people who like to read across genres, you can inform them of both titles to make that happen. Your own books will also all be shelved together permanently. If someone wants to see your other work, all they have to do is click on your name and get the lot.

As to branding? We can have a genre-free brand the same as we can cultivate a group of genre-free readers. Realm & Sands' tagline is "For Readers Who Refuse To Be Defined By Their Fiction." See what we did there? We turned what seemed random into a strength. I love this tagline because I'm not any one thing either, and don't want to be defined by a genre any more than our readers.

Protecting Your Copyright

Remember that legal section earlier in this book? We totally phoned it in. In fact, we only included it because we thought we should, because people would expect it.

Personally — and this is simply our non-legal opinion, and we're not lawyers giving advice, etc., etc. — we don't think that theft of your work is generally worth worrying about. That probably just made the hair on the back of your neck stand on end, but think about it for a second:

Your work has a copyright the minute you've written it. It's automatic and requires no effort. So, what we're really talking about here isn't protecting your work. We're talking about the way most writers sweat the issue of copyright, which is going to all sorts of extra lengths to register and reinforce it. We're not suggesting you're not protected; we're simply invoking the 80/20 Rule and arguing that taking those extra steps are firmly entrenched in the 20 percent.

Out of all the work out there to be stolen and infringed upon, do you really think that *yours* is going to be the one some poacher steals? Oh, you know someone it happened to? Did the poacher turn your buddy's work into a blockbuster and cost them a ton of money? Or was it just some random asshole?

If your copyright *is* somehow infringed and turned into a huge breakout hit, don't you think whatever it would cost you to get your fair share of that huge breakout hit would make it worthwhile?

Of course, copyrights are infringed upon from time to time. So what? Once you get your sense of artistic indignation out of the way, what harm was *really* done? The chances of someone doing something terrible to your rights are so incredibly remote that in our opinion it's simply not worth the expense, hassle, or mental space to consider. It could happen, but you could also be hit by a bus. We don't think that means you shouldn't cross the street.

Piracy

People sweat piracy as much as they sweat copyright, but in our opinion, obscurity is a far bigger issue. You'll never stop piracy. You can try, but before you do, we suggest you call the film, music, and porn industries and ask them how that strategy is working out for them. You could spend valuable hours scouring Internet file-sharing services and torrents to see if anyone is stealing your stuff, then try to stop them, but your efforts will net you a shuffle. If you're popular, people will always share your stuff.

We think this is a good thing. The people who read pirated books are never going to *buy* your work anyway; it's a totally different audience than purchasing readers. Even if you could scrub your stuff from the Internet, you'd only be keeping your book from pirate readers. You wouldn't convert those readers into buyers. They'd simply read something else that was free.

People staying interested in your work — even if that means stealing it — is a good thing. The more people who see your books, the more likely they are to talk about it. Remember the story about the two girls our friend Kyeli heard in line at Target, talking about *Unicorn Western*? They probably weren't pirates, but they could've been. We'd rather hear about as many of those conversations as possible, even if we don't get paid for every sale. Money lost to piracy is almost a sensible marketing expense. The more people who are talking, the more people who will hear. Some may become buyers.

How Much Money You'll Make

We'll answer this now so you can stop worrying: *Not much at first.*

You'll work really hard for months and months, and won't make much money at all. Keep at it, and that should turn around, but in general, this stuff takes time. But you knew that, even if you hadn't read this book. Only deluded people think they will publish one book and retire.

The fact that everyone spends so much time thinking about something they already know the answer to reveals the "How much will I make?" question to be not much more than a delay tactic. Get over it and move on. You won't make much at first, but the sooner you start, the sooner "not much" will become "more."

The issue of money does matter, but how much is the wrong question to ask. Don't think in terms of dollars and cents (euros, pounds, whatever) in the beginning. Think about creating books that are truly worth buying, doing it over and over, and getting it into as many hands as possible. Think about creating better funnels and gaining a better understanding of what makes prospective buyers tick. Think about forging better connections with your readers and growing your list.

Do those things faithfully, and money will (eventually) follow.

What Anyone Else Thinks

You're probably going to get pushback as you build your indie writing business. You may get it from well-meaning family and friends, or from fellow writers who think you should try to publish traditionally, that your decisions about what to write are somehow incorrect, or that you're going about your marketing all wrong. You'll get advice on your work, your titles, your funnel structure, the genres you write in, your pricing, and so on. Some of it will be good, and you should listen to it all. But in the end, once you know what you're going to do, cut it off and stand firm — and at that point, some of the advice and pushback will start to sound like criticism ... or even pity.

We've had our share. We appreciate everything that podcast listeners have debated with us and all of the contrary opinions, but ultimately this is our business, and we're going to make the decisions we're going to make. We suggest you approach your business the same way. Don't worry if your friends think you're wasting your time. Don't worry if you write some saucy, horrific, or profane scenes that Grandma wouldn't approve of. Don't worry if your writing group disagrees with your marketing or branding. Once you've listened, assessed, and decided, your decisions are yours to make. They are no one's business but your own.

This isn't about selfishness or bullheadedness. Once you have a group of ideal readers and true fans, you'll be making those decisions based on what you know about them that the critics don't. Your job is to serve your audience and yourself. If you've done your job and cultivated a group of readers that are indeed *ideal* readers, your aims and your readers' desires should nicely align.

You're an adult. You've earned the right to do what you want, regardless of what anyone has to say.

Making Your Book Perfect

Hey, have we told you to read *The War of Art?* Yeah … go read it if you're worried about making your book perfect.

Your book will not — and cannot — ever be perfect. Even if you get all of the grammar and spelling and punctuation in line with the official rules, your plot could always be a bit more exciting or heartfelt. You could always foreshadow better. You could always make the dialogue ring more true.

Worrying about perfection sounds noble. That's how you justify holding a book back: "I owe my readers the best, and this can still be better." But it's not noble; it's self-indulgent. You aren't refraining from publishing because you care about readers; you're refraining because you're afraid. You aren't ceaselessly revising and tweaking your book to improve its selling potential; you're doing it to avoid writing the next one. This is all fear and resistance, not quality control.

As Seth Godin wrote in *Linchpin*, "The only purpose of starting is to finish, and while the projects we do are never really finished, they must ship."

Your book will never be truly finished or perfect. Competent indies understand that while that may be true, you must publish anyway, so you can move on to the next one.

Hourly Changes in Your Rank, Sales, and Reviews

As I write this, Sean and Dave just ran a big promotion on Season One of *Yesterday's Gone*. At 1:42pm yesterday, I get this text from Sean:

> *Watching the promo is painful. Our sales rank is getting worse, not better. I know that will turn around but crap, what the fuck is taking so long?*

Now, I'm a forward-thinking, level-headed guy, so I replied:

> *Dude, FUCK YOU. You're watching it that closely? Get to work!*

I had to chastise Sean that harshly because he was doing what most indie authors are guilty of: obsessing over stats and sales on an almost hourly (or minute-by-minute) basis. It's distracting. It's inevitably demoralizing when things take brief dips. We wholeheartedly recommend against worrying about your stats. Check them only once per day if you must.

This morning, I got this text:

We cracked the top 100 but dipped back down. Right now we're at 101, so hopefully we go up again.

This was getting intolerable. Sean is my partner. He's supposed to be a mature, long-term-thinking self-publisher, and here he was obsessing over a three-point drop in sales rank, from 98 to 101.

I told him to relax. Not only was he being obsessive; he was being unrealistic. I knew for a fact that sales rank always dips a bit in the morning hours because I'd had my own promo on *Fat Vampire* the week before and had faithfully refreshed my stats every 15 minutes or so in the name of research.

Yes, we're as weak as we're telling you not to be. It's hard to resist watching those stats, and equally difficult to refrain from becoming emotionally tormented by their ups and downs. If you can, try to do as we say rather than as we do. Stats, sales, and ranking only really matter in the long term, on a weekly or monthly basis. We suggest you save yourself a ton of anguish and ignore them.

But of course, you won't.

20 Percent Activities

To close this section, let's cover some things that fall firmly into "the 20 percent" for most independent writers — activities that may give you *some* results but will likely require too much time relative to what your efforts will yield.

We're not discouraging you from doing these things, or saying they won't generate results. We're saying that in most cases, the potential returns are small enough that your time would be better spent writing — the one activity from which almost everyone reading this book stands to reap the most benefit.

Print

We love print. There's something about holding a book in your hand that makes you feel like a real writer.

But wanting to feel like a real writer isn't enough of a justification to set aside new production to create print versions of existing books, so we only do it when we can shove it in or when there seems to be another reason. As mentioned earlier, there can be value in handing out or selling print books in person, and the way Amazon makes your e-book price look better if there's print on the page for comparison is a nice psychological anchor. But even with all of that, print is still firmly in the 20 percent for us — and is probably closer to 5 percent or less for writers with only a few titles.

If you choose to spend time on print, just know you're not doing something likely to yield large monetary results.

Book Trailers

Book trailers are like movie trailers, but for books. They typically have dramatic still photos creeping across the screen and dissolving into one another, and higher-end trailers will include video. They may or may not have a voiceover, and usually have theatrical-looking text moving around and/or quotes from the book. The idea is to stick the trailers on YouTube or your website and use them to fuel anticipation for your book among an audience that's more visual than your core reader group.

Personally, I don't understand book trailers at all and have no interest in them despite hearing that they can be worthwhile. Sean and Dave have done them, and Lexi had an intro video made for herself as an author. Sean and Lexi both report that while the trailers have their value, they are, unsurprisingly, something that's firmly 20 percent or less. Ryan Holiday has a fantastic and effective trailer for *Trust Me, I'm Lying*, and Jonathan Fields has one for *Uncertainty*. But they are rare. Ryan Holiday is a born marketer and Jonathan Fields' trailer mined perfect emotion. Both look like they had a substantial budget behind them. Odds are that your trailer will only be a waste of time and money.

As with print, you can do them, but know what you're likely to get. Make sure the time, expense, and effort is something you'd rather spend on trailers than on writing more books.

Algorithms

We've spent a lot of time talking about various platforms' algorithms on *SPP* — mainly Amazon's ranking and recommendation engines — and we do suggest you know something about how they work. But as with all of these 20 percent activities, we recommend you minimize time spent thinking (or ruminating) about them.

Luckily, understanding most of what you need to know about algorithms doesn't take a ton of time. If you're an auditory person, you can search for episodes of *SPP* featuring Ed Robertson or David Gaughran, who we consider to be our algorithm guys. Or you can pick up David's excellent book *Let's Get Visible,* which is all about understanding the various ways that Amazon puts recommended books in front of prospective readers.

Once you've done your initial research, we suggest incorporating "algorithm thinking" as a by-the-way thing. *Let's Get Visible* has a great section on choosing categories for your work, so maybe you'll decide to tweak those categories. Maybe you'll wonder at the algorithms when you publish and keep them in the back of your head. Beyond that, we suggest letting it go. The title of this chapter is *Things You Can Probably Stop Worrying About,* and beyond the basics, you can probably stop worrying about algorithms.

Think about them, yes. But don't put algorithm optimization above writing good books and bonding with your readers. As with checking sales rank, trying to ride algorithmic waves is usually a procrastination tactic. You can increase your visibility by spending five minutes thinking about algorithms, but beyond that your best strategy for increasing visibility is to write more books, hence making your publishing footprint harder to ignore.

CHAPTER TWENTY:
How To Kill It

YOU'RE WRITING MORE BOOKS (*WRITE. Publish. Repeat.*), you're thinking of your books as products that are organized into product lines and funnels, you're building a mailing list and bonding with fans, and you're constantly refining your CTAs and strategies, keenly focused on heading toward where the puck is going to be.

That's all very necessary, but we also have a few ideas on how to kill it in self-publishing beyond the basics. Most of it has to do with attitude, and is therefore tricky to quantify. But make no mistake: This chapter's concepts can make the difference between a mediocre publishing career and a stellar one. You're about to read things that will take you from the place where you're following instructions and getting results to a place where your readers love you and you're a name that commands attention.

These are probably the closest things we have to "secrets to success," but of course they're not *secrets* at all. Some of what follows is subtle, so let it sink in. The more you own it, the faster you'll develop goals worth having.

Have Guts

We've lived through some scary stuff — separately, before we were even writing together. We've both had homes foreclosed on. We've both been down to our last few dollars. There have been plenty of times when we've had no reason other than blind faith and guts to keep moving forward. We just had to keep on, because we believed if we kept working and thinking and doing, things would work out. We're both unfortunately afflicted with a firm conviction (don't tell our wives) that we'd rather be broke and doing what we wanted to do rather than secure and hating life.

We've also done many things that others thought were stupid because we trusted our internal compasses more than the opinions of others. Sometimes, it can be an arrogant way of thinking, always listening to friends and family but ultimately deciding we know better. We've made plenty of missteps; we're certainly not saying that we've always had everything right.

That's the difference between people with guts and people who wish they had them: the need to feel entirely certain of a decision before it's made. It doesn't take courage to do things if you're infallible, or certain. Courage comes from knowing you could fail. We don't think we ever took stupid risks in our careers (everything has operated within a margin of acceptable risk, and the worst that could happen, while uncomfortable, would be far short of starvation or death) but we did know we could fail. And we did. Many times.

Today, sometimes, people will tell us that we're making bad choices as we build our product catalog and business. They'll tell us that we're pricing too high, that we shouldn't hop from genre to genre, or that we shouldn't structure or name our books in certain ways. The nature of these protests are often desperately helpful, eager to save us from making a mistake. But one reason I think we often confuse our helpful detractors is that we ultimately agree that we might be wrong. They'll say, "You could be wrong, so you shouldn't do it." And we say, "We could be wrong, and we're going to do it anyway."

Taking acceptable risks is a key ingredient for success. If the path was easy, everyone would take it. Ballsy people, if they're intelligent and learn from their mistakes, shape the world. The thing that few people get is that ballsy people aren't any more certain than anyone else. They know they could fail, but also know that if they don't take a shot, they can't succeed either.

We've already quoted Wayne Gretzky once. Here he is again: "You miss 100 percent of the shots you don't take."

We'd never encourage anyone to take stupid risks. Please do *not* interpret this section as us suggesting that you surrender your secure job and resolve to make it as an indie or die trying. *Do*, however, take *small* risks. Risk being incorrect. Risk being laughed at. Risk your mother disapproving of your latest book. Risk confusing the marketplace. Risk alienating some of the people in your audience during an attempt to foster better relationships with others. Do that, and you'll learn what small failures feel like, and realize that they aren't the end of the world.

Let's say you write an experimental book, like *Plugged*. People might tell you the idea is ridiculous and that it'll never sell. So what? If you believe in the project, write it anyway. If it doesn't sell, it was made with words, and you have a bottomless well. Go write another.

Let's say you want to make a profitable book free for an extended period of time in an attempt to build your readership. Will it fail? Will your decision be for naught, costing profits you'd otherwise have? Maybe. But so what? It could also succeed, and you could soar to new heights with your next release.

When Sean and Dave released the fourth season of their popular *Yesterday's Gone* series, they decided to mix up their release model. Instead of launching the full $5.99 bundle at once, they opted to publish the six episodes at 99 cents each, thus cutting their commissions in half because on Amazon, you only receive 35 percent commissions instead of 70 percent for prices below $2.99. They thought that if they had six distinct releases to cover a highly anticipated work, they'd get more attention and make up for the lower commissions. They were wrong, and made much less money than they should have. Some people would say they failed and shouldn't have taken the risk, but they didn't fail at all. Failure is a big-picture thing, and you can't fail unless you give up. Sean and Dave are still publishing, and what they learned from that launch influenced later strategy that has allowed all three of us to learn what to do in the future. Specifically, it was this exact experiment that led Sean to suggest I release *my* anticipated book *Fat Vampire 5* at $2.99 instead of bothering with 99 cents. We'd all learned something about 99 cent promotion, and never would have learned it without the guts to experiment.

If you want to kill it in self-publishing, you need to set goals that matter to you no matter what anyone thinks, then hit those goals without flinching. Be willing to experiment even if you might fail. Understand that life and your career are bigger than one incident or decision, and that sometimes, you have to hold your breath, take the leap, and see what happens.

If you act when there's no downside and you're not afraid, that's not courage. Courage is taking action in the *presence* of risk, in *spite* of fear.

The more comfortable you get with having guts and learning to trust yourself even if you're alone, the better off you'll be in the long term.

Do the Work

Do you know what truly, honestly separates people who succeed from those who fail? It's simple:

People who do the work succeed. People who don't fail.

I realized something sad, disheartening, and desperately frustrating back when I was teaching online courses: *Most people simply aren't willing to do the work it takes to get what they want, and don't even realize it.*

At first, before I had the second part of that realization, it was maddening. Someone would ask me how to do X, and I'd tell them. A week later I'd ask how they were doing, and they'd tell me they hadn't made progress. I'd repeat what to do, and a week later they'd still have done nothing. Eventually, they might half-ass something just so I'd leave them alone, but it was a hollow effort. And then they'd surrender, nothing would change, and they'd loudly declare that X was impossible.

By contrast — because everyone loves a success story — I know maybe two or three people who actually *did* do the work. One was my friend Jess, who first came to me as a coaching client. Jess did everything I suggested, then much more. I worked with Jess for years, mostly as a partner rather than as a coach. She's tireless. She exceeds expectations. She does nothing halfway, and takes every detail within a project as her personal responsibility even if it's not. She keeps trying to give me credit for eventually landing her dream job, but the truth is that I did less for Jess than I did for plenty of other clients who failed. *She* did it. *She* beat success into submission through sheer, workmanlike effort and grit.

Most people don't realize this is happening, and that's sad because if you can't see it, you can't fix it. We've been conditioned to believe that everything can be accomplished through a series of simple steps, and as a result, we tend to look for systems to do things. We want to push a button, pull a lever, then sit back and wait for achievement to manifest. If it's not that easy, most people will decide it can't be done.

If that last sentence seems absurd, think about people you know who want to lose weight or get in shape, including yourself. There isn't much more to it than "burn more calories than you consume," and that holds true for almost everyone. Weight loss takes effort and willpower, but it's not complicated. Yet, when people declare that they "can't lose weight," it's rare that they've faithfully and rigorously recorded their caloric intake and expenditures for months. They know what to do, but can't find ways to make themselves do the hard work required to make it happen.

Almost everything you'd ever want to achieve is *simple*, but that doesn't mean it's *easy*. Know the difference. Embrace it, and you'll have a chance of breaking free from the hypnosis.

"Simple" refers to complexity of the steps involved. Self-publishing — even after this entire book's worth of detailed how-to — at root isn't that complicated. There are a lot of details and possibilities, but this book's core message is to write a lot of good books and connect with your readers. That advice is simple, but it isn't *easy* at all — which is why most people who decide to make a career of self-publishing will ultimately quit.

Very few people will ever do the work required to get what they want.

The good news is if you're one of the few who *will* do the work, the world is your oyster.

Over-Deliver

Here's an obvious truth: If you're awesome to your readers, they will want to read more of your stuff. If you want readers who stick around and keep buying — and readers who tell their friends and hence gain you more readers — you should do your best to give them exactly what they want ... then give them more, and more, and more.

The book you're holding was originally on the Realm & Sands production calendar as a 50,000-word project. That's a decent length for a nonfiction how-to book, and we figured we could cover the basics of what we knew about building a publishing business in that space. We were wrong, and quickly realized that 60,000 words was a safer bet. I adjusted my schedule accordingly. Then Sean wrote the outline, and when we both worked our way through it in one of our meetings, we realized it would have to be 80,000 words.

I wasn't pleased from a scheduling standpoint, because we already had an insane amount of stuff to finish before year's end. Those 30,000 extra words hurt, especially after the project before *Write. Publish. Repeat.* (our *Beam*-world book *Plugged*) went several days longer than planned. I knew I'd have to work a few weekends to make it all happen, and I *hate* working weekends. But I sucked it up.

At around the 65,000-word mark, I e-mailed Sean a screen shot showing him the structure of my Scrivener file, detailing what I'd covered in the first draft so far. We compared the screen shot to the original outline and decided that the book would need to top 100,000 words just for our portion, plus Dave's interviews.

We couldn't afford to spend the time, but couldn't afford *not* to, either. As much as we wanted to rein in the project, it would have been an asshole move to withhold large sections of content from our readers, so we made it happen. And although we'd originally planned to sell a 50,000-word book for $4.99, we decided to raise the price by just a dollar for the finished book that was more than twice as long.

We love you guys, but this wasn't purely an altruistic move. In part, we made the decisions we made — increasing the book's length and taking a decent dollars-per-word hit — because we wanted this book to be as simple of a yes for readers as possible. We want this to be *the* guide to self-publishing, and in order for it to be *the* guide, it's not enough for it to be good. It must be outstanding. It must make readers say, "Wow, this is so much more than I expected."

If you keep that in mind, your readers will find ways to reward you, with repeat sales, loyalty, and sterling word of mouth.

Don't Buy Into Writer's Block

Writer's block is usually a habit, or a manifestation of resistance.

We don't want to be dismissive, because for a writer who's felt writer's block, the experience can be downright painful. But in our experience, you can reduce it to a species of fear that has nothing to do with the story itself. You might be afraid of finishing the story and having to show the world — or have to admit your fear by sticking it into a closet forever. You might be afraid of being judged. You might be afraid of writing a story or a plot that's stupid by your definition, as if you wouldn't later be able to revise the stupid right out of it.

A writer's best friend is momentum. For this reason, Sean recommends writing every day, and I recommend writing no fewer than five days a week. We both recommend writing fast for reasons having to do with momentum. Writing fast isn't about producing a lot of words as much as it's about outrunning doubts. Keep moving. And moving. And moving. Just keep putting words on the page, even if you think they suck. Commit to getting words down onto the page, even if they're awful. Why do you care? No one will see them. If you give yourself that permission to suck, you might find that simply getting those words out clears your blockage, and paves the way for better words.

If you can get used to doing those things — refusing to stop moving even if you start to feel blocked, maintaining your momentum, and writing through the suck — pretty soon, your sense of flow will feel like habit, too.

One of the biggest questions any writer is asked — and if you've ever told someone you're a writer, you may have heard it yourself — is, "Where do you get your ideas?" We get that a lot, and I think it's because we write in so many different story worlds. At first glance, it seems like we must have a lot of ideas. *Greens* is about a grocery store worker who decides to sell pot, but ends up selling something entirely different in a teetering house of cards. *Cursed* is about a man who becomes a chupacabra and must kill to purge. *Namaste* is about a monk from a peaceful but highly trained order who snaps and goes on a rather Zen homicidal rampage.

If you're a Realm & Sands fan, you're going to think a lot of these turned out to be pretty great ideas, and you might put your face in your palm, lamenting the fact that you didn't have those great ideas first. But the truth is the other way around: we don't have great ideas; we have random ideas and then make them great. The idea of a gunslinger riding a unicorn or an out-of-shape vampire were incredibly stupid when we came up with them, but we like to think that by the time *Unicorn Western* and *Fat Vampire* were finished, they were damned cool ideas.

Here's the Realm & Sands secret for coming up with good ideas for your writing. Are you ready? It's pretty complicated.

Anything is a good idea.

Got that? *Anything.* An idea is a concept. It's what you do with that idea — the directions you take it and how you articulate the story world — that fill it out and put meat on its bones. This was such a delightful epiphany for Sean and me that we started to take requests.

After our Outlaws suggested that we write *Caveman Timecop* for their free weekly serial, we had to figure out what tale we would tell. We tossed ideas around, and Sean came up with the idea that a future member of the time police could be sent back in time to restore the work of criminals in prehistoric times. We wanted it to be light and satirical but not absurd, so we based it in logic (there's a very definite reason he goes back, and a very definite mythology) but filled it with funny situations, most involving ridiculous caveman antics. Then I wrote it, filling in details and discovering new aspects of the story as I went along.

And in the end, yes, we thought it was a pretty good idea.

411

Consider Outside-the-Box Income

If you want to truly kill it in publishing, think outside the box. You can make money publishing, but you can also make money — and grow your name and brand — in ways that are related to and supported by writing and publishing but that aren't writing and publishing themselves.

This is all highly optional, but if you have the time, inclination, and bandwidth, diversification horizontally (into other disciplines) can make for great synergy with — and add a degree of stability to — your ongoing vertical expansion (getting deeper into publishing with more books).

Here are a few ways you may want to consider broadening your base:

Consulting

This is mostly for nonfiction authors, but if you have expertise in an area, you can often make good income by consulting. Certain disciplines are more amenable to consulting than others (business management authors will probably get more consulting clients than authors who write about making macaroni art), but this can make for a great sideline if you truly know your topic and can help the people who hire you to succeed.

Speaking

One of the many reasons Sean and I have for writing this book is that we want to expand into public speaking. We want to do this in order to diversify our income, but we also love to speak and like the idea of getting paid to travel. Speaking, for us, is a natural outgrowth of what we do each week on *SPP*. And hey, if you want to be paid to speak, you need authority in an area, and a portfolio piece. This book works as both. *Write. Publish. Repeat.*, in turn, was possible because we were already podcasting about self-publishing. (And, to add to the chain of veracity, we can really only speak with any authority on the podcast because we're successfully publishing as much fiction as we are.)

If you're writing in an area amenable to getting speaking gigs — sorry again, macaroni art authors — your books may help you land them. To bring things full circle, you can usually also sell books at your speaking gigs. Now *that's* synergy!

Affiliate Income

This a minor point, but if you go back to the section where we describe using Scrivener as a writing tool and click on that link, it will take you to a tools page on the *Self Publishing Podcast* website. Some of the tools on that page have affiliate links to the tools themselves. If you buy something from the page and use any given item's affiliate link, we will receive a commission for referring you.

Affiliate selling is its own field, and we won't go into it here, but if there are ways to get those kinds of referral fees in your topic area, you might as well take advantage of them. Just be honest with your readers that you'll earn if they buy, and always keep things non-pushy and aboveboard.

Supplementary E-Products

Again for nonfiction authors, if readers in your topic area might benefit from a digital course (video instructionals, audio content, comprehensive how-to, and best tips), creating those courses can be a great way to earn income. Joanna Penn does this on her website at TheCreativePenn.com, and suggests that other authors consider doing the same.

Like affiliate marketing, creating e-products is a topic in itself, and we won't go into it here, but there's plenty of information out there. Don't spend a fortune; both fields are rife with good, honest teaching and dodgy scams in equal measure.

CHAPTER TWENTY-ONE:
Write. Publish. Repeat.

WELCOME TO THE CHAPTER WHERE we bring this whole thing full circle.

We've given you a lot of details about what has worked for us throughout this book, because writing it all out was like opening a series of nested Russian dolls. We started with the question, "What do we know about self-publishing?" but inside that question were thoughts on production, marketing, mentality, and tactical distribution across multiple platforms. Within marketing, we had to explain funnels, but within funnels we needed to explain CTAs. And so on and so on, down what felt like a maze with a million branches.

Given the amount of detail in this book — and given how it's sprawled to over twice its original intended length — it would be easy to feel overwhelmed and think that self-publishing is complicated. But it's *not* ... or at least, it doesn't need to be. Within the universe of this book, 80 percent of what matters to your publishing career is encapsulated by the book's title.

Write.

Publish.

Repeat.

As we draw this book to a close, we want you to keep that in mind. Nothing in this book works if you don't have at least a few books and/or keep producing more. Nothing happens if your work sucks, or if you get mired in indecision and analysis paralysis and refuse to push the "publish" button.

Always be writing the next book. That's your best move at most times, especially when you're new.

The rest is details.

So, in closing, let's cover a few of the ways — at a nice, high, strategic and non-tactical level — that you can write, publish, and repeat.

Series vs. Serials vs. Standalones

We write in three primary structures.

Standalone books are what they sound like: books that don't relate to others and hence "stand alone." Of all of our books, only Sean's memoir *Writer Dad,* my first novel *The Bialy Pimps*, and *Write. Publish. Repeat.* are true standalone books. *Plugged* is a hybrid — it's almost a standalone, but it's also written in the world of *The Beam,* as if it were a kind of unofficial sequel in the series chain. Sean and Dave have standalone books coming before the end of the year, both ghost stories (*Crashed* and *Threshold*), but because the Collective Inkwell publishes in the same genre, all their titles feed into each other. Same with all the kids' stuff we publish under the pen name Guy Incognito.

Series novels or **novellas** follow one another in a logical chain. Series novels should open and close a major storyline or adventure in each book and have a satisfying conclusion for the reader — but beyond that story, there is a larger story arc. Some sequels are merely one-after-the-other tales with recurring characters and motifs but without much of a story beyond them, such as the old *Nancy Drew* books for kids. Others have a major story that evolves slowly behind the plot of any particular book, such as Harry's percolating relationship with Voldemort in the *Harry Potter* novels. Each of those books has its own arc, but the series isn't over until Harry and Voldemort go toe-to-toe. *Fat Vampire* and the core *Unicorn Western* novellas are series books. Series books can end in soft cliffhangers as long as the main plot of the book is resolved. The idea is to close one story and then open a small "wound" that makes readers curious about the next book.

Serials are stories with continuing plotlines — usually several — which are ongoing and are never truly resolved until the series ends. At the end of an installment (or episode), all plotlines pause, to be resumed within the next episode or two. At least one storyline ends in a cliffhanger that is pretty aggressive. The idea is to make the reader say, "WHAT THE HELL; I HAVE TO KNOW WHAT'S NEXT!" like they would at the end of a tense TV show. If you do this in a series novel (a hard, unresolved cliffhanger rather than a softer one that comes after the book's main storyline's resolution), readers will be pissed. We organize serials in collections called "seasons," again using the television metaphor. As with TV, seasons conclude the serial for a while, resolve a few of the season's big questions, and open something new to fester until the next one. At least one of the story lines will end on a season cliffhanger. Season cliffhangers are serious ball-busters and should feel urgent enough that your reader will simultaneously love you and want to punch you in the face. You've written a great season cliffhanger if, when in the same room as a beta reader, you hear that reader say, "OH, YOU SON OF A BITCH!" Readers of *Yesterday's Gone* were angry with Sean and Dave in the most wonderful way after the end of that series' second season. *The Beam* is Realm & Sand's biggest serial.

All three structures have their place, and readers want and will buy all of them. We tend to trust the project, seeing what it feels like as we create it. We thought *Namaste* and *Cursed* would both be serials (the first bits of each were written at around the same time as *Robot Proletariat*, which did become one), but *Namaste* felt like a standalone novel and *Cursed* felt like a series. All have their place, but serials and series have the most compelling "gotta get the next one," and that's the sort of thing you want to drive sales. For the opposite reason, standalones are often harder to sell, and you may choose to only write them for a specific reason, as we did with *Plugged* (to have more in the world of *The Beam* without writing a full second season).

Fiction vs. Nonfiction

We've already talked about some of the writing and marketing differences between fiction and nonfiction, but let's talk a little here about why you might choose to write one or the other.

To start with, you may not have a choice. You may not consider yourself a storyteller, but may know a ton about birdwatching. In that case, you'll write nonfiction about birds, and build your business, marketing, and brand accordingly. Alternatively, you may not think of yourself as a left-brained, organized, fact-oriented writer, and may only write fiction.

Just as we love to hop genres, we like to leap modalities as well. If you're like us, you may find which to write is a choice no different from writing in a genre — or writing a standalone, series, or serial novels. In that case, you'll need to identify your goals, ask yourself how each book will serve you, serve your readership's interests and needs, and what you feel most like writing.

Plugged was mostly fiction, but much of it was based in current, modern-day reality and required research. It was also written like nonfiction and was designed to, through fictional means, address real, nonfictional truths about the world. For us, the decision to write *Plugged* felt like a decision to write nonfiction. We wrote it be because it suited our needs at the time: to answer "world questions" raised by our *Beam* die-hards as well as to answer those questions for ourselves. Because *The Beam* world is so big and realized, we wanted to approach it as cultural anthropologists rather than as novelists, so it became what it is.

This book had a different goal. Sean and I have two audiences: our fiction readers at Realm & Sands and our podcast listeners at the *Self Publishing Podcast*. We wrote this book to satisfy the second group, but we also did it with the ninja intention of cross-pollinating those two audiences. We figure that some of our fiction readers might like this book and our podcast (which both exist to give us credibility as speakers), and we similarly figure that some of the writers who read this book will be interested in checking out the fiction they've been reading about. Publishing this nonfiction book also allowed Sean and I to tap our substantial experience and networks in the nonfiction writing and marketing worlds, which we could never do with our fiction. Smart new-wave authors use the tools at their disposal — and if they can't use those tools using their current M.O., they'll find a way. (Like, say, writing a nonfiction book that allows for all of those juicy nonfiction promotion avenues.)

If you're a multi-discipline, multifaceted writer who's interested in and able to write both fiction and nonfiction, consider your choice about which to do as you'd consider any other creative and marketing decision. Write to your muse and your enjoyment, with an unblinking eye on the market.

Produce Like a Maniac

The one thing we haven't explicitly addressed in this book is exactly *how* we produce as much work as we do. We've told you all about the tools we use and how we script story beats, write product descriptions, craft product funnels, and do our promotions. Behind all of that, we've given you examples, and those examples amount to around 1.5 million published words in 2013. But we haven't told you how we do it.

We toyed with the idea of including a big productivity section in this book, explaining the tools and techniques we use — me to write 35,000-50,000 words of first draft copy per week and Sean to write several thousand words a day while storyboarding and editing not just my work, but his work with Dave, himself, *and* other writers (including some mentoring with Lexi). But we also knew, given the way the rest of this book has unfolded, just how deep that rabbit hole would go. (For instance, I've told you that I write with a timer — but how specifically I use it and how I trained myself to beat it are both subtopics, each with subtopics beneath them.)

We decided to save our energy and your precious time, and to end this book here — at its already enormous size — instead of droning on for another 100,000 words. We have a lot more stories yet to tell, and every hour you spend reading this book is an hour you aren't writing your own. The title of this book isn't *Read. Analyze. Read Some More.* It's *Write. Publish. Repeat.*

We've already said the difference between success and failure in most things — and self-publishing is no exception — is a matter of keeping your butt in the chair and doing the work.

And so with that said, we'll finish up here. We *will* write that book about "how to write like a machine" in the next year, though, so if you'd like it, be sure to join our list so that we can let you know when it's ready, at SelfPublishingPodcast.com/repeater.

You have work to do.

Now get to writing.

APPENDIX:
Interviews With Successful Indie Authors

Introduction

THROUGHOUT THIS BOOK, YOU'VE READ our thoughts on what it takes to be successful. But what about the other self-publishers out in the trenches, getting the job done? What are *they* doing? What makes *them* successful?

We've had some amazing, full-time indie authors on the *Self Publishing Podcast*, so Dave asked if he could interview them for this book. We thought that was a great idea, and we've included those interviews here.

All of the interviews were conducted via email, so we've pasted all responses as they were sent. This is what it takes to build an indie career, folks — straight from the self-published horse's mouth!

Hugh Howey

HUGH HOWEY SPENT EIGHT YEARS as a yacht captain before giving up the seafaring life and taking up writing. His *New York Times* bestselling *Wool* series has been translated into more than thirty languages and was optioned for a feature film by Ridley Scott and Steve Zaillian. He lives in Jupiter, Florida with his wife Amber and their dog Bella. When he isn't writing, he's taking pictures or talking to strangers.

DAVE: What is your daily writing/work schedule like? (Please feel free to include non-writing tasks which are integral to your writing success.)

HUGH: I do most of my writing in the morning. I get up, collect the newspaper from the driveway, eat a bowl of cereal while I catch up on what's going on in the world, and then I write until lunchtime. I take my dog for a walk on the beach in the middle of the day, and this is when I clear my mind and think about where my current story is heading. In the afternoon, I answer emails and do all the business-related stuff. These days, my routine is broken up quite a bit with constant travels, but I hope to wind that down soon.

DAVE: What are the hardest and easiest parts of writing a book for you? How long does the typical book take you from start to final draft?

HUGH: The hardest part is the first draft. I like having words to manipulate, a plot to improve, sentences to rewrite. I have to really motivate myself and force myself to get that first draft done, which is why I set daily word count goals. Once I have this draft, I love performing revision after revision. I edit the book from beginning to end eight or nine times until I can't find anything else to change.

As for how long it takes, I've written novels in a month before, but the typical time from start to completion is now around three to four months. This has stretched out as I've become busier and have been traveling more. I also have a healthier work/life balance these days, though I probably still work harder than I ought to.

DAVE: What have been the key factors to your success?

HUGH: Stubbornness and ignorance. I never gave up, and I didn't have decades of experience in the publishing industry to tell me that my ideas were dumb. I went with what seemed logical to me, which is a huge boon in any industry experiencing turmoil. The experts are too busy trying to salvage the old way. It's the naïve and eager noobs who forge a new path and thrive. We are the tiny shrews cowering in the trees when the meteor strikes. Wide-eyed and following our noses, we find our way blindly and brilliantly.

DAVE: What's the best writing advice you've ever gotten (or read somewhere)?

HUGH: Just write. It was Caroline Todd who told me this. Well, she told an entire room full of aspiring writers this, but I swear she was yelling at me. Someone asked what they needed to do to become a writer, and Caroline slapped the table and yelled at us to stop dreaming of becoming writers and talking about becoming writers and just sit down and write. It's obvious advice, but it worked on me. I went home and pounded out my first novel. I haven't looked back.

DAVE: What's been your biggest mistake as a writer and how did you bounce back?

HUGH: I didn't hire an assistant a year ago when I needed one. I haven't bounced back from this, as I haven't remedied the mistake. The regret runs deeper every day, but now I don't even know where I'd find the time to train someone up. There's also the problem of trusting someone to put the same care and energy into even simple tasks that I like to pour into them. This is one of the (many) reasons I prefer self-publishing over traditional publishing. I've watched major publishing houses get the simplest of things dead-wrong while thinking they're doing them correctly. It's painful to place your art and career in the hands of others when you are willing to put in the long hours and hard work to do it the best you possibly can for yourself.

DAVE: What do you think traditional publishers should learn from indie writers? What things should indie writers learn from traditional publishers?

HUGH: That could be an entire book. Indies are doing well because of their willingness to experiment, their willingness to share data and lessons with other writers, and their unflinching habit of placing the reader first.

Publishers should experiment with free titles, especially first books in a series. They should lower the price of backlist titles (and do more price-pumping). They need to get rid of non-compete clauses and celebrate more prodigious output from their authors. They need to stop worrying about media reviews and stop placing primacy on sending ARCs out to critics and bookstores and instead release the ebook as soon as the copyediting is done. Allow readers to signal and build demand.

They should release paperbacks and hardbacks simultaneously and discover what every other retailer knows: upselling works. People will buy the hardback and calculate the cost of the book as the difference between the two formats, not the actual cost. They need to bundle formats for readers by giving away ebooks and audiobooks with hardback purchases. Man, I could go on for ages.

What can indies learn? That polished work breeds trust. Gorgeous cover art and mistake-free interiors are the way to draw readers in and have them come back for more.

DAVE: How has the success of *Wool* changed your life (and your writing?)

HUGH: *Wool* allowed me to become a full-time writer, which has been great. I get to sit around in my underwear at work, which used to get me into a lot of trouble. For the most part, it means being at home with my dog and keeping up with house chores during the day. But it has also meant a lot of time on the road of late. I've been on over 50 flights this year to as many cities in nearly a dozen countries. My life has turned right-side-up in a most violent manner.

I don't know how it has affected my writing. I like to think I'm growing as a writer. I work hard on my craft, and it helps to know that a ton of people are going to read my scribblings.

DAVE: Where do you see the state of publishing in the next 5 years?

HUGH: I think it depends on how books compete with other forms of entertainment. Television and the Internet are gushing fonts of entertainment. And this entertainment is practically free, because hardly anyone goes without TV and Internet. Both are seen as necessary as electricity and water these days, and sadly, books are not.

Our industry is heavily reliant on the avid readers that gobble down dozens of books a year. If we lose them to some other form of entertainment, the book industry will go the way of theater and opera. If that seems crazy to consider, get in your time machine and see how nuts people were over opera not that long ago. We never believe in change until years after it happened.

If I had to bet, I would wager that Barnes & Noble will be gone in 5 years. Indie bookshops will survive by catering to their communities and inviting readers and writers to come together for more planned events (and selling lots of coffee). Books will be printed on demand to cut the waste of predicting print runs, and the returns system will be abolished to save on needlessly shipping unread books back and forth. Ebooks will account for 70% of books sold. Digital and interactive textbooks will finally be the norm in American universities. And vampires will be hip again.

DAVE: Obviously having the success you've had opens doors to you. But do you find that it's also limited you in any way? If so, how do you deal with the limitations or heightened expectations?

HUGH: A lot of doors have opened, for sure. I've stepped through a few of them, taking up offers to attend conferences, speak at libraries, bookstores, and museums. I've traveled all over the world for my foreign publishers, and I've been blessed to work with some amazing people at some of the largest publishing houses.

But many of the doors that opened for me, I have decided not to walk through. I've had offers from publishers that I would have killed for a few years ago, and I've turned them down. I have publishers making offers on the next thing I write, but the next thing I write might be so completely different that I know better than to take them up on the offers.

The challenge is to just be myself, ignore the success, disbelieve it, and continue to write for the love of writing. I write for my wife and my mother and myself. I tell myself every single day that this is the apex of my career, to enjoy it while it lasts, because tomorrow I will sink back to reality. And that expectation both helps me appreciate where I am and stay grounded to where I feel I deserve to be.

DAVE: What do you want your legacy to be?

HUGH: I don't want a legacy for myself. My books, maybe. I'm going to leave behind a handful of stories that I hope people will read long after I'm dead and find some sliver of enjoyment. I'm still trying to cope with the idea that I entertain strangers. To imagine that I might leave behind something that entertains a person who is not even born yet, who will read my stories long after I'm gone, that's a mark on the world I never dreamed I would make. And it's more than enough.

Find out more about Hugh and his work at hughhowey.com

CJ Lyons

CJ LYONS IS A *NEW York Times* and *USA Today* bestselling author of twenty-one novels. As a former pediatric ER doctor, CJ has lived the life she writes about in her cutting edge "Thrillers with Heart."

Winner of the International Thriller Writers' coveted Thriller Award, CJ has been called a "master within the genre" *(Pittsburgh Magazine)* and her work has been praised as "breathtakingly fast-paced" and "riveting" (*Publishers Weekly*) with "characters with beating hearts and three dimensions" (*Newsday*).

CJ is also what we call a "hybrid" author. She has both self-published and traditionally published novels.

DAVE: What is your daily writing/work schedule like? (Please feel free to include non-writing tasks which are integral to your writing success.)

CJ: I'm terribly undisciplined—I don't plot or outline, I don't keep track of my word count, I don't write every day, I don't even write in order! I actually have written entire novels literally backward, starting with the final scene! All I need is a deadline—give me that and I'll beat it every time. I spend very little time marketing—my belief is that my best marketing is writing the next book, so I concentrate my time and energy on new projects.

One thing people should keep in mind is that this is hard work. I actually work more hours a day and more days a week as a writer than I ever did as a physician.

DAVE: What are the hardest and easiest parts of writing a book for you? How long does the typical book take you from start to final draft?

CJ: The first draft is the easiest part—I tend to blitz write it, have fun, not worry about false starts or logic pitfalls since this draft is selfishly for me, me, me. It's where I get to play and discover the story.

The second draft is the toughest part. This is where I actually need to work and divorce my ego from the process. This draft is when I re-envision the entire story (now that I've discovered it in the first draft) and slice and dice and rework it any way necessary to make it worthy of my audience. At every step of the way I ask myself: is this decision going to delight and excite my readers?

My goal is to take my story and turn it into something so great readers won't think twice about spreading the word. I want it to have such impact that they WANT to talk about it with their friends.

DAVE: What have been the key factors to your success?

CJ: Because my writing career had a disastrous start (my debut novel was cancelled by my NYC publisher 90 days before publication because of cover art issues) I quickly took control of my career and immersed myself in the business side of things: learning how to write copy, following marketing blogs, understanding branding, etc.

Then the light bulb moment came: if I'm CEO of Me, Inc, then any publishers I work with, work FOR me ... they're strategic partners, subcontractors. My challenge wasn't would I ever be published but HOW would I be published.

To answer that question, I began with my WHY (thanks to the wonderful Simon Sinek's book explaining this concept). Why do I want to write? Why this book? Why would my readers fall in love with this story? Why would they want to take the time to share it with friends?

That's when I realized what my brand was: Thrillers with Heart. In other words, my stories, no matter where in the thriller-suspense genre they fall, aren't about the fast-paced action or adrenaline rush, they're about ordinary people facing the worst day of their lives and finding the courage to stand up and become heroes.

My stories explore the grey area between the black and white of good and evil. My brand, Thrillers with Heart, is the emotional promise I make to my readers. As long as I keep that promise, I can easily cross genre boundaries without disappointing my readers.

In sum, start with your WHY, use that to take control of your career, build your global publishing empire, and build your brand.

DAVE: What's the best writing advice you've ever gotten (or read somewhere)?

CJ: The best advice I've received came after the publication of my first book, LIFELINES. I was sitting beside Jeffery Deaver at an awards banquet (both of our books won, yeah!) and asked him what advice he had for someone at my stage: one book out and a second due to be released.

His reply: *Always remember, the reader is god.*

Simple. Easy to think, oh sure, of course …but then I realized what an absolute game-changer those words were. Since then they've guided every decision. Should I spend time blogging or writing? My readers want more books, so I spend my time working on the next book.

I also keep this piece of advice foremost when I'm revising. My first draft is selfishly for me, me, me. But the second draft is totally focused on the reader. What will inspire and delight and surprise them? What will evoke emotion? Is it the emotion I'm aiming for? What will pull them into the story and make them miss their bus stop?

Suddenly, thanks to that advice from Jeffery Deaver, every fork in the tortuous path from idea to finished novel, is clear. Given that writing a novel and guiding it through the labyrinth that is publishing is a complicated and chaotic process, having these simple words to light the path has been invaluable.

DAVE: What's been your biggest mistake as a writer and how did you bounce back?

CJ: My biggest mistakes have all revolved around trusting people (and publishing companies ARE people) to do what they say (or what their contract says) they'll do.

I put 120% into everything I do — my readers deserve it. I don't make a promise I can't keep, I don't miss deadlines, I will always show up with my best work and yet ready to take any suggestions that I feel will make it better.

Not everyone is like that, from established traditional publishers who don't abide by their own contracts or do their jobs to independent contractors. But why should they be? Why should they care about your readers or your book?

You have to take responsibility for anything that has your name on it. You need to take ownership of your career.

No one else on the face of this planet is going to care as much or as passionately as you do.

Once you understand that, you realize your mistakes are simply necessary course corrections and that what you learn from them is more valuable than anything you might have lost.

DAVE: What do you think traditional publishers should learn from indie writers? What things should indie writers learn from traditional publishers?

CJ: I think traditional publishers need to learn how to connect with readers—most of them have no clue who their readers are! All they know are the handful of distributors they sell to. Sadly, even now many publishers simply don't care about the people who spend their time and money on their authors' books. Whereas indie writers not only care about our readers, we're devoted to them, encouraging conversation, constantly striving to write books of our heart that will inspire and empower our readers.

But traditional publishers do do one thing right. They know how to make a book, especially a printed one, an event, like what one of my publishers, Sourcebooks, has done with my YA debut, BROKEN. It's been a delight partnering with them and I've learned so much! We can learn a lot from traditional publishers on how to do that—or better yet, partner with them.

DAVE: Where do you see the state of publishing in the next 5 years?

CJ: I see a web of strategic partnerships bridging the gaps between traditional publishers and indies; indies and a community of freelance artists, editors, formatters, and marketing experts; indies branching into joint venture type partnerships with translators, media producers such as TV/film and video games; and readers reaching for stories in whatever container they most enjoy (audio, video, ebook, print) and immersing themselves in rich, brilliant new worlds, reaping the benefits.

Wait … most of that is happening today! But in small islands scattered around the world. I think in a few years this will not only be commonplace but instead of the hard work it takes now to establish these partnerships, there will be an easily accessed marketplace where authors can communicate, share advice and knowledge, and form these essential partnerships.

Last year someone asked me what the key word in publishing would be for 2013 and I answered "strategic partnerships." I think next year it will be "synergy."

Because despite the misnomer "indie" or even "self-published" you can't truly succeed in this business without forming a team. In fact, the only real difference between indie publishing and traditional publishing is who leads that team: a CEO in NYC or the author acting as his own CEO of his own Global Publishing Empire.

Unfortunately, I see another of my predictions from last year coming true: market saturation. As traditional publishers encroach on what was originally indie territory using price pulsing and loss-leaders and as indie publishers increase the quality of their packaging to rival traditional publishers, readers can no longer tell the difference.

Which is great for them—they can gleefully load their e-readers with free and heavily discounted books, saving tons of money and having enough reading material to last them years ... only now readers are showing signs of fatigue. They think twice about buying even free books, knowing how many books are sitting unread in their devices.

And with so many writers discovering the ease of indie publishing, there is also more supply than there is demand.

I always say that writers aren't in competition with each other—readers read faster than any one writer can write. BUT for the next year or so, we will be in competition with ourselves in the form of the books already bought and waiting to be read. And we'll all be in competition for audience attention.

That's why it's so important to build your brand: your emotional promise to your readers that you keep with every book. Focus on keeping THOSE readers happy (not every single person on the planet with an e-reader or smart phone) and even in the dry times, you'll have a base income that can support you while you write the next great book.

DAVE: You've developed quite a community of readers and reviewers. What are some things that writers should do to better connect with their audience?

CJ: There is no right answer to this, other than do what will give you so much joy and energy that your writing sings and your readers leap for joy. Play to your strengths.

For me, that means focusing on the next book. It's by far my best marketing tool and the best way I can excite and engage my audience.

Along the way I've tried blogging for readers—I don't have the voice and the time and energy drained me so it was difficult to write on days I blogged. It simply wasn't my strength or my passion, so I quit. Same with twitter and Facebook. I use them very rarely.

But I can manage a once a month newsletter, chatting with my readers—I also love answering my fan mail (I mean, who wouldn't? How cool is it to actually even get fan mail everyday?) and since I'm also an avid reader, I love stopping by when readers are chatting about books (not necessarily mine) so I began a Goodreads Thrillers with Heart group.

Follow your bliss, your passion, your strengths. It's the best way to be authentic and protect your time and energy so you can do what your readers really want: write more great books.

DAVE: You talked about wanting to write sci-fi again. How much pressure do you feel to stay within the genres where you've found success? How would you deal with reader expectations?

CJ: I don't feel any pressure about genres—I do occasionally get pressure from readers who fall in love with a series or character and want more stories faster than I can write, but that's not necessarily a bad thing. A little anticipation can lead to increased excitement around a release.

I knew from Day One that I didn't want to be pigeonholed into writing any one genre, whether it was medical suspense or romantic thrillers or mainstream. That's why I created my own genre, Thrillers with Heart, and have built my brand around it. I always give my readers that essential "heart," characters who are ordinary people finding the courage to stand up and make a difference, sometimes with a romance, sometimes with a family at the center, sometimes it's one character struggling as they face their greatest fear.

I also work very hard not to allow my books to become at all formulaic—another way to keep my readers on their toes and give them the unexpected with each book. For instance, my bestselling Lucy Guardino FBI Thriller series starts with SNAKE SKIN, a straightforward police procedural; then BLOOD STAINED, a very dark and devious psychological suspense novel; followed by KILL ZONE, a high impact thriller that takes place in less than four hours; and the new story, AFTER SHOCK (out Jan 7th, 2014) ricochets back and forth between two timelines eight hours apart as it builds in intensity.

But despite the different techniques and storytelling styles, each of these stories is at its heart the tale of a Pittsburgh soccer mom struggling to balance work and family—only when your job is catching predators and saving lives, where do you draw the line?

That universal "heart" increases readers' identification with Lucy—her struggles are their struggles—and keeps them coming back asking for "More Lucy, please!"

DAVE: What do you want your legacy to be?

CJ: Ironic that you ask that since the name of my publishing "label" is Legacy Books. I did that both as a play on words and because my books are my legacy to my family. The awesome thing is that thanks to my readers, I've already created my legacy: my family is provided for and I've been able to establish the Buy a Book, Make a Difference program that has raised over $74,000 for charity and provided 54 scholarships for police officers from underserved communities to receive CSI/forensic training.

In other words, my readers and I are helping to keep the bad guys from getting away with murder right here and now! Who could ask for a better legacy?

Learn more about CJ's Thrillers with Heart at CJLyons.net and everything she knows about being a bestseller at NoRulesJustWRITE.com

David Gaughran

DAVID GAUGHRAN IS AN IRISH author, living in Prague, who spends most of his time traveling the world, collecting stories. He's the author of the South American historical adventure *A Storm Hits Valparaiso* and the popular self-publishing guides *Let's Get Digital* and *Let's Get Visible*. He blogs about writing and the book business on his authority site "Let's Get Digital."

DAVE: What is your daily writing/work schedule like? (Please feel free to include non-writing tasks which are integral to your writing success.)

DAVID: My process is so borked that I'm kinda loathe to share, but here it goes. When writing non-fiction, everything is pretty smooth. I bash out a chapter or two on the laptop in the morning, and then print it out and clean it up in the afternoon. Books tend to get written pretty quickly.

I find fiction more challenging and production is much slower. For starters, I write it by hand. I've tried writing fiction straight-to-laptop but it tends to be much drier, and riddled with plot holes. When all is going well, I tend to write new chapters in the afternoon, and type them up the following morning to let my brain get to grips with the story again before the next writing session. Often that takes place outside the house, and away from the internet... for obvious reasons.

When I get blocked, or write myself into a corner, I try and work on something else. If that doesn't work, or if the well has run dry, feeding the cultural parts of the brain always helps, whether that's with some clever TV, a terrible book, or just a long walk with some time alone in my own head. Good books work too, but reading something that's badly written often teaches you more. Maybe it's because the seams are visible, I don't know. But try it!

If all that fails, embrace boredom. I've had some of my best ideas, and untangled some of the worst plot knots, staring out the window of a bus. Smartphones are your enemy. Try and leave the internet at home when you venture into meatspace.

DAVE: What are the hardest and easiest parts of writing a book for you? How long does the typical book take you from start to final draft?

DAVID: It's all pretty atypical, to be honest. I can write a non-fiction book in a few weeks, but fiction can take forever. I am speeding up though, and trying to force myself to transition away from writing by hand.

What's hard or easy changes with each book. I guess you look at the last thing you wrote and try and identify the weaknesses and make sure you have improved with the next book. Otherwise, what's the point?

The ever-present challenges are ones of my own making. I get bored quite easily, which means that I switch genres a lot, and haven't (yet!) written a series. As such, I don't get to recycle characters or settings, and each "world" must be built anew. I'm not against the idea of writing a series, it's just that I haven't come up with an idea (yet!) that could keep me motivated across three, four, or five books. And if I'm bored writing it, you can be damn sure that readers will be bored reading it.

DAVE: What have been the key factors to your success?

DAVID: I think the Irish naturally bristle at the idea of being called successful; we don't embrace it naturally like Americans tend to. But my aim when starting this a couple of years ago was to make a living from books, and I've been doing that for about a year now, so I guess I've achieved some level of success. A lot of it is luck, but you can increase your chances of getting lucky by putting out a professional product, and being smart about how you set about attracting readers.

Don't be afraid to give your work away for free; it's a great, cheap way to build an audience. Don't be afraid to price your work cheaply, or promote yourself or your work. That's pretty basic stuff, but I'm amazed how many writers refuse to do any of that, thinking that they are somehow sullying their art. If that's your attitude, you might as well leave the book on your hard-drive. It will reach roughly the same amount of people. If you want to be read, you gotta hustle.

DAVE: What's the best writing advice you've ever gotten (or read somewhere)?

DAVID: It was from an amazing blog post by Austin Kleon, a blog post so amazing that he turned it into a book *(Steal Like an Artist)* which became a *New York Times* bestseller. The best bit was simple: write the book you want to read. The blog post is, sadly, no longer online, but it had a profound effect on me.

DAVE: What's been your biggest mistake as a writer and how did you bounce back?

DAVID: What a fiendish question! Off the top of my head, I guess I spent too long trying to perfect my first novel. I was so much in love with the story, and it was such an ambitious idea, that I took forever trying to pull it off.

I didn't know then two important things that I have since learned. First, there's no such thing as a perfect book, and if you try and write one you will never finish it. Second, and *much* more importantly, you will never step up as a writer until you start the *next* book. It's as if all the skills you learned writing one particular book don't get activated until you move on to something new.

DAVE: What do you think traditional publishers should learn from indie writers? What things should indie writers learn from traditional publishers?

DAVID: There are a million things publishers could learn from indies, if they weren't so snooty about grubby self-publishers, but I'll stick to the highlights: price cheaply, advertise, use social media to connect instead of broadcasting, run regular 99c sales, make the first book in a series free, don't use DRM, treat readers with respect, release in each format as soon as it's ready, publish quickly, treat Amazon as a partner in the business of selling books instead of an enemy who is trying to destroy the world, never treat the first book of a series as backlist but promote the hell out of it alongside each new installment, and format your books with care because nothing will bug power readers more.

And what can we learn from publishers? I struggle to answer that as the self-publishing hive mind seems to have already internalized everything that was worth learning, like having covers which speak to genre. There's a reason why chick-lit books tend to have a cartoonish blonde weighed down with shopping bags, or thrillers have a body or a gun or a crime scene on the cover, and it's not because publishers lack imagination. It's because you have two seconds to grab readers' attention and tell them what genre the book is. I think, a couple of years back, self-publishers tried to be a little different, but they learned that lesson pretty quickly.

DAVE: Where do you see the state of publishing in the next 5 years?

DAVID: More chaos! The publishing establishment seems to have convinced itself that it is managing the digital transition well, that ebooks are plateauing, and that Amazon Publishing has been something of a failure. None of this is based on anything that you or I would describe as reality. Things aren't settling down, far from it. I expect more disruption, the pace of change to increase rather than decrease, and for all of that to suit fast-moving, crowd-sourcing indies much more than unwieldy, insular publishers.

DAVE: How much has your writing blog affected your writing career? Do you feel that you've got a larger readership for your fiction because of the blog?

DAVID: I think people are generally surprised when they find out that popular blogs shift way less books than they think (and with Amazon affiliate tracking you can get a pretty clear idea). Obviously, my blog helps sell more of the non-fiction stuff, but, even then it's less than people suppose. I'm firmly of the opinion that author platforms (mailing list aside) don't really sell books. But boy can they *launch* them.

The distinction is crucial and kind of obvious when you think about it. If you have a few thousand people reading your blog every day, they can only buy your book once. They can't keep buying it, and they certainly won't still be buying it a few months later. But if you can get a decent chunk of them to buy your book in the first few days it's out, that concentration of sales will launch you up the charts, where you will suddenly become visible to thousands more readers who troll the charts looking for new reads. The same effect is present when you run a 99c sale or anything else like that.

So, yes, it helps, but not in the way you might think (but does in another cool way that I'm totally grateful for and shamelessly exploit!). I think you have to love blogging for its own sake, and not as some means to an end. I must say, though, that the blog has opened some doors for me, and I've got to meet a whole bunch of cool peeps.

DAVE: You talk a lot on your blog about predators taking advantage of writers. What are some of the things writers should beware of when it comes to self-publishing?

DAVID: Self-publishing is big business, and there are a whole bunch of companies that will promise to do it faster, cheaper, and better than you can do it yourself. And they are all full of it. At best, you will end up paying over the odds for basic services of questionable quality. At worst, you could get scammed for every penny you have, and be left with a shoddy book that no-one will read.

None of the successful self-publishers use one of these service companies to self-publish. All of them upload directly to Amazon themselves. The reasons: you get paid more, you get paid quicker, you have access to live sales reports (crucial for marketing), and you can make changes in hours instead of days or weeks (crucial for promotions).

This DIY approach doesn't mean you have to do *everything* yourself. You can hire help where needed (usually editing and cover design, and sometimes formatting).

DAVE: What do you want your legacy to be?

DAVID: Well, Hunter S. Thompson got his ashes shot out of a cannon to the tune of *Spirit in the Sky*, so that's taken. Like most writers, I want to write stories which make people laugh, or cry, or just forget the crap in their lives for a few hours.

Often there's a deeper message in the story, something I want readers to consider, or think about differently, or whatever, but I'm totally okay with readers simply enjoying my stuff and building statues of me when I die. Giant statues. Colossus of Rhodes size.

Be sure to check out David's excellent the self-publishing guides Let's Get Digital *and* Let's Get Visible, *as well as his blog about the book business at davidgaughran.wordpress.com*

Ed Robertson

ED ROBERTSON IS A SCIENCE fiction and fantasy author based in the LA area. His ebooks are available in stores around the world and his short stories have been published in a couple dozen magazines online and in print. He blogs about self-publishing.

DAVE: What is your daily writing/work schedule like? (Please feel free to include non-writing tasks which are integral to your writing success.)

ED: My fiancee's schedule varies every week, so mine does, too. But at the moment, I get up around 5, then spend the first couple hours catching up with my writing group, reading the self-publishing forum at KBoards, and getting fiancee off to work. I start writing around 7:30-8 AM and wrap up around 4-5 PM. The typical day is good for 2500-4000 words of first draft material.

I do that four or five days a week. On the other days, I get up a little later and quit a little sooner in the hopes fiancee will be less likely to murder me. So far, so good.

On these half days, I try to write at least 1K. It adds up. I'm not the world's fastest writer, but this gets me about 15-20K of new material a week, and 60-80K a month.

DAVE: What are the hardest and easiest parts of writing a book for you? How long does the typical book take you from start to final draft?

ED: The hardest part for me is probably the wool-gathering stage when I'm plotting a new book before I've dived into the actual draft. When I'm just sitting around trying to come up with ideas, there's less structure, and I lose focus. Editing is a bitch, too. I do a lot of sentence rewrites, it takes forever, and I'm always fighting to come up with the magic pixie dust to elevate the whole thing. It rarely hits the level I want it to and then I get cranky.

Easiest part is the beginning. I'm all excited to get into a new character's voice, and I don't have to sit there pounding my fists on the desk trying to figure out how in the heck I'm supposed to connect all these plot threads to the overall arc because there are no threads yet.

Typically, it takes me three months to finish a book: two months of first draft, one month of edits. Except when I'm being stupid and writing giant epic fantasy novels. Then it takes longer and I get to enjoy the feeling of watching my empire crumble before my eyes.

DAVE: What have been the key factors to your success?

ED: Writing every day. Where "writing" can include editing, formatting, publishing, etc. When you come up through the creative writing system, it's inculcated in you that writing is a sort of sorcery where each book may take years.

But the creative side is a developed skill, too; you can teach yourself how to break down plots piece by piece, generate new ideas, etc. If you put in full-time hours, you can get an incredible amount done. Multiple books a year, even if you're kind of slow like me.

On the business side, the key for me has been to try a whole bunch of different junk, then be super aggressive when I find something that's working. I try my best not to have any preconceived notions about my books' "value" or that Sales Idea X is a horrible idea that will leave the entire publishing landscape a cancerous wasteland. Right now, I'm selling a three-book set of my most popular series for just $0.99, because it's working. When it stops, I'll try something else. And probably fail a whole bunch. But if you keep trying, something new generally crops up to get you back on course.

DAVE: What's the best writing advice you've ever gotten (or read somewhere)?

ED: In terms of craft? I dunno, that every scene should be driven by conflict? That one was pretty useful.

DAVE: What's been your biggest mistake as a writer and how did you bounce back?

ED: My almost biggest mistake presented itself when a book I thought of as a standalone novel had a giant free giveaway followed by weeks of awesome sales. It clearly had lots of commercial potential, but I considered the story finished and

452

thought it would be selling out to write a sequel. Ha ha ha!

Fortunately, my writing group convinced me I was being an idiot. It took me a little while to figure out a way to continue the series in a way that excited me, but I might not have a career right now if I hadn't listened to them. I guess I bounced back by getting over myself and being open to opportunity.

DAVE: What do you think traditional publishers should learn from indie writers? What things should indie writers learn from traditional publishers?

ED: Indies have to fight tooth and nail because we have to or we'll starve. This giant anthill of struggling indiedom exposes all kinds of emergent behavior that trad publishers are already adapting to their own abilities — they're publishing series faster, being more daring with sale prices, etc. We're forced to work on the edge and take risks (often because we have nothing to lose) and that turns up all kinds of amazing information.

Trad publishers can serve indies as a constant reminder of how good we can be. Obviously they've got their share of duds and mediocrities, but trad houses publish some remarkable work, in terms of both packaging and content. The most successful indies seem to be those who make their work indistinguishable from those of a big publishing house. We can be that good, too.

DAVE: Where do you see the state of publishing in the next 5 years?

ED: Not much different. Maybe I lack imagination, but I think it just went through a phase transition and is now at a relatively stable equilibrium. It will fragment some more in the next few years, but I don't think it will be completely reinvented again for some time.

DAVE: What are some of the things that writers should pay attention to when it comes to other writers? I know that you track sales and rankings looking to find ways to get the most out of book sellers.

ED: Yeah, I like the numbers. I have less time for it now, but I used to do a lot of public analysis of how the various ebook vendors rewarded books with visibility. Indie authors are incredible about sharing information. Go take it from them!

I pay attention to what successful people are doing different and what they're doing the same. For instance, if everyone who's built a lasting career is using great covers and building a mailing list, you should probably do that too. And then if someone comes along and starts destroying the world with something new, like when you guys rode in on the Legion of Serials, it's supremely interesting to dive into that, try to figure out exactly why it's working, and see if there are any lessons you can apply to your own work/business.

DAVE: If you could go back in time to before you published your first book and give yourself one piece of advice what would it be?

ED: Pay for a real cover and make sure it is instantly recognizable as whatever genre it belongs to. Then immediately start writing the next book. I cheated! That's two advices.

ED: What do you want your legacy to be?

DAVE: Not a guy who died in a ditch. I dunno, in my dream world, I'd leave behind a body of cool SF/F stories for readers. For writers, it would be great to be someone who, in the early days of self-publishing, helped introduce a few analytical processes to a business that often feels like the Wild West. Is this a trick question to make us all sound like asses?

To check out Ed's books (including his hit Breakers series) or read his amazing self-publishing blog, visit www.EdwardWRobertson.com.

Joanna Penn

JOANNA PENN, WRITING AS J.F.PENN, is the author of the bestselling *ARKANE* thriller series, including the recent *One Day In Budapest*. Her new crime series begins with *Desecration*. Joanna also writes non-fiction, including the bestselling *How To Market A Book*.

DAVE: What is your daily writing/work schedule like? (Please feel free to include non-writing tasks which are integral to your writing success.)

JOANNA: I have a sign on my wall, "Have you made art today?" That drives me to create something new in the world every day — so that may be word count for a first draft, or editing, or production tasks on a book, or creating a blog post or podcast. It can also be a speaking event as I feel that is also art. It must add to my body of work in the world, which is how I see my career as an author, speaker and entrepreneur. So basically, I don't have a set schedule, but mostly I create in the mornings and then do marketing stuff in the afternoons, unless I'm speaking which often involves travel and a different type of day.

DAVE: What are the hardest and easiest parts of writing a book for you? How long does the typical book take you from start to final draft?

JOANNA: The hardest part for me is the first draft. It's still extremely painful for me getting words on the page. I love the research, idea generation and dreaming, and even plotting. I love the editing process, particularly the second major draft where I really mold the book into what I want. Currently, it's taking me around six months to turn a fiction book around, and three months for non-fiction. I'm slowly learning my craft, so I hope to speed up, although part of what I enjoy most about my creative process is the research and associated travel, so that will always take time (which I revel in!)

DAVE: What have been the key factors to your success?

JOANNA: Becoming a successful author drives me daily, and for the last five years it has been my passion, my hobby and my obsession. I really want this. People ask how many hours I spend on this or that, but it doesn't matter to me. I want this so bad that I got rid of all the extraneous stuff in my life to follow this dream. So hard work and persistence, and wanting it badly enough to ditch the TV, spend every hour I have working towards my goal (happily, because it's pleasure as well as work). The definition of success is a tough one though, and I haven't reached my goals yet, but I see this as a lifetime pursuit!

DAVE: What's the best writing advice you've ever gotten (or read somewhere)?

JOANNA: "It's not writing, it's rewriting" - Michael Crichton, "and Write shitty first drafts" - Anne Lamott.

The moment I realized that the words didn't have to emerge perfectly onto the page, I decided I could write, because I knew that I could edit. That changed my life!

I also highly recommend 'The Success Principles' by Jack Canfield which starts with 'Take 100% responsibility for your life'. I read that every day when I was a miserable IT consultant, and tried to put it into action. It took three years from that day to when I resigned my job and became a full-time author-entrepreneur.

DAVE: What's been your biggest mistake as a writer and how did you bounce back?

JOANNA: It was more a mistake with self-publishing, than with writing. When I self-published my first book, I did a print run of 2000 books because I was certain I could sell them all and make money as well as change people's lives. That was about 6 months before the Kindle or print on demand went global. I made it onto national TV and radio, but still only sold about 100 books. In the end, they went to the landfill and I moved my publishing and marketing online. I bounced back by getting straight into writing another book, and also by sharing my lessons on my blog, The Creative Penn, in order to help other people. There's a fantastic community of writers sharing lessons learned online these days, so people can avoid these mistakes.

DAVE: What do you think traditional publishers should learn from indie writers? What things should indie writers learn from traditional publishers?

JOANNA: Traditional publishers have already shown that they are learning from indies — and very fast! We started the 99c price point, and now big publishers do this too. We started with novellas, and now you see big name authors doing the same between their main books. We used targeted email marketing first, and now publishers are creating niche audience hubs, to attract segmented audiences. So I think publishers can continue to learn about experimentation, agile marketing and pivoting from us indies.

I also think we can, and do, learn from traditional publishers. Successful indies are modeling the best practices of publishers by using professional editors, professional cover design and distribution models. For example, some of my books are now available in audio as well as print and ebook. Plus, I'm doing joint venture deals for translation into foreign languages. I'm emulating the traditional publishing/agenting process for exploiting all the rights associated with my creative work. In the past, it was impossible, but every day, we see new opportunities for entrepreneurial indies.

DAVE: Where do you see the state of publishing in the next 5 years?

JOANNA: I'm massively excited about the growth of markets outside the US and UK, which are already considered mature ebook markets right now.

For example, there are twice as many English speakers in India than in England, and they are the educated Indians with a middle class income. When that market explodes, it will be amazing. My books are currently selling in 22 countries, via Amazon and Kobo. I even sold a book in Burkina Faso the other day. These are small volumes, for sure, but that's an early indication of ebook penetration into the most surprising of places. So in the next five years, I see indies selling to a growing global market and doing joint venture deals to reach people in their own languages. I see the Kindle in Arabic and Mandarin, which will reach a greater portion of the world. Basically, I see growth, and that is exciting as hell!

DAVE: What made you decide to podcast, and how has it affected your career?

JOANNA: I started The Creative Penn podcast in early 2009 in order to learn from other people. I'd listened to a few interview shows and noticed how the host could ask whatever they wanted from these amazing people. I was desperate to learn more about writing, publishing and marketing, so I just started to ask people to come on my show. I was amazed when they said yes, and I started with an mp3 recorder held next to a speakerphone, so I was NOT technically savvy at all!

Four years on and the podcast continues to be one of the best investments in terms of my time. I continue to learn from amazing people, and have made personal connections that have helped me in my own career. I also believe in social karma and the generosity of the Internet world, and the podcast is an excellent way to promote other people's work.

DAVE: What advantages and limitations do you face being based in the UK?

JOANNA: I started my journey in Australia, which was pretty difficult because it is a long way from anywhere, and I suffered for lack of a creative, physical network. I would do Skype interviews for the podcast at strange times of day, but I still felt quite removed from the hub of the literary world.

But I'm now in London, and it's fantastic to be here at this point in the history of publishing. Indie is just turning the corner, from stigmatized to trendy, and there's a great network of creative people in this brilliant city. My own writing is steeped in European culture, history and art, so being here is a distinct advantage. Every day I find something new that sparks story ideas, and my fiction is steeped with a sense of place. My next novel, *Desecration*, is a real homage to a curious side of London.

I don't think there are any limitations really, because the online community is so strong now and I continue to connect with my American author friends via Skype.

DAVE: What do you want your legacy to be?

JOANNA: I have two major goals in terms of legacy. I want to be as well known and loved by readers as Stephen King by the time I am in my 50s (I'm 38 right now). So I want to be primarily known as a storyteller with a following for my fiction. But I am also passionate about empowering authors to become entrepreneurs, to take control of their creative lives. So I am also building my speaking practice, investing in becoming a world-class speaker, in order to reach and inspire more people through that avenue. These two things drive everything I do.

You can sign up for pre-release specials and receive a free short story and audio at JFPenn.com. Joanna also writes non-fiction, including the bestselling How To Market A Book. Her site, TheCreativePenn.com has been voted one of the Top 10 Blogs for Writers 3 years running. Connect with Joanna on Twitter @thecreativepenn.

Are You a Repeater?

WE HAD MORE FUN WRITING *Write. Publish. Repeat.* than we expected and plan to write a lot more books like this, including our "how to write like a machine" book, a book on collaboration, and our upcoming *The Fiction Formula (There is No Formula)*. If you'd like to know when those come out (along with the other ones after that), then just sign up for our list at:

http://SelfPublishingPodcast.com/repeater

If we do it, so can you.

OTHER BOOKS BY THE
SELF-PUBLISHING PODCAST
SUPERFRIENDS

TO SEE ALL THE BOOKS AT REALM
AND SANDS:

http://realmandsands.com/books

TO SEE ALL THE BOOKS AT
COLLECTIVE INKWELL:

http://collectiveinkwell.com/our-books

TO SEE ALL OF JOHNNY'S BOOKS:

http://johnnybtruant.com/books

TO SEE ALL OF SEAN'S BOOKS:

http://seanmplatt.com/books

About the Authors

Johnny B. Truant is an author and podcaster who, like the Ramones, was long denied induction into the Rock and Roll Hall of Fame despite having a large cult following. He makes his online home at RealmAndSands.com and is the author of the *Fat Vampire* series, the *Unicorn Western* series, the political sci-fi thriller *The Beam*, and many more.

You can connect with Johnny on Twitter at @JohnnyBTruant, and you should totally send him an email at johnny@johnnybtruant.com if the mood strikes you.

Sean Platt is co-founder of the Realm & Sands and Collective Inkwell, speaker, and author, with breakout indie hits such as Yesterday's Gone, WhiteSpace, Available Darkness, and Dark Crossings, plus two traditionally published titles with Amazon's 47North, Z 2134 and Monstrous – all co-authored with David W. Wright. All the Inkwell's existing pilots can be found in one low-priced volume in "The Serial Box."

You can find Sean at SeanMPlatt.Com, Follow him on Twitter at @SeanPlatt, or email him at seanmichaelplatt@gmail.com.

Johnny and Sean, along with David Wright (the guy whose curmudgeony stance on western research inspired the Unicorn Western series) host two podcasts: the horror/comedy show Better Off Undead and the Self Publishing Podcast. Both podcasts are available on iTunes and the other podcast directories, as well as on Stitcher Radio.

1. make a good –
   excellent –
   product

2. no one markets
   a book like its
   author

3. marketing =
   daily time + focus
   _____
   long term

4. write a lot

5. the best way to sell a
   book is give a book